Integrating Cleveland
Baseball

Integrating Cleveland Baseball

Media Activism, the Integration of the Indians and the Demise of the Negro League Buckeyes

STEPHANIE M. LISCIO

Prof. Dessants —
Thanks for all of
your help. I hope
you enjoy the book!

McFarland & Company, Inc., Publishers

Jefferson, North Carolina, and London

All photographs were provided by NoirTech Research.

LIBRARY OF CONGRESS CATALOGUING-IN-PUBLICATION DATA

Liscio, Stephanie M.
    Integrating Cleveland baseball : media activism, the integration
of the Indians and the demise of the Negro League Buckeyes /
Stephanie M. Liscio.
        p.   cm.
    Includes bibliographical references and index.

    ISBN 978-0-7864-3690-3
    softcover : 50# alkaline paper ∞

    1. Cleveland Buckeyes (Baseball team) — History.   2. Negro
leagues — Ohio — Cleveland — History.   3. African American
baseball players — Ohio — Cleveland — History.   4. Racism in
sports — Ohio — Cleveland — History.   5. Discrimination in
sports — Ohio — Cleveland — History.   6. Mass media and
sports — Ohio — Cleveland — History.   7. Cleveland Indians
(Baseball team) — History.   I. Title.
GV875.C695L57   2010
796.357'640977132 — dc22   2010024311

British Library cataloguing data are available

Front cover: 1946 Cleveland Buckeyes (photograph provided by
NoirTech Research). Players identified on page 179.

Manufactured in the United States of America

McFarland & Company, Inc., Publishers
  Box 611, Jefferson, North Carolina 28640
  www.mcfarlandpub.com

To all of my friends and family
for their love and support, particularly
my little buddies, Sweet William and Torrey.

Table of Contents

Acknowledgments

"Don't worry, it's just a game." I've heard those words spoken many times throughout my life, a friend or family member's attempt to convince me that it's really no big deal that my favorite baseball team — the Cleveland Indians — just suffered a crushing loss. Deep down I knew they were right, yet why did I still feel terrible? It is because baseball and sports in general play such a large role in my life and the lives of countless others. They represent an opportunity to step away from your responsibilities and your problems, and to focus your energy on an event that has no direct impact on your day-to-day life. For many during the 1940s, baseball took on a much greater meaning. It was not an escape but rather a way to confront segregation and inequality. While it might be "just a game," it is a game that changed attitudes and changed lives.

There are numerous people that helped me throughout this process, which actually started as my master's thesis at Shippensburg University of Pennsylvania. My thesis committee — John Bloom, David Godshalk, and Betty Dessants — provided me with countless bits of helpful advice and suggestions. I presented various versions of the chapters in this book at several different conferences including the Baseball in Literature and Culture Conference at Middle Tennessee State, the Jerry Malloy Negro League Conference and the NINE Journal of Baseball History and Culture Conference, and received many helpful suggestions from conference participants. Ike Brooks provided a detailed list of statistics on the Cleveland teams, including won/lost records and team owners. I'd also like to extend a special thanks to Leslie Heaphy, who read a full draft of the book and offered excellent advice, as well as Larry Lester, whose NoirTech Research provided the wonderful photos throughout the book. I'm proud to say that I have been a part of the history department at Case Western Reserve

University for nearly three years, and I am thankful to those in the department for their support and encouragement. I created entries on all of Cleveland's early Negro League teams for the *Encyclopedia of Cleveland History* under the guidance of Professor John Grabowski. From Professor Grabowski I was able to expand my knowledge of Cleveland history and sports history. For that, I am grateful.

I would also like to thank my family for their support, as I worked on this book and as I pursue my graduate studies in history. I'd like to thank my mom, Cheryl Fleet, for her support and encouragement. Even though the subject matter was not among her interests, she always listened and asked questions. My mother-in-law, Sherry Liscio, and my brother-in-law, Patrick Liscio, read several chapters and provided helpful feedback. My father, George Fleet, read a draft of the entire book and gave me advice on several chapters. He has roughly a half-dozen jobs between his sales work and college teaching positions, and I know his free time is basically nonexistent. I appreciate the fact that he used his few spare moments to take a look at the manuscript for me. And last, but certainly not least, I'd like to thank my husband, John Liscio. Not only did he agree to move to Cleveland so I could pursue a Ph.D. at Case Western Reserve University, but he also helped me with anything pertaining to the book whenever I asked. John, who sometimes seems like he was a born complainer, never complained once about anything I asked of him. I know I'm not always the easiest person to live with, so his patience and willingness to help meant a lot to me.

Preface

This book covers Negro League baseball in Cleveland, particularly the Cleveland Buckeyes of the 1940s. During the decade of the '40s the Cleveland Indians integrated, becoming the first team in the American League to do so; however, integration proved detrimental to the city's Negro League team. The African American press of Cleveland acted as a cheerleader for integration and encouraged the Indians to add black players to its roster.

As an Indians fan, I became interested in the integration of Cleveland baseball after reading about the 1948 team which won the World Series. I wanted to learn more about Satchel Paige and Larry Doby, as well as how their presence on the Indians affected the Negro Leagues, yet when I looked for books on the topic, I found that there were none. There were books on African Americans in Cleveland, and biographies or autobiographies of Satchel Paige and Larry Doby, but nothing that included the entire experience. Books like *Alabama North* by Kimberley Phillips and *Black Americans in Cleveland* by Russell Davis explore the experiences of Southern migrants and the daily lives of African Americans in Cleveland yet do not extensively analyze how the integration of baseball impacted these same citizens. An excellent biography of Doby, *Pride Against Prejudice* by Joseph Thomas Moore, examined the player's life and personal experiences in integrating the Indians, but did not go into great detail about the impact that integration had on Cleveland's African American community, nor how it affected Cleveland's Negro League team. I wanted to follow the experience through the eyes of the media, due to their encouragement of integration.

In the course of my research I read almost thirty full years of African American newspapers that operated in Cleveland, focusing not just on sports but also on editorials and general news. Most of the microfilm I used was obtained through the Kent State University library and the Cleveland Public Library. I also researched various topics and items at the National Baseball Hall of Fame and Museum's library in Cooperstown, New York, and items at the Western Reserve Historical Society in Cleveland. I also employed numerous secondary sources on related topics.

Introduction

As the United States entered World War II, many Americans were well aware that as the U.S. worked to secure democracy on the world stage, there were glaring inequalities among its own citizens. African Americans were segregated or completely excluded from many aspects of society. When it came to informing the public of these injustices, and campaigning for their end, the African American press played a decisive role. These newspapers fought for the desegregation of the military, fair housing standards, fair employment practices, and the end of segregation at public facilities, such as stores, restaurants and swimming pools. The *Cleveland Call and Post* fought these battles within its pages, and focused some of its energy on the integration of one specific aspect of society — baseball. Other African American publications, specifically the *Pittsburgh Courier* and writer Wendell Smith, also targeted this sport. Writers with the *Call and Post* believed that the successful integration of baseball, often referred to as "America's pastime," would prove to whites that integration was beneficial. Even though the paper began its integration campaign in 1942, the Cleveland Indians did not integrate until 1947, becoming the first American League team to field a black player just eleven weeks after Jackie Robinson integrated the Brooklyn Dodgers and the National League. This campaign was often waged at the expense of the city's Negro League team, the Cleveland Buckeyes.

It should come as no surprise that baseball was targeted for integration since sports had great meaning for African American citizens. In *Sandlot Seasons: Sport in Black Pittsburgh*, author Rob Ruck discussed the importance of sport to the black community in Pittsburgh in the first half of the twentieth century. Sport helped to foster a sense of community among blacks in Pittsburgh and provided an outlet for expression and creativity.

According to Ruck, African Americans in Pittsburgh developed a sense of pride in their sports teams and brought together native-born and new migrant black residents in the city. Aside from providing a release from work and the concerns of daily life, sport provided African Americans with heroes to cheer for. Ruck quoted Mal Goode, Homestead native and the first African American to work as a national television news correspondent, who spoke about the importance of sport to the black community when he said, "Sport was segregated in those days ... but when you found blacks were playing white teams, our pride was showing. It had to be. There was so much negative living that we had to do, over which we had no control." Goode added, "Anything that we could hang onto from the standpoint of pride, it was there, and it showed."[1]

Even though segregated sports meant a lot to the African American community in Pittsburgh, the *Call and Post*, while itself a segregated institution, did not openly support segregated sport in Cleveland. The newspaper grudgingly accepted the Cleveland Buckeyes throughout the team's existence in the city, yet always believed the team was secondary to their primary goal of integrating the major leagues, specifically the Indians. A point of irony in the *Call and Post*'s push for integrating the Indians was the team's racist name and image, a lightning rod for criticism from many Native American groups throughout history. The primary image associated with the team is Chief Wahoo, a grinning, red-skinned Indian with a feather sticking out of his headband. Despite this, the *Call and Post* never questioned these racist overtones, and the Indians actually gained a reputation as a pioneer in race relations with African Americans. In fact, the team was invited to participate in major league baseball's inaugural Civil Rights Game in Memphis, Tennessee, on March 31, 2007, against the St. Louis Cardinals. Major league baseball explained its selection, stating, "The Indians ... were chosen for their history in contributions to integrate the game — specifically, the 1947 signing of Larry Doby, who became the first black player in the history of the American League, and the 1975 naming of Frank Robinson as baseball's first black manager."[2]

When it came to race relations and integration, many believed that Cleveland was a pioneer compared to other major American cities. In fact, in 1950 *Ebony* magazine said, "Cleveland has better race relations than any other big city in America."[3] In 1945 the city established the Community Relations Board, the first municipally-sponsored body designed to handle issues of race in the Cleveland community. Aside from being the first American League team, and second overall, to integrate, the Indians hired Frank Robinson as the first African American manager in baseball in 1975. Carl Stokes became the first African American mayor of a large American city when he was elected to lead Cleveland in 1967. However, the experiences of Stokes and Robinson may never have been possible without the advances made in Cleveland during the 1940s. One of the major driving forces in the creation of the Community Relations Board was the fact that African Americans lived in deplorable conditions and Cleveland leaders were afraid the situation was a powder keg waiting to explode. As of 1945 there had been no significant race riots, no great instances of racial unrest. Detroit experienced severe rioting in 1943, which may have led Cleveland leaders to examine their own city for potential problems.

During this rather turbulent time, several African American newspapers, the *Call and Post* included, were often critical of baseball's Negro Leagues within their pages. The leadership of the Negro National and Negro American leagues had a rocky relationship with the press, with poor communication between league and team officials and writers. While some newspapers offered sparse coverage of Negro League games, it was not always for a lack of trying. It was not unusual for writers to receive little information about Negro League contests, and teams provided almost no information on individual player statistics. While major league baseball had organized publicity departments, radio and later television coverage, Negro League teams were considered to be doing well if they communicated an accurate schedule to the public. Official league contests were often mixed with exhibition games, and teams would often play nine straight days in nine different cities in an attempt to maximize their earning potential. Almost no Negro League team owned its own stadium, which meant that the clubs were at the mercy of other teams' schedules in making arrangements for their games.

During the 1940s the Negro American League Cleveland Buckeyes played their home games at League Park, located in the eastside community of Hough. The Indians usually split their home games between League Park and Cleveland Municipal Stadium, which opened downtown on the shores of Lake Erie in 1931 as the first stadium in Cleveland built with municipal funding. The Indians moved exclusively to the downtown facility by the late 1940s.

An exploration of the *Call and Post* of the 1940s confirms there were many instances where the team took a backseat to other, more important issues. Because writers at the newspaper believed they should take an active role in advancing the civil rights of African Americans, they often ignored the Buckeyes in favor of promoting an integrated Indians team. Baseball was viewed as a reasonable starting point for integration, a public venue where the success of African Americans on the field could be tied to success in integration.

The first chapter explores the troubled start for Negro League baseball in Cleveland prior to the formation of the Buckeyes. Between 1922 and 1940, the city had ten different Negro League teams; most lasted only a year and struggled to win games. The failure of the ten teams demonstrated the challenges that Negro League baseball faced in Cleveland and across the nation. Not every team that folded in Cleveland failed for the same reasons, but many failed due to a combination of mediocre players, poor game venues, a bad economy and turmoil in the league. By the time the Buckeyes were formed in 1942, it was possible that some people in Cleveland were fed up with Negro League baseball. Through my examination of the first ten Negro League teams in Cleveland, I offer theories as to why these teams failed where the Buckeyes were able to succeed. The early teams also had less exposure in the local Cleveland media, which may have aided their demise.

The second chapter explores the creation of the Buckeyes in late 1941 and follows the team during its first full season in 1942 through the pages of the *Call and Post* and sports editor John Fuster. While he appeared pleased to have a Negro League franchise in Cleveland, Fuster often ignored the accomplishments of the team as he fought for most of the season to earn Indians tryouts for three Buckeye players. The third chapter further explores the *Call and Post*'s push for integration, and discusses the unique impact of World War II on baseball and integration. Military enlistments left holes on the rosters of many major league teams. Writers in the black press believed this was a perfect opportunity for African Americans to join major league teams; black players could replace the men that left for the war. The Negro Leagues were also vulnerable to military enlistments, as well as player defections to high-paying Mexican leagues.

The fourth chapter examines the 1945 world champion Buckeye season, as well as its appearance in the Negro League World Series. This was one of the last times the Buckeyes enjoyed the spotlight before an integrated Indians team stole the show. The fifth chapter looks at the 1946 and 1947 seasons and examines some of the challenges the Buckeyes faced following their Negro League World Series title in 1945. By 1946 Jackie Robinson already played for the Brooklyn Dodgers' minor league club in Montreal; it looked like integration of the major leagues was closer than ever. The Buckeyes returned to the World Series in 1947, but the excitement and anticipation from the 1945 season was gone. This was the last time the Buckeyes were able to field a competitive team in the Negro American League.

The sixth chapter focuses on the 1947 integration of the Indians, as well as a comparison of the *Call and Post*'s coverage of the 1945 Negro League world champion Buckeyes and the 1948 world champion Indians. I also compare the paper's portrayal of the Indians' first African American player, Larry Doby, with legendary Negro League pitcher Satchel Paige, who joined the Indians in 1948. Doby was portrayed as a role model and a trailblazer in the local media, while Paige was seen as more of an entertainer and an attendance draw.

The seventh chapter focuses on 1949 and 1950 in Cleveland, as Fuster returned to the newspaper as sports editor after a six-year hiatus. Throughout these two years Fuster reflected on the racial advancements made in Cleveland during the last decade, as well as his role in these accomplishments. Fuster promoted further integration of the major leagues, and hoped to see the Negro Leagues integrated in the near future. While strictly a venue for entertainment in the past, the real purpose of the Negro Leagues in the post-integration era, according to Fuster, was to serve almost as a minor league system to the major leagues. This would give teams a chance to scout young African American talent and integrate more major league teams.

The eighth and final chapter looks at a forgotten event in the history of the Cleveland Buckeyes and the integration of baseball: the addition of a white pitcher to the Buckeyes' roster in 1946. Even though Fuster continually pushed for the integration of the Negro Leagues, he never mentioned the fact that the Buckeyes already integrated several years before he wrote his columns. While it was entirely possible that Fuster did not realize the Buckeyes signed a white player in 1946, he may have known and yet chose to ignore the event for numerous reasons. I list several explanations that suggest a willingness to conceal or downplay the event in the years following the white player's departure. The epilogue discusses the Buckeyes' all-star outfielder, Sam Jethroe. Two major league teams offered Jethroe auditions prior to the signings of Jackie Robinson and Larry Doby. Even though he was not one of the first African Americans to integrate baseball, he did integrate two different National League teams.

As mentioned in the preface, while there have been books and articles written on the Negro Leagues and Jackie Robinson, there is virtually nothing written on Larry Doby and the effect the integration of the Indians had on the African American community in Cleveland. Books like *Alabama North* by Kimberley Phillips and *Black Americans in Cleveland* by Russell Davis describe the experiences of Southern migrants and African Americans in Cleveland in general, yet do not consider in depth how the integration of baseball affected these citizens. An excellent biography of Doby, *Pride Against Prejudice* by Joseph Thomas Moore, looks at the player's life and personal experiences in integrating the Indians, but does not delve into the impact that event had on Cleveland's African American community. I examined the *Call and Post* over a sixteen-year period, analyzing sports stories, editorials and general news coverage within the paper. When necessary, I compared my findings to other African American publications as well as white daily publications. I also looked at eighteen years of Cleveland's other African American weekly paper, the *Cleveland Gazette*. Started in 1883, the paper was under the editorial control of Harry C. Smith for most of its tenure, until it collapsed in 1945. While it did take an activist position on many issues in Cleveland and the state of Ohio, the paper paid less attention to sports. The *Gazette* spoke out against the use of municipal funds to build a new stadium in Cleveland if there were plans for that stadium to remain segregated. The *Gazette* also fought segregation at Luna Park in Cleveland and tried to arrange for boycotts of the property.[4]

Throughout my research I found that baseball, often viewed as strictly an entertainment medium, became so much more for the writers of the *Call and Post* and for African Americans in Cleveland. It was living proof that equality in society was not only acceptable, but preferable; integrated teams won championships and increased attendance, therefore increasing profits. Baseball was an integral part of a much larger picture as it provided many in the African American press with the opportunity to prove that not only could blacks coexist peacefully with whites, but were as talented, if not more talented, in many cases, on the baseball diamond. Baseball was a chance to earn respectability on a very public stage, and once that respectability was earned, the Negro Leagues would no longer be necessary in their current form, according to several African American sportswriters in Cleveland. In the minds of these writers, the Negro Leagues would function better as a minor league system for the major leagues, a place to showcase young, black talent that the white teams could scout. If this solution was not successful, then the leagues should dismantle.

1

Before the Buckeyes

Cleveland's Ten Negro League Teams, 1922–1940

The city of Cleveland received its first professional Negro League team in 1922 when the Tate Stars joined the Negro National League. The team, one of ten black professional teams in Cleveland between 1922 and 1940, was plagued by financial problems and a dismal record. It folded by the end of 1923. Within months another ownership group purchased the Tate Stars and rechristened the team the Cleveland Browns. When that team failed less than a year later, another took its place. This became almost an annual occurrence in Cleveland — a new team with high hopes for success in March found itself in complete disarray before October. There were a number of Negro League teams across America that failed and disappeared; Cleveland was not unique in that sense. What made Cleveland unique was the fact that a new team was always ready to take the spot of its predecessor as they bragged about how successful they would be. The new team always knew the mistakes of the old group and vowed not to commit the same errors (even though they almost always did). In some cases, the men whose team just failed were the same men that started the new team.

There were a number of possible reasons as to why these teams failed; some reasons fell within the greater landscape of Negro League and United States history. The city of Cleveland offered a few unique problems that likely contributed to the failure of several teams. In some cases the most likely reasons were incompetent ownership and a lack of talented players. The teams played at a number of different fields over the years, many of which reportedly provided substandard conditions. While the teams brought players from other parts of the country to Cleveland, many were comprised from a collection of local sandlot players. Even though these players excelled on the local stage, it was difficult for them to compete with powerhouse teams like the Kansas City Monarchs and the Chicago American Giants. Teams across Negro League and major league baseball felt the pinch caused by the Great Depression. African Americans in Cleveland suffered from difficult financial conditions as early as 1928, a full year before the stock market crash that triggered the Great Depression.[1] Fans with limited disposable income were reluctant to spend their money and their free time watching teams with dismal losing records. Each year Cleveland's two primary African American newspapers, the *Cleveland Gazette* and later the *Cleveland Call and Post*, always had the highest hopes for the city's teams. By the end of the season, most writers made their dissatisfaction with that year's Negro League entry quite evident.

Robert Peterson, in his book *Only the Ball Was White*, wrote, "Tracing the course of the organized Negro leagues is rather like trying to follow a single black strand through a ton of spaghetti. The footing is infirm, and the strand has a tendency to break off in one's hand and slither back into the amorphous mass." Teams often shifted cities, dropped their league affiliation mid-season and vanished into thin air (even though they likely returned to their city's sandlots). While Peterson admitted that it was difficult to make blanket generalizations about the Negro Leagues, there were a few issues that every city seemed to face. The leagues and the teams were underfinanced, and often lacked centralized leadership. Because of issues like these, the Negro Leagues never enjoyed the stability of major league baseball.[2]

The Negro National League was founded in 1920 by Rube Foster, who ran the league for much of the decade. A talented pitcher and manager of the Chicago American Giants, Foster ran the league from Chicago until he was hospitalized for mental illness in 1926. His hospitalization and subsequent death in 1928 left the league without a solid leader. Foster was vital to the operation of the Negro National League, as he often gave struggling franchises money from his own pockets and even paid for the transportation of some teams. What Foster expected in return for his generosity was "compliance with his will," to which most clubs agreed with limited complaints. The league had no umpires; the home team usually provided the officials for games. One point of contention was the fact that umpires across the league tended to be white men, which led to complaints about a "lack of race pride." According to Robert Peterson in *Only the Ball Was White*, Foster also acted as a disciplinarian of sorts toward players in the league. When he was no longer in charge of the Negro National League, the standard of on-field conduct seemed to disappear. Players supposedly knew that any type of retribution or discipline was unlikely.[3]

Foster's Negro National League stumbled after his death and managed to survive until 1932, while the Eastern League failed in 1930. Cumberland "Cum" Posey, owner of the Homestead Grays, founded the East-West League in 1932 with ambitious plans for league games on almost a daily basis. With the grim economic realities of 1932, the league barely made it off the ground and collapsed by the end of summer. In 1933 Gus Greenlee, the owner of the Pittsburgh Crawfords, started the second incarnation of the Negro National League, which lasted (with some changes) until 1948. It included cities in both the East and Midwest when it started in 1933 but became an eastern circuit once the Negro American League was founded in 1937. The NAL housed the midwestern and western teams for the Negro Leagues and lasted in some form until 1960.[4]

Cleveland had teams in both versions of the NNL, the East-West League, and the NAL. The Tate Stars were Cleveland's first professional black baseball team, and spent 1922 and part of 1923 in Foster's Negro National League. The team formed in 1918 and played against local clubs for several years before accepting a position as a league "affiliate" for the 1921 season. The Tate Stars were invited to join the NNL in 1922 after they paid their $1,000 league entry fee.[5] The team was started by a man named George Tate, who was born in Knoxville, Tennessee, and reached Cleveland via Detroit and Oberlin, Ohio. Tate had an interest in athletics throughout his life and was a "clever pitcher" with Oberlin. The 32-year-old Tate was a Cleveland businessman who supported a number of semi-pro teams in the city before his involvement with the NNL. The *Gazette* said the league chose Tate and his team "not only because of his ability as a baseball man but also as a compliment to the Cleveland fans." Tate rose quickly within the hierarchy of the Negro National League; by March of 1922 he was named vice president.[6]

The Negro League leadership considered Cleveland to be an untapped resource when it came to baseball. The city saw an influx of African American migrants from the South in the previous five to seven years. In 1910, African Americans represented 1.5 percent of the total population, and by 1920 were 4.3 percent of the population. By 1930 that number jumped to 8 percent and reached 9.6 percent by 1940.[7] The majority of these migrants came to Cleveland to work in the city's various industrial jobs. In the boom years immediately following World War I, many of these residents had disposable income for the first time in their lives. Baseball games were the ideal activity on which to spend some of that hard-earned money.

The Tate Stars were set to play their home games at a park owned by Tate, located between Woodland and Central avenues, near East 55th Street, christened Tate Field. The team played its games at the park starting in 1921. In regards to Tate Field, Rube Foster once called it "one of the finest baseball stadiums owned by our people in the country."[8] Bill Dismukes, the manager of the Pittsburgh Keystones, said the Tate Stars played in "the most spacious and beautiful park, owned by members of the race."[9] Dismukes thought the Tate Stars could be a dangerous team in 1922 because of the leadership of "Candy" Jim Taylor and the team's powerful offense. He thought that Taylor, Claude "Hooks" Johnson and Fred Boyd would carry the offense and that their young catcher, John Barnes, was one of the best backstops in the league.[10] Prior to the season Tate acquired a few additional players to help the team — George Britt, a pitcher from the Columbus Buckeyes, and three players from the Dayton Marcos in Mitch Murray, Eugene Keeton and Edward "Boots" McClain. The *Gazette* reported that McClain was a favorite among Cleveland fans by midseason yet never explained the reason for his popularity.[11]

The team ran a series of advertisements in early January in the *Gazette* where it offered stock for $10 a share, and a few weeks later for $15 a share.[12] Prior to the spring, the Tate Stars offered season tickets for $11; friends and family of the ticket holder could enter the park for free.[13] The team hoped to sell $3,000 to $4,000 in tickets prior to the start of the 1922 season. Since the Cleveland Indians sold $70,000 worth of tickets in the two months prior to the start of the 1921 season, the team felt its goal was reasonable.[14] The Tate Stars neglected to acknowledge the fact that the Indians sold that large quantity of tickets in the wake of their 1920 World Series championship. It was never determined if the team met its pre-season sales goals, but they did report 6,500 fans in attendance for one late April game which was a rather large crowd for a regular-season Negro League game in the early 1920s.[15]

By May of 1922 creditors and stockholders began to clamor about outstanding debts owed by the Tate Stars. The first court complaint claimed the team owed one Cleveland man $4,302.41.[16] In June of that year treasurer Col. Jacob E. Reed publicly complained that he was not allowed to review the team's finances despite his position with the Tate Stars. The *Gazette* reported, "Treasurer Reed's character, standing and reputation as a business man are far and away above those of any of the other officials of the company, and it is 'like a clap of thunder in a clear sky' for the general public to learn that The Tate Baseball Co.'s business affairs are apparently not being handled in a regular and proper way." The paper feared that without a dramatic change in the financial management of the team, the Tate Stars would inevitably fail.[17] Stockholders called a meeting in June to express their dissatisfaction with Tate's handling of the finances, even though Reed was elected for that purpose. The *Gazette* was shocked that even though Tate and Reed were supposed to handle thousands of dollars, neither man was officially bonded.[18] Tate spent most of the summer in and out of court fighting the claims against him while the public wondered what happened to the "thousands of dollars" the Tate Stars earned at the gate.[19] In addition to Reed, the team had a full board of directors, which included at least one white businessman.[20]

By the end of the 1922 season the finances weren't the Tate Stars' only problem; the team was near the bottom of the standings in the eight-team league.[21] They finished tied for seventh with a record of 17 wins and 29 losses.[22] After the season their financial affairs were in shambles and many in the community believed the Tate Stars were nearly $20,000 in debt. Creditors were told that if they received twenty-five percent of their initial investment, they could consider themselves lucky. Soon the creditors and stockholders learned that even Tate Field suffered financial problems; part of the Tate Field grandstand was on leased ground and there was a large, second mortgage on the park. Tate owed his players almost $1,000 in back wages after the 1922 season ended.[23] When the league hierarchy met in December, they dropped the Tate Stars from the NNL. The team actually made $8,000 in profits during the 1922 season but was hindered by the $20,000 needed to pull the team out of debt.[24]

In February of 1923 Rube Foster came to Cleveland for a dinner in his honor held by "Candy" Jim Taylor and Phil Fears, owner of a local black semi-pro team. Taylor spoke highly of the team he built in his two years as manager but said he wanted to leave his position for unnamed reasons. There was no mention of Tate's presence at the banquet, but J.E. Reed and Tony Strunko both spoke about the financial difficulties of the club and their hopes for the team's future. Another "director" of the Tate Stars, Russell Cross, was less kind to Foster than the other men. Cross harshly criticized Foster for his "disinterestedness in the local company's struggles" and claimed that Foster treated the Tate Stars players poorly, provided the team with a bad schedule, and that Foster had a general sense of disregard for teams that owned their own parks. The toastmaster tried to smooth over the disagreements between the men, and the banquet reportedly ended on a conciliatory note.[25]

Tate continued with plans for the team in 1923 and announced that the Tate Stars planned to start their spring training schedule on April 2 at Tate Field. Claude Johnson was named the manager and the Tate Stars became an associate member of the Eastern Mutual League.[26] Even though there were fewer complaints about the team's finances in the media in 1923, a group of stockholders publicly pressured Tate to return their money. Sparked by rumors that Tate planned to sell the club, the stockholders feared they would lose their money, or that it would end up in the hands of local whites.[27]

By the end of June things looked a bit more promising for the Tate Stars. George Tate traveled to Chicago to meet with Rube Foster, and after they settled their differences, Foster let the Tate Stars back into the NNL. When a team from Toledo folded, Foster and Tate arranged for the Tate Stars to play the rest of their scheduled games.[28] Even though the team was supposed to begin July on the road, Foster and Tate arranged for the Tate Stars to play at home for the Fouth of July holiday crowd.[29] In 1922 Tate complained that the league gave the Tate Stars an unfair and inconvenient schedule. By allowing the team to play the holiday at home, Foster was able to placate Tate and provide the team with a holiday attendance boost.

Whatever boost the Tate Stars received from the Fourth of July series, they still struggled to put fans in the seats in 1923. During a mid–July game the manager of the Rochester, Pennsylvania, Terminals refused to let his team take the field for a scheduled doubleheader against the Tate

Stars. He said he did not want his team to play before such a small crowd (rain was supposedly a contributing factor) unless George Tate promised the Pennsylvania team an established amount of money. Tate refused, and the game was called.[30] Without modern money-makers such as broadcast rights and licensing agreements, Negro League teams were completely reliant on the gate receipts to pay their costs. The Rochester team likely required a minimum sum in order to pay their players and their transportation costs to Cleveland. While this particular situation was likely frustrating for the players involved, it caused the small crowd to lose faith in their hometown team.

The Tate Stars managed to stumble through the rest of the season in financial disarray and with a dismal 7–14 record. Tate fully intended for the team to return to the league for the 1924 season, but he seemed to vanish after the 1923 campaign concluded. The team was purchased by new ownership, which changed the name to the Cleveland Browns. Tate also sold his baseball park to a man named George Hooper, who renamed it Hooper Field. In preparation for the next season, Hooper added seats and remodeled portions of the park.[31]

Despite posting several early exhibition victories, the Browns struggled for much of May, which prompted manager (and Hall of Fame member) Sol White to tinker with the team's roster. The *Cleveland Gazette* seemed optimistic about the Browns despite four straight losses to the Cuban Stars, reporting, "It takes more than a week or two to build a team that will beat the American Giants, the Detroit and Cuban Stars, all three old organizations and good ones, very good clubs."[32] The *Gazette* thought the Browns looked good in early June, when they split a series with the St. Louis Stars before a crowd of 4,500.[33] For a short time the changes appeared to work and it seemed as if the Browns had pulled it together. In late June the Browns won three games in one week against the Pittsburgh Keystones, one of the league's top teams with a 12–1 record.[34] Unfortunately, the Browns were never able to pull together a solid streak of victories.

In early July "Candy" Jim Taylor returned to Cleveland as manager of the St. Louis Stars and led his team to victory over the Browns in both games of a doubleheader. The *Gazette* appeared baffled by the Browns' inconsistency since the paper believed the team was strong offensively and defensively.[35] Former star outfielder for the Tate Stars, "Bobo" Leonard, joined the Browns for one game while the team was in Chicago. Leonard was now with the Lincoln Giants of New York City and planned to tour Cuba with that team during the winter of 1924–1925. Leonard claimed he made $190 a month with the Giants but did not mention how that compared to his salary as a Tate Star.[36] He spoke as if his new salary was a large upgrade over the old.

There was a great deal of promotion and excitement when the "greatest ball-team in America," the Kansas City Monarchs, were scheduled to come to town in July. The *Gazette* anticipated the largest crowd in the history of Hooper Field for the game. Fans were encouraged to see the "star array of players" on the Monarchs and to "boost our baseball in Cleveland."[37] The *Gazette* reminded fans that the Browns attempted to improve their roster and that locals should support them. This language likely implied that the Browns were already struggling to survive in Cleveland. The Browns won only one of the four games against the Monarchs, but fans were encouraged to ignore the defeats since the Monarchs were such a good team. The *Gazette* was pleased with the turnout for the series, as fans nearly filled Hooper Field to capacity. The paper criticized a large number of fans for cheering for the Monarchs and told the patrons to be loyal to their hometown team.[38] This was the second time fans reportedly gave up on the hometown team and cheered for the visitor. During a June game against the Memphis Red Sox, loud cheers were heard coming from Hooper Field. People in the neighborhood believed the Browns were doing well; it turned out the fans had turned on them and were rooting instead for the Red Sox.[39] The Browns finished in last place in 1924 with a 15–34 record.[40]

Early in 1925, the Negro National League was thrown into chaos when Rube Foster temporarily resigned as president.[41] The Cleveland Browns initially planned to return for the 1925 season, but uncertainty within the Negro National League called such a return into question.[42] The *Gazette* suggested that the Browns and their regional competitors start their own league, which never materialized. Under the management of pitcher "Slim" Branahan, the Browns opened the season against a semi-pro team from Lorain.[43] The Browns learned they had no home field for the 1925 season after their deal with Hooper Field fell through. The team's directors complained about the "raw deal" they received from George Hooper, owner of Hooper Field, and Hooper's former business partner,

L.L. Yancey. Hooper was no longer directly involved with the Browns by this point. The Browns complained that the two men "hamstrung" them all winter and then showed up with their own "all-star" team for the 1925 season that would replace the Browns as Cleveland's primary black baseball team. Several of the Browns directors bragged that they convinced fans to stay away from this new team's games at Hooper Field. The "all-star" team, also referred to as the Star-Giants or Giants, supposedly played to poor crowds.[44]

During the 1924 season the Browns reportedly made $23,000 and set money aside for the 1925 season. While there were claims the team avoided a deficit, supporters of the team stressed that many established teams lost money in 1924. Detroit, Birmingham, and Memphis lost several thousand dollars during the season, supposedly due to "awful weather and business conditions." One fan said, "The smart manager-gang running things out at that park have just about killed our baseball in Cleveland thru [*sic*] their inexperience, ignorance, amateurism, greed and raw-dealing." This fan said that the small crowds that came to see the Star-Giants were evidence of the widespread disinterest of black Cleveland fans. There were a few reported contests that involved the Star-Giants, but the team was never officially affiliated with the Negro National League.[45]

If the fan was correct, and black professional baseball in Cleveland was on life support, Sam Shepard did not realize it. Shepard was the owner of the next Negro League team in Cleveland, the Elites, who played in the city for the 1926 season. "Candy" Jim Taylor returned to manage for part of the season after his stint with the St. Louis Stars, while Frank Duncan led the team for the rest of the season. The Elites played their home games at Hooper Field and, like the teams before them, the Elites were not successful on the field, notching an abysmal 6–38 record.[46] Prior to the start of the 1926 season, Shepard traveled to Texas, Arkansas, and Memphis, Tennessee, to recruit players for the team. His travels led to the signing of six players, and Taylor brought two players from St. Louis to Cleveland with him. The *Cleveland Gazette* said an infielder named Beard and a catcher named Spearman came from the Texas and Arkansas trip, while pitchers Ralph "Squire" Moore and William Spearman came from Memphis. No other names were mentioned. Frank Duncan was charged with helping new players get into shape for the regular season.[47]

By the end of June, only five players from the Opening Day roster were still on the Elites, three of whom were pitchers. Due to the team's poor play for much of the season, management decided to completely dismantle and rebuild the club mid-season. The Elites were almost unrecognizable to fans, as they replaced their entire infield and most of their outfield. The *Gazette* even asked "'The Elites' or 'Derelicts' — Which?"[48] The team managed to win a couple of games in the week after the roster changes, but one of the victories was due to forfeit. The manager of the Dayton Marcos, angered over an umpire's call, pulled his team off the field and gave the victory to the Elites. This incident was one of many examples of an umpire's inability to control a game. With Rube Foster hospitalized, the league lacked a central authority figure that forced players and teams to play by the rules. Despite the victory by forfeit, the *Gazette* complimented the Elites for playing a "snappy brand of baseball."[49]

The Elites had a few flashes of brilliance during an otherwise dismal season. In early September the *Gazette* called one of their recent victories "one of the most sensational rallies ever witnessed at Hooper Field." The Elites scored six runs during the ninth inning to beat the Detroit Stars, 9–7. The *Gazette* gave credit to Duncan, who took sole control of the team midway through the season. The paper said that Duncan took command of a team "that had not been able to define the word victory ... pulled it out of its lethargic state and made it one of the most feared diamond outfits in the vicinity."[50] Even though the Elites had a good record against local semi-pro teams, their record in league contests remained lackluster. The team folded at the end of the year, and Cleveland was offered the Indianapolis ABC franchise for the 1927 season.

Cleveland often benefited from another city's inability to maintain a Negro League for the entire season. The entire Indianapolis franchise moved to Cleveland except for the team's manager, "Bingo" DeMoss. Frank Duncan remained in Cleveland to lead this new franchise.[51] Originally called the Buckeyes at the beginning of the season, the team was referred to as the Hornets by July of 1927. A group called the Cuyahoga Amusement Co. was responsible for bringing the team to Cleveland. This organization included many men that were (or would be) familiar names in the world of black professional baseball in Cleveland, such as S.M. Terrell, Col. Jake Reed, and L.S.N. Cobb.[52] The team appeared to have better connections with the media, as L.S.N. Cobb and S.M. Terrell often acted in a public relations capacity. The Hornets even offered at least one Ladies' Day pro-

motion during the season, which showed they sought to improve attendance among certain demographics.[53] The leadership of the Hornets often
reassured fans the team was run in a professional manner, an apparent
swipe at some of their predecessors in the city.[54] The *Gazette* predicted the
Cuyahoga Amusement Company was going to give Cleveland fans the best
Negro League baseball to date.[55]

The team trained for the season in Birmingham and Montgomery,
Alabama, but the preparation did not keep them from playing mediocre
baseball through the month of May. During one of the team's losses against
the American Giants, in front of 2,500 fans, the Hornets committed seven
errors.[56] In July the Hornets withdrew from the Negro National League
because they were unable to earn enough money as league members. The
team barely broke even after the transportation costs were taken into
account, and blamed bad attendance on a rainy spring and early summer.
Instead of cancellation, many games were moved to the visiting team's
city.[57] Since league cities were relatively spread out, teams incurred large
transportation costs while traveling to league matches. Many teams found
it more profitable to maintain a schedule against semi-professional teams
closer to home. This was exactly what the Hornets did for the rest of the
season; they played exhibition games against other NNL teams or played
against semi-pro teams. The Hornets decided to play the 1928 season as
an independent team under the name Euclid-13th St. Recreation Co.[58]

Cleveland had another team — the Tigers — ready to step into the
Negro National League limelight for the 1928 season. One of the primary
backers for this team was a white man named M.C. Barkin, who wrote a
check for $10,000 to purchase the franchise.[59] The Tigers decided to leave
Tate/Hooper Field, the home of the prior Negro League teams, for a field
at Cleveland's Luna Park. One of the reasons the team selected the Luna
Park field as their home grounds was due to the park's large capacity. It
could seat 26,000 people, and five street car lines ran to the main entrance
of the park. Luna Park's facilities were also considered better because of
the large number of restrooms for men and women, three clubhouses, and
parking that could accommodate up to 2,000 vehicles.[60] The *Gazette* complained frequently about instances of segregation at Luna Park, including
an ad with the headline "Color-Line Luna Park" that said, "'Negroes' only
are barred from Luna Park's dance-hall, roller skating rink and bathing
pool. That ought to be enough for all self and race respecting 'Negroes.'

Do not be coaxed to go to Luna Park for any celebration or anything else!"[61] The *Gazette* added in a later story, "There are THOUSANDS of our people in this community who have too much self and race respect to go to Color-line Luna Park, or its stadium, to see or hear anything."[62]

While Cleveland's Negro League teams struggled to find a suitable facility for their games, the Cleveland Indians pushed for a new stadium in the city. The *Gazette* was upset that the city considered providing public funds to the Indians for the new ballpark, despite the fact the Indians were a segregated team. Cleveland Municipal Stadium, completed in 1931 on the shores of Lake Erie near downtown, was the first stadium built with public funding in Cleveland. The *Gazette* believed that if public tax dollars were used toward the stadium, the Indians should be forced to field African American players. The *Gazette* also pointed out that the Indians and other major league baseball teams wanted to add Jewish players to their rosters in order to increase the number of Jewish fans that attended games. The *Gazette* asked the Indians, "Why not give the Afro-American ball-players the same chance, President (Alva) Bradley?"[63] Teams eventually rented the Indians' facilities for their games, but not until the mid–1930s.

In the meantime, the Tigers had to settle for the field at Luna Park. This park was popular among Cleveland residents, but enacted a policy in 1910 that only allowed African Americans into the park on designated "Jim Crow days." Even on these specific days, the Luna Park management did not let African Americans use the bathing facilities. One African American citizen claimed the park was somewhat discrete when it came to their prejudicial rules on bathing facilities. This man said that on the "Jim Crow days" the pool was always oddly "out of order."[64] Despite these negatives, the fact remained that Luna Park's field offered improved amenities for fans.

In addition to a field upgrade, the Cleveland Tigers also attempted to hire superstar Negro League first baseman Oscar Charleston to manage the team. This plan fell through when O.J. Gilmore, one of the Negro National League's commissioners, reportedly offered Charleston the largest salary ever for an African American player to play for the Harrisburg, Pennsylvania, team. The Tigers settled for Judy Gans, a former manager of the Lincoln Giants, and added "home run king" Oscar "Heavy" Johnson when Barkin outbid five other teams for his services.[65] During the 1927 campaign, Johnson hit 42 home runs and batted .364 in just 88 games after injuries ended his season. In a full season, Barkin thought Johnson could hit 60 home runs, Babe Ruth's record-setting figure from 1927. He also believed Johnson had the potential to be "the biggest box office attraction in the league."[66]

S.M. Terrell, a veteran baseball official with the Tate Stars and the Hornets, served as a general manager for the team. The players Terrell signed came primarily from the South and the West, with only one player from Cleveland (catcher John Barnes). The Tigers performed poorly during the first part of the season and were referred to as a "consistent loser" on their first road trip of the year. At the beginning of June, Terrell resigned and Barkin took over sole control of personnel decisions. He announced dramatic changes in the team's roster. In his first move Barkin fired Frank Duncan and replaced him with third baseman Harry Jeffries. Despite his expressed interest in controlling the team's personnel decisions, within a week of Terrell's firing Barkin named Lem Williams as general manager. Williams, formerly the booking and publicity agent for the team, planned to release a number of players who were playing "indifferent ball."[67]

Williams, who also worked as a policeman for the city of Painesville, had a long history in organized black baseball prior to his work with the Cleveland Tigers. For sixteen years he served as the captain of New York City's Cuban Giants. When the Tate Stars were organized, Williams was involved with the construction of Tate Field, later known as Hooper Field. He was one of the first men chosen for an African American all-star team that played before the king and queen of England. As a young man, Williams attended Hiram College for three years, where he was an athlete in multiple sports.[68] Despite the changes Williams instituted, such as the release of four players and the signing of two new infielders, the second half of the Tigers' season was almost as bleak as the first. One bright spot among the number of lopsided losses came during an exhibition game with a white Triple-A all-star team when Nelson Dean pitched a perfect game.[69] By the end of 1928 the Tigers were out of the Negro National League and disappeared from the public eye.

Cleveland went without a team for a couple of years before the Cleveland Cubs joined the Negro National League in 1931. There were likely several reasons for the absence of a team, including the collapse of the economy in 1929 and the uncertainty in the Negro National League caused by the death of Rube Foster in 1928. Kenneth Kusmer claimed that economic conditions for African Americans in Cleveland deteriorated as early as 1928, which meant that many blacks in the city had less disposable income to spend on baseball games.[70] The Cubs already seemed to have two strikes against them when they started the season, but the team was much better on the field than the prior black professional teams in Cleveland. The Cubs won both games of a late-April doubleheader against the Nashville Elite Giants, which prompted the *Gazette* to say, "Both teams showed fine form for so early in the season, pulling off many fast plays. The Ohio club has a strong array of talent and is likely to hold its own in National league competition." Aside from the Buckeyes, the 1931 Cubs were the only Negro League team in Cleveland to finish the season with a winning record, at 29–24.[71] The team also had a young pitcher by the name of Satchel Paige, although the media in Cleveland never mentioned this fact.

In general, the media in Cleveland provided little information about the Cubs in 1931 but managed to dedicate space to another umpire-related incident. Supposedly the Cubs and the St. Louis Stars narrowly averted a riot on June 2, when the Stars walked off the field in the fifth inning of a game at Hooper Field. Umpire Cummings ejected Young, the catcher from the Stars, for his use of profanity during the game. When Young refused to leave the field, the umpires called time in an attempt to remove the player. By this point the rest of the Stars were angry and refused to return to the field to finish the game, which the Cubs led, 4–3. The umpires waited for five minutes for some type of resolution to the situation; when nothing changed they called the game a forfeit in favor of the Cubs. Fans supposedly started a "stampede" to the ticket box office in an attempt to get their money back. Cleveland police were called to maintain the peace and prevent further trouble. Even though it was technically an official game, the Cubs agreed to give the fans rain checks for any other game played by the team. The *Gazette* said that if incidents such as this continued, the strife and "poor grounds" could completely kill black baseball in Cleveland. Negro League baseball was already pressured by increasing unemployment numbers and the "economic depression." The team could not afford to anger the small number of fans that could afford to attend a game.[72]

Even though the Cubs were a good team, they were no match for the powerhouse teams of the league, on the field or in attendance totals. When the Homestead Grays played the Cubs in June at Kinsman Hardware Field, the Grays beat them "decisively." Attendance was less than 1,000, but the poor playing conditions at Kinsman Hardware Field were blamed rather than the teams.[73] The Homestead Grays drew about 4,000 fans when they played the Kansas City Monarchs at the new Cleveland Stadium downtown in August. Even though 4,000 was a big improvement over the figure at Kinsman Hardware Field, that size crowd in the cavernous Stadium likely seemed like nothing. The Grays returned again in September for a game at the Stadium against the Baltimore Black Sox and in October for a game against a group of white major and minor league players. Reportedly, the Grays drew about 4,000 for all of these matches at Cleveland Stadium.[74]

The Cubs planned to remain a team for the 1932 season but the league crumbled around them. A group of the leading men in Negro League baseball gathered at the Majestic Hotel in Cleveland before the season and attempted to salvage Cleveland as a site for organized black baseball. The men, led by Cum Posey from the Homestead Grays, formed the East-West League. Instead of maintaining the current Cubs team, Lem Williams and Artie Savage acted as sponsors for a new Cleveland team, the Stars. The *Chicago Defender* bragged that the East-West League planned to use African American umpires.[75] The Cubs were offered a spot in the Southern League in place of the Rube Foster Memorial Giants and were run by Jim Brown, who moved his team of "star" players (that included future Hall of Famer Cristóbal Torriente) to Cleveland to finish the Cubs' schedule. The *Chicago Defender* claimed, "Local fandom is all agog over the coming of Jim Brown's Cubs, who play here this season as associate members of the Southern league. Jim has some of the best men from the South and West in his lineup and figures his outfit will come through in the first half."[76] Despite this plethora of talent, the team no longer existed in Cleveland after the 1932 season.

The Stars attempted to stumble through the 1932 season under the direction of Lem Williams, but since the East-West League did not survive the summer, the Stars had little chance of success. The team appeared to play most of their games at Luna Park, and the *Defender* actually had high hopes for them when it reported, "With the full strength of the team finally assembled, the Stars exhibited a brand of ball that bids fair to take them far along the East-West pennant chase." The Stars went 8–14 in league play and were in last place when the East-West League folded.[77]

In 1933 Gus Greenlee stepped forward to help establish the second incarnation of the Negro National League, and owners gathered to brainstorm for ways to make it through the Great Depression. The owners wanted to place star players in management positions across the league to draw fans in struggling markets. Cleveland qualified as one of the cities in need of a boost from the management of the league. Another issue the NNL hierarchy tackled at their pre-season meeting was the topic of pay cuts. Major league players like Babe Ruth already accepted a pay cut for the 1933 season, and the owners wanted some of the Negro League stars to accept similar cuts.[78] Cleveland actually received the most focus at this meeting, as Gus Greenlee sent a telegram to the *Defender* that said, "All hands were out to strengthen Cleveland, recognized as the weak sister of the group." Greenlee called Cleveland an "experiment" and said that "something must be done to have a great team there." While the *Defender* claimed that no team owner wanted Cleveland to win the pennant, they at least hoped that "the Ohioans come through with a strong team and at least trouble the other winners."[79]

The *Defender* said that "the most sympathetic outfit in attendance" at this January meeting was the group that represented Cleveland. The Cleveland faction supposedly wanted to field a strong team but realized it "must rebuild from the bottom up." Negro League and Cleveland officials thought that signing a strong figure as manager would automatically help the club. They talked about sending Oscar Charleston to Cleveland and rumors were rampant that this move would happen.[80] All of the planning and rumors, however, were for naught. By the end of February, George Mitchell, the representative from the Cleveland squad, said his sponsors were unable to secure a ball park and would not join the new Negro National League for 1933. The absence of a Cleveland team left a vacancy in the league; Detroit was offered this now-empty position.[81] Supposedly when Cleveland expressed interest in joining the league, the other owners considered giving Cleveland some of their star players to help the team's development. The league was encouraged to offer the Detroit team the same deal, but by mid–May the club struggled and left the league.[82]

Even though Cleveland did not start the 1933 season with a professional black baseball team, there was a semi-pro team in Cleveland, the Giants, who bragged about their new second baseperson — a young woman named Isabelle Baxter. During the season opener at Hooper Field against the Canton Clowns, Baxter fielded the ball in five different plays. Her only "miscue," according to the *Defender*, was when she pulled the first baseman off the bag with an errant throw, following a lunging stop. As a hitter, Baxter singled and stroked two "hard-hit" balls to the outfield.[83] Baxter's days with the team were numbered; in July Prentice Byrd took control of the Giants and ran them for the rest of the 1933 season with the assistance of manager "Scrappy" Dixon. Baxter did not survive the roster changes that Byrd and Dixon instituted.[84]

When the Columbus Blue Birds left the Negro National League in August, the Cleveland Giants took the team's spot. There were several roster changes from the semi-pro sandlot Giants that played in Cleveland. The *Defender* said the Giants were engineered by Gus Greenlee and assembled by Bingo DeMoss as a consolidation of three clubs — Cleveland, Akron and Columbus. Prentice Byrd was still in charge of the team with help from Bill Ford. The Giants were the first local professional Negro League team to play regularly at Cleveland Stadium. Unfortunately the Giants drew nothing close to the crowd that came to see a game promoted by Lem Williams between the Pittsburgh Crawfords and the Philadelphia Stars that drew a reported 10,000 fans. The crowd was the largest for an African American sporting event to date in Cleveland. The Giants were no better on the field than the other Negro League teams in Cleveland; in early September they were in dead last with a record of 2–14. They even supposedly forfeited four games to Nashville when they failed to show for a series. [85]

* * *

There was a new Negro National League team in Cleveland, the Red Sox, to take the place of the Giants in 1934. Coincidentally, this was the same year records for the *Call and Post* were readily available. Throughout the season, sports editor Bill Finger frequently complained about the lack of information he received from Red Sox personnel. Finger was unable to relay game scores and schedules to fans, which likely made it difficult for people in Cleveland to follow the Red Sox. Finger instead used the space in his columns to voice his thoughts on Negro League baseball in Cleveland and the reasons for black baseball's struggles in the city. He also used the opportunity to offer to advise Negro League teams in Cleveland and encouraged teams to listen to this unsolicited advice. While the writers at the *Gazette* occasionally criticized teams, Finger was the first to really call out people affiliated with Negro League baseball in Cleveland. For example, in his first column of 1934, he criticized the Negro Leagues' publicity skills, specifically the Cleveland teams. In a later column, Finger criticized segregated sports in the United States. Midway through the 1934 season, he bashed the Red Sox for their lack of communication with the media. Finger complained that he was unable to obtain specific details on games and players, adding that he had to chase the Red Sox for information.[86]

Prentice Byrd and Dr. E.L. Langrum were the owners of the Red Sox and Lem Williams was in charge of business operations for the team. The group hired Bobby Williams, a protégé of Rube Foster, to manage the team. Williams received high praise from the *Call and Post*, who thought he had an enviable record as a player and later manager with the Pittsburgh Crawfords. Williams, who was credited with signing most of the star Crawfords players, also played for the Cleveland Tigers in 1928 during the twilight of his playing career. Finger thought Williams was a "veteran of the old school" and that he had a tall order to build a new organization in Cleveland. Even though Finger said Williams had the full support of ownership, he thought it might take a few years to establish a successful team in Cleveland. Finger believed it would take time to develop the young players that the Red Sox signed for the 1934 season. It is likely he wanted to set the bar low for the team so that fans would not be disappointed if the Red Sox did not perform well. Finger also regretted that Williams' playing days were behind him, because the Red Sox could use such a solid player on their roster.[87]

Finger believed the Red Sox could surprise the league in 1934, but thought that the Nashville Elite Giants, the Kansas City Monarchs, or the New Orleans Crescents were probably the teams to beat. Finger firmly believed that Cleveland "can be made one of the best, if not the leader of colored ball towns." He noted that several black infielders would improve the Indians' roster and make them contenders. The Red Sox spent the first part of the year barnstorming through the South, and opened the season on Sunday, June 3 at League Park.[88] This was the first black professional team to share League Park with the Cleveland Indians and Finger said that African American players were equal to or better than the white players on the Indians. While attendance figures for most of the Red Sox games were unclear, they drew an estimated 2,500 fans on a couple of occasions.[89]

In September the Red Sox left the league and chose to play the rest of the season independently, primarily due to dissatisfaction about how the league was run. Both Dr. E.L. Langrum of the Red Sox and Cum Posey of the Homestead Grays were upset about how the Negro National League spent money. There was some displeasure over how certain teams were treated, specifically Baltimore, Newark, Cleveland, and Atlantic City. The complaint was the league hierarchy forced all of the teams in these cities to follow their will; Finger referred to these teams as the "goats of the League." Posey said that Cleveland was shunned after the team complained about the cancellation of a game in Pittsburgh against the Homestead Grays. The Red Sox continually protested their unbalanced schedule, but supposedly the secretary of the Negro National League refused to deal with Lem Williams. Even though the major clubs like the Chicago American Giants and the Pittsburgh Crawfords offered to help the smaller clubs succeed in 1934, they still neglected to provide them with assistance. Finger thought the powerful figures in Negro League baseball could help the entire league if they made sure all of the teams were strong. A strong league would draw attention and possibly help African American players reach the major leagues.[90]

Finger believed the Negro Leagues should aim to draw white fans and suggested that a successful franchise could attract both white and black fans. He also thought that teams needed to focus on promotion, advertising and the players' on-field conduct.[91] Teams in Cleveland received failing grades for most of these suggestions from Finger, who actually compared black sports in Cleveland to a desert. Like a desert, Cleveland had fertile soil if one knew how to use it properly. It seemed like every year there was someone who claimed they could give Cleveland "one of the best teams of its kind anywhere in the country," and that "owners have spent large sums of money in order that the fans might enjoy the comforts of a vastly improved place to play." During most years, the teams played terribly, crowds stayed away, and there were no financial rewards for the owners. Finger accused the owners of the past Cleveland teams with a lack of thought toward the future. These owners were primarily concerned with finding enough players for their rosters, without much thought to a field, transportation, or the crowds their team would draw. Finger claimed that owners never put themselves in the fans' shoes; instead, they were worried about what promoters thought. If the teams managed to promote themselves, they did so only at the beginning of the season. Cleveland was a good location for a team, according to Finger, but an owner needed to exhibit patience while starting their team.[92]

The two main culprits for the string of team failures in Cleveland, according to Finger, were a lack of promotion and mediocre play. While fans, specifically migrants from the South, were eager to see early teams like the Tate Stars play, their interest dwindled when they were forced to watch a consistent loser. Many of the teams were comprised of young, local players with one or two veterans added for balance. None of them were able to compete on equal footing with teams like the Indianapolis ABCs, the Chicago American Giants or the Detroit Stars. While it was exciting for fans to see the star players from these teams, the experience lost its luster when fans were forced to sit through a number of lopsided beatings.[93]

The other factor that hindered Negro League baseball in the city of Cleveland was its lack of suitable ballpark facilities. Even though Tate/Hooper Field was highly touted in the African American press throughout the 1920s, Finger admitted the park was a mess. Some of its faults included a poorly covered grandstand whose roof had no paint and a lack of "compact construction." Many seats were uncovered and were at the mercy of the sun on a hot summer day. The baseball diamond was "skinned," the outfield grass was sparse, and the ground was rocky. The restroom facilities were reportedly "atrocious and backward," and long lines of men actually chose to urinate on the right field wall in full view of the fans rather than brave the bathrooms. Players and some fans frequently used foul language, which supposedly drove "decent" fans away from the ballpark.[94]

Finger offered solutions for the major problems that affected Negro League baseball in the city of Cleveland, many of which were relatively obvious. He thought the teams needed a satisfactory ballpark, preferably one that they did not have to share with anyone else. This ballpark should have nicer facilities for the fans and a better playing surface for the teams. If teams were unable to afford grass, they at least needed to grade the field and make sure it was level. Teams needed to use publicity to promote themselves in the newspaper, radio, and "every agency possible." Rather than a sole reliance on the local weeklies, such as the African American papers, teams needed to reach out to the white dailies to ensure that they did not just lump Negro League games in with all of the local sandlot contests.[95]

Finger believed teams needed to cater to fans in order to attract their interest and to get them to return to games. Teams should provide personal stories and histories of their players, as well as plenty of pictures of the team's members. These pictures could go to the newspapers, public officials, or anyone that could spread the word about the team. Finger even went out on a limb and suggested that fans needed to feel as if they had an ownership stake in the team. An easy and inexpensive way to accomplish this was to hold a contest to name the new Negro League team in Cleveland. The teams could also provide free passes to children, and could hand out as many as five or six thousand free tickets. This would serve two purposes: It would put fans in the seats and create a small army of dedicated fans. These children could convince their parents to come to games with them, and the parents would be forced to buy tickets for themselves. The Negro League teams could also make black baseball universal in appeal to both white and black fans. More fans in the seats equaled increased revenues, which could be used for better players, equipment, and more publicity.[96]

African American baseball in Cleveland received a big publicity boost in October of 1934 from a barnstorming match headlined by Dizzy Dean and Satchel Paige at League Park. Finger thought such games were important because they increased the visibility of Negro League players and showed fans they were talented enough to compete against white major leaguers. Black stars like Paige "never get their due" in Finger's opinion. In fact, Finger criticized Oscar Charleston (manager of the African American team) because he removed Paige from the game after six innings. Paige was in the midst of a perfect game — no hits, walks or errors allowed for the first eighteen batters — when Charleston removed him. A perfect game against Dean's team could have drawn national attention.[97] Finger drew parallels between Paige and Dean, sparked by Dean's decision to hold out for more money from the St. Louis Cardinals at the beginning of the 1935 season. Finger lamented that Satchel Paige would like to hold out for more money but like most Negro League players, "he probably shall never see a well-padded pay envelope."[98] Paige actually fared quite well in a monetary sense during his time with the Negro Leagues. While one may understand the point that Finger tried to make, Negro League owners were almost always willing to pay handsomely to receive Paige's services.

Barnstorming matches between famous teams were a large attendance draw in Cleveland, but these games were not immune to problems. In September of 1935 the Pittsburgh Crawfords were scheduled to play the Homestead Grays in a night game at Cleveland Stadium. When it was time for the game, the Nashville Elites walked onto the field instead of the Crawfords. The story around the mishap was convoluted, and seemed to stem from a personal argument between Gus Greenlee and the Grays' business manager, Sonny Jackson. Jackson reportedly worked for Greenlee for a while and sued the Crawfords' owner for back pay. Greenlee claimed he would not play the Grays until they agreed to fire Jackson, which the Grays refused to do. When the Crawfords backed out of the game, Cum Posey was able to bring the Nashville club to replace them. When Greenlee heard the teams intended to play the game anyway, he was suddenly willing to play the Grays. Posey was hesitant to turn the Elites away after they traveled all the way to Cleveland for the game.[99]

Barnstorming matches, such as a Crawfords-Grays game, were the only professional black baseball Cleveland saw in 1935. Cleveland had no hometown team to follow and had to satisfy their desire for Negro League baseball by watching teams from other cities. The Red Sox folded after the 1934 season and Dr. E.L. Langrum, former co-owner of the Red Sox, and Wilbur Hayes, a local promoter, attempted to assemble a semi-pro team to play on local sandlots. Finger was disappointed by this, primarily because he thought that young players developed skills in the more stringent league contests.[100] A July game between the Pittsburgh Crawfords and the Chicago American Giants at League Park drew an estimated 8,000 fans, so there were people in Cleveland that wanted to watch Negro League baseball. Finger thought the league should bring more of these types of games to Cleveland.[101]

It was five years before Cleveland saw another professional Negro League baseball team. In 1939 the Jacksonville Red Caps transferred sixteen players to Cleveland after a spring training stint in Jacksonville and Daytona, Florida.[102] Marceilus Mason, secretary and treasurer of the new team, named Alonzo Mitchell, a former Negro League pitcher, as manager. Mason planned to hold a massive pre-season event so that fans could help select a name for the team and meet the new players. It was unclear how much influence the fan input had over the name choice of "Cleveland Bears," which the team announced in April. Lem Williams supposedly helped secure the franchise deal and was considered a candidate for Negro League commissioner by the *Call and Post*. The paper hoped that the beginning of the new team's season would "be one of the outstanding sporting and social events of the season." Many speculated that the new Cleveland club would be one of the strongest in the country and could finish high in the league standings for 1939. Wilbur Hayes, the future general manager of the Cleveland Buckeyes and a local sports promoter, was appointed as the umpire of the Bears and was responsible for the team's publicity. It seemed like the Bears recognized the importance of better publicity and fan relations. They heeded Finger's advice when it came to team name selection, and also announced that they planned to place the Bears' uniforms on display for fans to view before the season started. The *Call and Post* and the Bears' officials never said why it was important to put the team's uniforms on display for the public. It seems as if they hoped the uniforms would generate excitement about the team prior to the start of the season.[103]

Ken Jessamy, the new sports editor for the *Call and Post*, was cautiously optimistic about the new Negro League squad before the season started. He admitted he knew almost nothing about the Bears players and that he based his opinions on statistics from the previous season. While Jessamy said that the Bears looked good on paper, unfortunately the team does not play based on their performance from the previous season. Jessamy was glad to see a Negro League team return to Cleveland and thought the fans would support it. He admitted, "We have learned from observation however, that they are interested in seeing the real McCoy and anything short of that interests them as much as another piece of coal would a tenant of Hades." Jessamy said that Cleveland fans were smart enough to realize a team was a failure, and added, "In the past one or two local lads have attempted to pass off damaged goods and wake up holding the bag." He advised the Bears' leadership to heed the mistakes of their predecessors to keep from making the same mistakes.[104]

Before the season even started the Bears had trouble finding a location to play their home games. The team initially planned to share League Park with the Indians, but after they were unable to settle on financial terms with stadium officials, they instead agreed to play their home games at

Cleveland Stadium during the 1939 season.[105] This was a less desirable location for two reasons: the location of Cleveland Stadium and its massive size. League Park was located on the east side of Cleveland at the intersection of East 66th and Lexington avenues, surrounded by residential neighborhoods. Cleveland Stadium was downtown along Lake Erie, a further distance from where people lived and a larger inconvenience. Most Negro League games in Cleveland at this point had an average attendance of 3,000 to 6,000 fans. Even a large crowd by Bears standards was dwarfed by the cavernous Cleveland Stadium, which held nearly 80,000 people. Jessamy thought the Bears made a big mistake when they failed to secure League Park but understood the rent costs were prohibitive. The owners were willing to spend money on the team but thought funds were better spent on players.[106]

The Bears made the best of their situation, as they drew 7,000 fans to their season opener against the Chicago American Giants. Mayor Harold T. Burton threw out the first pitch, and the Bears won both games of the doubleheader, 5–3 and 5–1. Jessamy thought the young team hustled during the games and that Mitchell was a "capable and shrewd" manager. The Bears looked so good that some started to suggest an exhibition game with the Indians after both teams' seasons were over.

There were some complaints about the quality of the umpires at the games, but Lem Williams assured Jessamy that he'd solve the problems for future contests. There were no more public complaints about umpires following this statement, so either the situation improved or the media abandoned the subject. In the first few weeks of the season, the Bears continued to play hard and found success; at one point they won six games in a row. Attendance was reportedly steady at around 4,000, and Jessamy thought fans were treated to better baseball than they had seen in the past. He added that fans were used to seeing the team give up by the second game of a doubleheader, but the Bears continued to play hard for eighteen innings. Jessamy said, "Cleveland will support the squad as long as they continue to play the sort of ball that they are playing now and unless I overestimate the calibre [sic] of Alonzo Mitchell, the team's manager, they will." The Bears actually led the league in the standings at the end of May but fell behind the other teams after a poor road trip. The *Call and Post* blamed poor umpiring for a set of road losses in Chicago.[107]

The Bears took another piece of advice from Bill Finger in June when

Lem Williams gave away 50 tickets for the team's June 17 game. The tickets were for box seats and were reserved for the first 50 women that asked for them at Boyd's Music Store on Cedar Avenue in Cleveland. The Bears also planned to host track star Jesse Owens at Cleveland Stadium during the last game of the season. They offered any fan the chance to sprint against Owens in an exhibition race, and also planned to see if Owens could set a new record for rounding the bases. The Bears had a .500 record at the end of the first half, and were recognized by fans nationally when three players and the team's manager were named to the East-West All-Star Game. The players were pitcher Leo "Preacher" Henry, third baseman Parnell Woods and outfielder Raymond "Smokey" Owens; Mitchell was to serve as a coach on the team. It was quite a compliment to the young team, as all of the players were under the age of 30, with the exception of Mitchell, the manager. Jessamy reminded fans the team played hard every day and that a loss just meant things didn't go the Bears' way that particular day.[108]

In early August, J.L. Pickering, a representative of Bears owner J.B. Greer, announced that Lem Williams was no longer connected to the team. Williams, who worked as an advertising agent and a general manager for the team, was supposedly targeted by ownership because they believed he did not promote the team properly. Jessamy said the size of crowds dropped throughout the season for the Bears, and since the team was a good attendance draw on the road, the team's hierarchy blamed Williams for the attendance slide. Attendance figures were never publicly released, so it is difficult to determine the accuracy of that statement. Ownership also blamed Williams for the debacle with League Park, and thought he should have secured the facility for the Bears. A rift grew between Williams and Greer's group as the season progressed, and the two sides finally decided to terminate Williams' contract toward the end of summer. The split was so bitter, Pickering claimed that Williams was never officially the team's general manager even though numerous public statements listed him as such. Jessamy, who never publicly complained about Williams before this point, seemed elated over his dismissal from the Bears. When he learned that the Bears planned to return for a second season in the Negro American League, he said it "is as much good news as is the report that Williams is no longer connected with the club."[109]

When Jessamy reflected on the 1939 season, he did not blame

Williams for the drop in attendance. While he admitted that nobody knew the real reason, the best guess suggested it was due to "poor and inadequate promotion, faulty umpiring and poor management." Even Jesse Owens, a graduate of Cleveland's East Tech High School, failed to put a dent in the cavernous Cleveland Stadium when he offered to face any willing local fans in August. Ownership claimed they weren't discouraged by the first season's attendance and planned to make some slight adjustments to the team's roster for the 1940 season.[110] A fan named Arnold Brown wrote to the *Call and Post* after the 1939 season to complain about the lack of a solid African American baseball structure in Cleveland, both at the professional and semi-professional level. Brown claimed that he lived in smaller cities with better Negro League teams than Cleveland and added, "Your city is far behind the times when it comes to helping our boys develop into useful players, and be a credit to the city and the race from a baseball point of view."[111]

Before the 1940 season started, a "citizens committee" wrote to one of Cleveland's weekly publications to call for a boycott of the Bears. The unsigned complaint expressed anger over the fact that the Bears were owned by a white man. Jessamy did not call Lem Williams out by name, but implied that he was the culprit behind the letter when he said, "It is our belief that this 'citizens committee' was born in the none too fertile mind of a gentleman who last year was connected with the team, during the earlier part of the season, but was dismissed at the half-way mark." Jessamy was not concerned about the fact that the Bears' owner was white since there were several white owners in both the Negro National and Negro American leagues and with various sandlot clubs. Since Cleveland spent several years without a professional black baseball team, Jessamy said there was ample opportunity for an African American owner to organize a team. He complimented the Bears and said, "They played good, hard ball and gave the fans the impression that they were playing for all they were worth." Any criticism that Jessamy had was directed toward the umpires and the people in charge of publicity and promotions for the team.[112]

One of the reasons Jessamy thought Williams was behind the anonymous letter, was the large number of compliments it directed to Williams. The letter claimed that Williams could probably qualify as one of the officials of the Negro American League if he was willing to leave Cleveland. Fay Young, a writer with the *Chicago Defender*, pointed out the fact that

Williams had many opportunities to succeed in Cleveland but that he continued to fail. Young had a valid point; Williams' name was tied to professional black teams in Cleveland for at least ten years, and all of those teams failed after just one season. Jessamy challenged the anonymous letter writer to come public with his claims, and said if he wanted to sling mud he should not do it anonymously.[113]

J.B. Greer, the white owner of the Bears, responded to the anonymous criticism and defended his actions with a letter to the *Call and Post*. Greer, the station master of the Jacksonville Railroad Terminal Company of Jacksonville, Florida, said he oversaw about 80 red caps, and some of them decided to form a baseball team in 1925. Greer claimed that his management company at the railroad asked him to sponsor the baseball team as a "recreation advantage" to its employees around 1935. The team likely played on local sandlots in the ten-year period between the formation of the Red Caps and Greer's involvement with the team. Greer said he was more than happy to assist the players with their team since he was born and raised in the South and "understood their (African Americans') need for assistance and encouragement along such endeavors." Greer assured Cleveland fans that the Bears players were good men when he said, "These boys are well and orderly, good dressers and conduct themselves as gentlemen and good sports on and off the field." The players supposedly worked as red caps at the Jacksonville terminal during the off season. Greer bragged that he provided each player with a medical exam each year "to protect their health and welfare" and paid all of the men's expenses from the time they left Jacksonville until they returned after the season. Greer claimed he wasn't involved with baseball to make money since he had a good job and added that he didn't know of any other owner who did as much for their team as he did. Supposedly he just wanted to give Cleveland fans "a good honest clean game of baseball every time they come to the park regardless of who their opponents may be."[114]

Greer and the Bears made one major change for the 1940 season as they planed to play their games at League Park and abandon the cavernous Cleveland Stadium. Greer said he hoped this would make the team more accessible for fans and that it would allow fans to travel less in order to see a game. The Bears planned to charge a flat entry fee of 55 cents for each game, with children admitted to the park at half price. The team hoped to endear itself to Cleveland fans, according to Greer.[115]

The Bears opened the season on May 26 at League Park against the St. Louis Stars and lost both games of a doubleheader before 5,100 fans. Despite the losses, the *Call and Post* considered the home opener a success both "financially and socially." Jim Williams was named the manager for the 1940 season, and many believed the team had an excellent pitching staff and a roster that was an improvement over the 1939 club. One of the promising young pitchers was Lefty White, whose pitches had speed and control; Jessamy even went so far as to compare him to star Indians pitcher Bob Feller. Jessamy called new manager Jim Williams the "goat of the game" because of his terrible play at first base and at the plate during the home opener. Supposedly, Williams was not going to play during the game. When the regular first baseman was pulled from the lineup because of an injury, Williams inserted himself in his place.[116]

Williams felt the need to defend the Bears for their poor play against the Stars since the team seemed lethargic and lacked its usual hustle. He claimed the team's bus was involved in an accident on April 5, but the Bears never told anyone about the incident. Ernest "Mint" Jones, the regular first baseman, supposedly broke his arm in the accident and Al "Cool Papa" Frazier received eleven stitches in his foot. The Bears played without their first-string catcher, Joe Brown, who broke his leg during a pre-season practice game, and three other players who were reportedly injured in the bus accident. Williams claimed the team had an excellent record on the road before the home opener, and reportedly the Bears were 15-7 in pre-season play.[117]

By June the fans were losing patience with the Bears, according to Jessamy, who also admitted that the once promising young pitchers were terrible. After a four-game losing streak, Jessamy said, "The Bears were as sad as McKinley's funeral and linotypist Henry Jacobs, who attended the solemn rites, swore even the horses cried on that occasion." Jessamy said the team lacked confidence in itself, and in the same article said the Bears needed to play well the next week since fans were ready to walk away from the team. If the Bears' players thought they were in a do-or-die type of situation, it likely added to their stress and lack of confidence.[118] The Bears managed to beat the Crawfords during a doubleheader the next week, which prompted the *Call and Post* to say the team was "rejuvenated." Jessamy said the games against the Crawfords were the first time he saw any spark from the Bears during the 1940 season. Perhaps the rejuvenation was due to the firing of Jim Williams and the rehiring of Alonzo Mitchell. Jessamy said, "It did our hearts good to hear Mitchell riding the opposition pitchers from the dugout and yelling words of encouragement to his mounsmen [*sic*]." He also thought the players seemed to enjoy themselves more once Mitchell regained control of the team. Jessamy gave full credit to Mitchell for the team's victories.[119]

One of the figures that worked behind the scenes to salvage the Bears was a man by the name of Harry Walker. Walker was a prominent figure in African American sports in Cleveland who worked as an announcer for the Cleveland Indians during the 1920 World Series. He also worked as an announcer at other sporting events, particularly football, promoted sporting events in Cleveland, and worked as an umpire for Negro League games. In fact, Walker was an umpire for the 1939 Bears but was appointed the business manager of the 1940 team. Jessamy commended Walker for his promotional work with the Bears as their business manager and said that he "has been doing a yoeman's [*sic*] job trying to get people into the ball park on Sundays." Walker was supposedly able to work well with the radio stations, the newspapers and fans "simply because Walker is a pretty swell fellow and deserves a better break than the one he is getting."[120]

Despite Walker's promotion of the Bears and the "rejuvenation" Jessamy spoke of, the team was finished — by mid–July they were out of the league. The Bears were scheduled to play a game on June 29 at League Park against the Birmingham Black Barons but the Bears were no-shows for the game. The team, which last appeared in Cleveland on June 10, failed to inform Walker they would not be back. The departure "left a bad taste in the mouth," of fans who were already disgusted with the play of the Bears, according to Jessamy. Jessamy criticized the Bears for poor management and for starting the season with a large group of injured players. While the 1939 squad was repeatedly complimented for its hard work and hustle, Jessamy said the 1940 team "conducted themselves like a bunch of third rate sandlotters." Fan support dwindled throughout the season, which Jessamy attributed to the Bears' losing record and poor play.[121]

Despite the collapse of the Bears, Jessamy insisted that Harry Walker deserved high praise for his work with the team and that the business manager should not be blamed for the Bears' mistakes. Jessamy cited Walker's publicity work and said he got the team more "goodwill" newspaper and radio publicity than any other Cleveland sports venture. Walker believed the team owed fans an apology, not only for skipping town, but because they allowed an inferior team on the field in the first place. He went so far as to submit a letter to the *Call and Post*, where he asked for the fans' forgiveness and apologized for the poor play of the Bears. Walker claimed he begged ownership to add more players but they refused. He lashed out at J.L. Pickering, a representative for the owner in Cleveland, and claimed that the last time he saw Pickering, he seemed like a man who was ready to flee. Walker said he continued to work with Pickering because he wanted to make sure he received all the money that was owed to him. Unfortunately, the Bears still reportedly owed Walker money for his services and also had an outstanding bill at a printing shop in Cleveland. The *Call and Post* attempted to contact the Bears at their Jacksonville headquarters but received no response.[122]

As the Bears fell apart in Cleveland, even normal barnstorming events seemed to fail in the city during the 1940 season. In August a number of local men from semi-pro teams were selected to play an exhibition game against an all-star team from Puerto Rico; the game was scheduled for August 11 at Cleveland Stadium. The game was highly touted for several weeks in the media, and the local team hoped to earn enough money to pay the entry fee as an associate member of the Negro American League. Alonzo Boone, a former Bears player (and future Cleveland Buckeye), managed the local team. The Puerto Rican club was the reigning champion of the South American Winter League, and the *Call and Post* called them "one of the flashiest and best balanced clubs in the country." Unfortunately, the Puerto Rican team disbanded before it ever reached Cleveland. Since the weekly papers were printed by the time officials in Cleveland received notice of the cancellation, hundreds of fans showed up at Cleveland Stadium to see the game. The *Call and Post* cited "the baseball jinx that has plagued Cleveland since the opening of the present season," as far as black baseball was concerned. This "jinx" did not scare away all teams and fans in 1940. When the Cuban Stars and the Homestead Grays played an exhibition game at Cleveland Stadium in August, one unnamed couple was married on the field during a break in the action.[123]

Negro League baseball in Cleveland between 1922 and 1940 experienced a rather tumultuous existence. Ten different teams tried to survive in the city, yet all ten teams managed to fail in two seasons or less. Teams in Cleveland faced the same problems that all Negro League teams did during this time period but also needed to clear additional hurdles. The uncertainty of the league, particularly between 1926 and 1933, obviously hindered team development in Cleveland. The Great Depression challenged even the most popular and economically viable teams in both the Negro Leagues and the major leagues. The economy for African Americans in Cleveland began to deteriorate as early as 1928, which meant that fans had less disposable income to spend on a leisure activity. The Cleveland teams never found a satisfactory field at which to play their home games. They had to choose between prohibitively high rental rates at the Indians' parks or inferior conditions at the local fields. Some of these fields were either miserable places in which to see a baseball game or they were located at a distance that was inconvenient for fans. While the owners did their best to organize a team each season, the fact remained that most of these teams were terrible. Only one, the 1931 Cleveland Cubs, had a winning record, while the Cleveland Bears managed to finish at .500.

There were obviously a number of reasons to explain why so many teams failed in Cleveland. What was a bit more mysterious was why people were willing to start a new team almost immediately after their predecessor failed. During this eighteen-year period, Cleveland was either the fifth- or sixth-largest city in America in terms of population. The city saw a great influx of African Americans after World War I, particularly from the South, who now earned a decent living working in one of the city's many manufacturing plants. Many Negro League officials and city leaders thought that Cleveland was an untapped resource when it came to Negro League baseball. Even though many different men thought they had found the formula for success in Negro League baseball in Cleveland, they were always unable to overcome the standard problems that affected teams in the city. By 1942 the booming war-time economy and a second wave of Southern migrants gave Cleveland its best opportunity for Negro League baseball success. Once the Buckeyes established an agreement to play at League Park and proved that they could win baseball games, there was finally a recipe for success in Cleveland.

2

The Push for Integration
and the Formation
of the Buckeyes

In 1942, African Americans in the city of Cleveland capitalized on the wartime swell in popularity of Negro League baseball as the Negro American League added the Cleveland Buckeyes to its ranks.[1] The stage was set for the addition of a team in the city by the end of 1941, and while the African American weekly newspaper, the *Call and Post*, supported the new team, the writers made clear their preference for major league baseball as opposed to a Jim Crow version of the sport. Unfortunately for the Buckeyes, the writers for the paper were more concerned with arranging major league tryouts for Buckeyes players than they were promoting these same players as "Buckeyes," often overlooking the Negro League team in the push for integration. Throughout the early 1940s, the *Call and Post* viewed itself as a potential catalyst for civil rights advancement and believed that African American newspapers had a duty to promote integration and equality. The writers from the *Call and Post* and other black papers hoped that through their publications they could further equality in all aspects of American society. In addition to these larger concerns, many African American writers were already frustrated with the disorganized leadership of the Negro National and Negro American leagues and the leagues' lack of communication with the press. Game statistics were often difficult to come by, which made it hard for the press and fans to follow Negro League teams. Teams also had a confusing and hectic schedule that included many meaningless exhibition games scattered among league contests. Throughout 1941 and 1942, the *Call and Post* actively followed the exploits of pitcher Satchel

Paige, even though he had no official ties to the city until 1948. Paige was a symbol of the Negro Leagues — a popular player who earned a high salary in comparison to other African American players and who also increased attendance at league and exhibition games. Despite their obvious admiration for Paige, the famous pitcher did not escape criticism from the *Call and Post*, as well as African American writers with other newspapers. Paige frustrated writers with his penchant for breaking deals and his supposed lukewarm support of integrating the major leagues.

The Buckeyes fought an uphill battle as they entered the Negro American League, often considered weaker than its counterpart, the Negro National League. While both leagues struggled through financial hardships throughout their existence, the NNL had the benefit of proximity between its rival cities. The NNL (or "East" for the benefit of the annual East-West All-Star Game) had teams in New York City, Newark, Philadelphia, Baltimore and Pittsburgh. The NAL (or "West") had teams scattered throughout the South and West, in Cleveland, Memphis, Birmingham, Chicago, and Kansas City. This would become especially challenging once World War II rationing led to travel restrictions among Negro League teams. Aside from limits on gasoline and rubber for tires, teams were all but forbidden to use their buses for transportation to and from games. While train service was much more feasible for teams traveling between cities such as Philadelphia and New York, train transportation would not be as logical a travel option between cities such as Kansas City and Cleveland.[2] The NNL of the early 1930s was the second variation of the league (the other Negro National League started by Rube Foster failed during the 1920s), and while several NAL teams were also competing during the early years of the Depression, that league did not officially organize until 1937.[3] Both leagues lacked the structured authority and organized publicity that the white major leagues enjoyed, a point that left many observers, particularly the African American press, frustrated.

Pittsburgh Courier writer Randy Dixon was a frequent and vocal critic of the poor governance of the Negro Leagues and criticized the NNL in his "Sports Bugle" column from 1940 entitled "'Your Man' Makes Discovery Baseball Meeting is Merely a Scheme to Embarrass Newspapermen." In this column, Dixon went as far as to claim that the NNL did not hold a scheduled meeting to discuss business, but called the meeting just so they could have an opportunity to laugh in the faces of reporters and tell them they were not welcome. Dixon said that reporters were excluded in order to prevent publicity on league matters and said, "Isn't it the same public from which the league expects support, to pay the tariff so to speak? Yes, it is, but the league seemingly thinks that the public should please the league instead of the league pleasing the public."[4] It was possible the league wanted to avoid publicity in order to mask its disorganization and lack of structured leadership. In a column printed several months later, Dixon picked up his criticism of the NNL right where he left off and said that "the league is a downright nuisance, tolerated but not greatly valued." Fans tolerated disorganized African American sports in the 1920s because "money flowed easily" but those days were long gone, according to Dixon. He added, "Today, new economic and social forces have jelled to such point that the time-hallowed cry of "support a race institution" doesn't mean a thing unless that race institution is on or near a keel with its particular rivals."[5]

It was obvious that Dixon had grown weary of the disorganization and lack of communication with the leagues and felt that fans deserved a better product for their money. Since many African American fans chose to attend white major league games instead of Negro League games, Dixon felt that the Negro Leagues should provide a product comparable to the major leagues if they were to succeed with the public.

Al Sweeney of the *Call and Post* jumped on the Negro League criticism bandwagon shortly after the inception of the new team in Cleveland. In his weekly column, Sweeney admitted that Negro League baseball was often the target of sportswriters and said, "There have been so many vulnerable spots in baseball as played by the darker diamond players, that sports writers for want of a weekly topic for their pillars can always find an unexploited angle of the game to sling their typographical darts." Sweeney cited poor communication with team ownership across Negro League baseball as a reason for the bad coverage but said he was encouraged by the appointment of a publicity director in the NAL. The publicity director was to be in charge of notifying papers of scores and statistics on individual players. Sweeney said, "It is the first step towards giving the public a break." If this new director lived up to his assigned duties, the press would finally have batting and pitching statistics on all of the league's players.[6] There were varying theories as to why it was so difficult to obtain statistics for Negro League teams. Compiling statistics would likely cost owners money and these same statistics could later be used as bargaining chips for players who demanded a salary increase over the prior year. If there were no hard statistics to prove a player's skill, the owner could more easily justify withholding a raise. By 1944 the leagues finally settled an agreement with the Elias Bureau to maintain statistics.[7]

Other reporters, such as Wendell Smith from the *Courier*, favored a different approach. He chose to criticize fans for supporting major league baseball even while it refused to integrate. Smith is best known as the writer that advocated the signing of Jackie Robinson in the mid–1940s and who traveled with Robinson during his early days with the Brooklyn Dodgers. In a 1938 *Courier* article, Smith said:

> Why we continue to flock to major league ball parks, spending our hard earned dough, screaming and hollering, stamping our feet and clapping our hands, begging and pleading for some white batter to knock some white pitcher's ears off, almost having fits if the home team loses and crying for job when they win, is a question that probably will never be answered satisfactorily. What in the world are we thinking about anyhow?[8]

Smith criticized black fans' attendance at major league games as long as teams refused to integrate. Even though these teams refused to integrate, they were still more than willing to take the money of African American fans when they walked through the gate. Smith wished that fans would recognize this inequality and stop spending money at major league games.[9] John Fuster, the sports editor who replaced Sweeney at the *Call and Post* by 1942, followed the same path and criticized the white major leagues for their short-sightedness as he said, "Negroes spend thousands of dollars every year at big league baseball parks. Even in those big cities where there are jim-crow stands 'For Colored,' they flock in to watch their home teams. But regardless of the fact that thousands more of these dollars would flow into big league tills if Negroes were allowed to participate, the high moguls say 'nothing doing.'"[10]

Despite the various criticisms of Negro League baseball, the *Call and Post* and various Cleveland dignitaries were pleased to secure a new professional team by the end of 1941. While black professional teams had come and gone in the city throughout the years, the Buckeyes would be the first solid attempt at success in the city by a team that was a member of the major circuit of Negro League baseball. Events began to align during 1941 that made the possibility of a team a reality. African American and Erie,

Pennsylvania, native Ernest Wright came to Cleveland with the hopes of purchasing a baseball team. He eventually took over the Cleveland White Sox, a semi-pro team, and upgraded its uniforms and equipment. It was not long before Wright came into contact with local sports promoter Wilbur Hayes, who had been promoting sporting events in Cleveland since World War I. Wright placed Hayes in charge of the business side of his team.[11] By June of 1941, Hayes was promoting a game at League Park (home of the Cleveland Indians) between the Birmingham Black Barons and the Cleveland White Sox, for whom Hayes had secured an associate membership in the NAL. The contest was dubbed "Alabama Day" and promoters hoped that recent migrants from the South would be drawn to the game.[12] Within two weeks of this promotion, Hayes and Wright purchased half interest in the NAL St. Louis Stars. By merging players from the Stars with players from the White Sox, the two men hoped to hold a home game in Cleveland every Sunday the Indians were not scheduled to play at League Park. The two also had a rather ambitious plan to build the team its own stadium in Cleveland — a dream that was never realized. Hayes promised *Call and Post* writer Sweeney that the paper would receive NAL standings regularly as well as statistics on the new Cleveland team's games and players. Despite criticism in his weekly column regarding the leadership of the Negro Leagues, Sweeney appeared ready to give Hayes a chance when he said, "Hayes has given his solemn promise that the club will be handled in a business like fashion." For the remainder of 1941, the intent was for six of the St. Louis players to play with the Cleveland White Sox rather than move the entire team to Cleveland.[13]

Even though he appeared willing to give the Buckeyes a chance, Sweeney at times throughout the summer of 1941 referred to Cleveland as a dead sports town and cited a lack of interest in baseball among fans of the city. His explanation for this lack of interest was that Cleveland residents had lost confidence in promoters, who had given fans raw deals in the past. Sweeney stood behind Wright and Hayes and even went as far as naming Wright the "Gamest Guy of the Year" by mid–July, even though the year was only half over.[14] One must imagine that in a story that praises Wright yet barely makes mention of Hayes that the latter may be one of the "promoters" Sweeney believes fans do not fully trust. It was also quite likely that Sweeney, following in the footsteps of local writers before him, was taking a stab at Lem Williams. Within a week of this article, the *Call and Post* published a letter from Hayes that addressed local fans and assured them that he and Wright spent a lot of time and money assembling the new Negro League team in Cleveland. The men signed players from across the country and the local sandlots and hoped to finally have a winning team in the city of Cleveland. Hayes promised fans that they would not be disappointed in the new team and encouraged them to come see the new team play at League Park.[15]

Through this letter, Hayes may have extended an olive branch to fans who were frustrated by past athletic promotions in the city. He also placed some of the burden on the fans for the success of the team by stressing the talent of the team and its ability to win. In a story printed in the *Call and Post* in February 1942, an unnamed author (more than likely the sports editor, Sweeney) encouraged fans to come and see the team's upcoming season and noted, "There has been nothing cheap in the way that Wright has been going at building a baseball team. Something that is unusual for Negroes."[16] It was unclear whether or not the author meant the comment to be critical towards African Americans or if this was a jab against local promoters such as Hayes.

With the addition of a team in Cleveland, Hayes and Wright hoped fans would come to games to see some of the more famous Negro League stars that passed through the city, including Satchel Paige. A popular player throughout his Negro League and major league career, Paige had a colorful upbringing in Mobile, Alabama, the seventh of eleven children in a poor family. "I went around with the back of my shirt torn, a pair of dirty diapers or raggedy pieces of trousers covering me. Shoes? They was somewhere else," explained Paige in his autobiography *Maybe I'll Pitch Forever.*[17] When Paige was a child, his mother attempted to send him to school, but the family needed money more than he needed an education. Paige skipped school so frequently, it was a challenge for his mother to make sure he attended classes on a regular basis. When he was seven, Paige got a job hauling bags and satchels for passengers at the train station. To save time and to earn more money, he rigged a pole loaded with satchels over his shoulder and figured that the more bags carried equaled more money earned. The other children made fun of how Paige looked hauling the large quantity of bags and referred to him as "a walking satchel tree."[18] The nickname stuck.

Paige became interested in baseball after he began watching a local

African American semi-pro team in Mobile, not the white pros of major league baseball. He wanted to emulate the players but could not afford a baseball. Instead, he practiced by throwing rocks and learned that he had good control of what he threw. When he was ten, Paige tried out for the team at the school he occasionally attended, W.H. Council School. There, Paige claimed he pitched against children his own age up through high school students. However, when he was 12, Paige got into trouble for stealing from a store and as punishment was sent to the Industrial School for Negro Children at Mount Meigs, Alabama, where he would spend the next five and a half years.[19] When he reflected on the experience, Paige saw the school as a positive influence and the start of his very long career in baseball. "If I'd been left on the streets of Mobile to wander with those kids I'd been running around with, I'd of ended up as a big bum, a crook. That's what happened to a lot of those other kids. But Mount Meigs got me away from the bums. It gave me a chance to polish up my baseball game; it gave me some schooling I'd of never taken if I wasn't made to go to classes; it learned me how to pass time without getting into trouble."[20] After he finished school in 1926, Paige entered semi-pro ball at the age of 20. Some people disputed this claim over the years as Paige's true age and birth date were called into question. Several players claimed to have played with him as early as 1920. Paige stuck to the story that he first played with the Chattanooga Black Lookouts of the Negro Southern League in 1926.[21]

Promoters like Hayes and Wright often advertised the Cleveland visits of Negro League superstars like Satchel Paige and Josh Gibson in order to entice fans to the ballpark. An August 1941 game between the Cleveland club (now referred to as the Cleveland-St. Louis Stars) and Paige's Kansas City Monarchs drew an estimated 10,000 fans, a figure the *Call and Post* called "the largest group of fans to witness a Negro ball game in Cleveland in the past fifteen years." The paper said Paige was "the whole show" and described some comical antics that didn't even involve his pitching expertise.[22] In the run up to the game, the paper called Paige the "bad boy" of the leagues and said, "He has literally thumbed his nose at exploiting club owners and jumped contracts as he pleased." This preview story noted that Paige was supposed to pitch in Cleveland earlier in the season, but disgusted fans were let down when they arrived at the park and found out that Paige was not pitching that night. Supposedly, fans refused to come to League Park in large numbers following this disappointing event in which Paige was a no-show, and thus harmed black baseball in the city.[23] What was probably more likely is that fans only came out in large numbers to see Paige, and the lack of a promotional tool left fans with fewer reasons to attend games.

While it seems harsh for the *Call and Post* to blame Paige for poor attendance at black baseball promotions at League Park, it was nothing compared to the criticism Paige received from Wendell Smith and the *Courier* when he stood up Pittsburgh fans. Smith said that Paige made "suckers" out of the 10,000 fans that came to see him pitch at Forbes Field against the Homestead Grays. Smith continued:

> The "Great Satchel" ... the man who has received more than any other player in the history of Negro baseball for doing less ... didn't feel like putting on his uniform Wednesday night. He didn't feel like giving fans who had trudged out to Forbes Field a "break." So he just lolled around in the dressing room while his mates were out on the field taking a shellacking from the Homestead Grays.

The article goes on to say that Paige claimed he did not show up because he was not scheduled to pitch on this particular night. But Smith attempted to remind Paige that he made a lot of money playing baseball, and he earned this money due to his popularity with the fans. Even though some people claimed that Paige pitched in roughly 100 ballgames, sometimes in two or three games a day the prior year, Smith thought that was "a lot of publicity hooey." He argued that Paige probably only pitched enough innings to total fifteen games, yet he earned the rather large sum of $15,000 for his work. Smith said that Paige wanted to get away with pitching even less during the current year.[24] In both cases, Paige was criticized for disappointing fans, even though by this point Paige already had earned a reputation across the Negro Leagues for his tendency to jump contracts and skip scheduled appearances. The *Call and Post* encouraged fans to come see Paige despite the fact that he disappointed fans in the city earlier in the season. Smith did no such thing, as he ended his article demanding an explanation from the Kansas City Monarchs for Paige's absence and said the team would be welcome again with an explanation, minus Paige.[25]

Team owners were almost always more willing to forget Paige's indiscretions than the press was. The famous pitcher had no problem obtaining contracts for his services despite his reputation as a contract jumper. At one point, NNL executive and owner of the Homestead Grays Cumberland "Cum" Posey wrote a letter to African American newspapers saying (among other issues) that he had read a comment that said Paige was "running Negro baseball." Sweeney replied to this in his *Call and Post* column by saying, "We don't know whether or not he would want to run the messed up set that Negro baseball is, but we do know one thing. Satchel has got every Negro club owner in the country ready to plunge a knife into the back of a fellow owner for his services."[26] Owners were well aware attendance figures nearly doubled when Paige was scheduled to pitch. No matter what hassles Paige brought with him, he also brought money into the pockets of the owners.

The Cleveland Negro League team had to find a way to draw fans to the ballpark when superstar players were not in town. By the end of 1941, it was announced that the team would officially change its name to the Cleveland and Cincinnati Buckeyes for 1942 and would split time between the two cities. They would also play games in other Ohio cities, such as Youngstown, Columbus, Springfield and Dayton.[27] A spirited rivalry was also being touted between the Buckeyes and the Cincinnati Clowns (also known as the Ethiopian Clowns and later the Indianapolis Clowns), the team that performed comical antics on the field in addition to their baseball performance. Before beginning their regular season in June of 1942, the Buckeyes spent nearly two thousand dollars, a figure comparable with white major league teams, to perform their pre-season training in the South. New *Call and Post* sports editor John Fuster commended the move and said, "What we're trying to get over is the fact that there exists in Ohio a Negro team with enough organization and enough capital to invest two grand in training or for that matter, in ANYTHING."[28] Fuster expressed mock concern about the finances of the team when he later joked that during their first game in Cleveland, a Sunday doubleheader, there were sixteen balls fouled into the stands for a total of $32. Despite the fact that the Buckeyes split the doubleheader with the Jacksonville Red Caps, nearly 8,200 were estimated in attendance, including such dignitaries as Cleveland mayor Frank Lausche, who threw out the first pitch to councilman Gus Parker.[29]

The Buckeyes hoped to capitalize on the popularity of Paige early in the 1942 season as he and his team, the Kansas City Monarchs, were scheduled for a game at League Park. As they recalled the nearly 10,000 fans that Paige drew to League Park toward the end of last season prior to the official introduction of the Buckeyes, Wright and Hayes were probably anxious to crush their former attendance record. Fuster speculated that as many as 15,000 people might attend the game. However, only 2,600 fans came to League Park to brave conditions described as "the chilly wind which blew in from the North and the threatening clouds which overcast the entire sky."[30] Despite the drastic dip in attendance for Buckeyes games due to the weather, the Cincinnati Clowns still had large numbers of fans in attendance for their games. Although the *Call and Post* did not list figures, it did say that large crowds still attended despite weather that normally would have cancelled games due to poor weather.[31] Throughout the early portion of the season, the *Call and Post* often blamed the weather for poor Buckeyes attendance figures rather than search for an alternative cause for the lack of fans attending games. The poor turnout for Paige's appearance occurred despite a full-page spread in the sports section a week earlier pushing the visit of the famous pitcher. While Cleveland is known for chilly and dreary weather, the average temperatures for May and June are rather pleasant, with an average high of 68 degrees in May and 77 degrees in June. Average temperatures for these two months ran above average in 1942, as May was 2.5 degrees higher than normal and June 1.6 degrees above normal. Rainfall was slightly above average in May and below average in June. For the June 14, 1942, game starring Paige, the high was 65 degrees and the low was 56 with about three quarters of an inch of rain over a 24-hour period.[32] While it was probably not the most pleasant weather, it does not offer an explanation of why fans stayed away by the thousands.

Despite mediocre interest in the Buckeyes, the *Call and Post* did its best throughout the summer to convince fans to follow the team and attend their games. Fuster said, "It is shameful that Cleveland baseball, with the fine Cleveland Buckeye Club giving this town the best ball it has ever seen, should need a 'shot in the arm,' but such, judging by the scimpy [*sic*] crowds which have supported the Bucks in the team's appearances here, is surely the case." Fuster said star players like pitchers Eugene Bremmer and Willie Jefferson, catcher Ulysses "Buster" Brown, third baseman Parnell Woods and first baseman Archie Ware should be reason enough to draw at least 10,000–15,000 fans to see the team each time it played. Fuster attempted to explain why the Buckeyes never seemed to draw more than a couple thousand fans per game, writing, "Whatever the reason, Cleveland just has not cottoned to the Buckeyes. We think it is because Cleveland has never seen the Bucks in action; that is, no large number of Clevelanders have yet showed up at the park." Again, poor weather was suggested as another cause for fans staying away from the park, but by the time Fuster made the argument, it was July and probably considerably warmer and more pleasant.

A number of promotional tactics were used in the attempt to draw fans, including the appearance of Homestead Grays slugger Josh Gibson (often billed as the black Babe Ruth) or the Grays themselves.[33] The Grays were the powerhouse of the Negro Leagues for much of the 1940s, often compared to major league baseball's unstoppable New York Yankees teams of the 1940s and 1950s. When tactics like these still did not create much success, the Buckeyes developed promotions such as "Wilbur Hayes Day" in the hopes that people would want to head to the ballpark to thank Hayes and show their support of him. Despite reservations about promoters in Cleveland, the *Call and Post* still respected Hayes and all that he did to promote black sports in Cleveland. The newspaper commended him for his promotion of football, baseball and boxing events in Cleveland and said that events were always the best that he could pull together for a small sum of money. Even during the Great Depression Hayes managed to organize events for the fans in Cleveland despite the economic uncertainty of the times.[34]

Not even a large gathering of the most famous players in the Negro Leagues could draw great numbers of fans to the ballpark in Cleveland. The city had a chance for potential attendance records at a black baseball event known as the famous East-West All-Star Game which was scheduled to take place in Cleveland in 1942.[35] While Negro League players often barnstormed across the country, the East-West game boasted a large number of superstars in one place. All of these popular and famous players being together in a place where there also happened to be a large migrant population fueled hopes for a large attendance. The East-West All-Star Game, played annually from 1933 to 1953, was often considered the showpiece of black baseball each year and tended to draw anywhere from 30,000–50,000 fans.[36] Some years, due to the great popularity of the East-West game, there were actually two games played, one in an eastern city and one in a western city. In 1942, two western locales hosted the game, as Chicago (annually one of the participant cities) hosted the event on August 16 and Cleveland on August 18. Instead of the game being played at League Park, the home of the Buckeyes, it would be played at the much larger and lighted Cleveland Municipal Stadium, which held an estimated 80,000.[37] The *Call and Post* bragged that the same players participating in Chicago would be playing in Cleveland. However, they would be paying their own transportation, hotel expenses and admission to the park so that all of the money from the game could be given to the Army and Navy Emergency Fund.[38] While the game ended up raising a decent sum of money for the relief fund ($9,499) and had good attendance for a black baseball event in Cleveland (10,791), it fell short of the optimistic estimates of 30,000–50,000 spectators.[39] White newspapers often took notice of the East-West All-Star Game, and the games drew many white and African American fans. John "Buck" O'Neil, Negro League player and later coach, said the event was "something special" for black fans and "a matter of racial pride." O'Neil said that whites did not come out in any great numbers to the event until after Jackie Robinson integrated major league baseball in 1947, but others suggest differently.[40]

As the Buckeyes continued their hectic schedule into the final month of the 1942 season, nobody could have predicted the tragic end to the campaign that would trump concerns about the popularity of the team. At three in the morning on Monday, September 7, the Buckeyes were returning to Ohio following a Sunday doubleheader in Buffalo, New York, against the New York Black Yankees. Team members, traveling in three cars due to their broken bus, were attempting to arrive in Akron, Ohio, (nearly a 200-mile journey from Buffalo) by Monday afternoon in time to play another exhibition against the Black Yankees. By Monday evening the team would be due in Meadville, Pennsylvania, (about 100 miles from Akron) for yet another exhibition against the Black Yankees, their third match-up with the team in a period of 24 hours. However, one vehicle got a flat tire on Route 20 near Geneva, Ohio (a town about 50 miles east of Cleveland along Lake Erie) and the men stopped to change it. As catcher Ulysses "Buster" Brown pulled the car back onto the road, a large truck and semi-trailer crashed into the back of the players' car, pushing it across the road and into a tree. Brown and pitcher Raymond "Smokey" Owens were killed instantly as they were pinned against the tree, while business manager Wilbur Hayes and pitcher Alonzo Boone were mildly injured as they were thrown from the car. Pitcher Eugene Bremmer and pitcher Herman Watts were critically injured, Bremmer with a potentially fractured skull and Watts with a possible fractured pelvis. The other two vehicles

Several Buckeyes players stand outside of their bus in 1946. Transportation issues plagued many Negro League teams, the Buckeyes included, during the 1940s. World War II rations of rubber and fuel made travel difficult at times. In 1942, after the Buckeyes' bus broke down, two players were killed and several others were injured in an automobile accident. Left to right: unidentified, Johnny Cowan, Jesse Williams, Sam Jones (exiting the bus), and Quincy Trouppe.

were not involved in the accident and continued the trip to Cleveland unharmed. Despite the loss of at least five players due to death or injury, Hayes announced the team would complete the remainder of its 1942 schedule. The Buckeyes had dates arranged through the remainder of September, including a stretch of exhibition games against the Black Yankees that included nine different cities over nine straight days. Hayes said the team planned to schedule more dates beyond those in order to play right up to the beginning of October and hoped to acquire two more pitchers in order to help fill the void left by the death of Owens and the injuries to Bremmer, Boone and Watts.[41] What made the end of the season even more difficult was the fact that the Buckeyes had already completed all of their home dates in Cleveland and would spend the remainder of the slate on the road. It was possible that the distance from Cleveland was one reason the *Call and Post* did not provide many updates on the team following the accident. The paper printed only one story — a tribute to the Buckeyes' resolve to "stagger through their few remaining games like true sportsmen" despite a series of disappointing losses. No further updates were provided on the status of the injured players.[42]

One issue that was covered frequently by the *Call and Post* during 1942 was Paige; the famous pitcher contradicted many of the paper's goals through comments to the media. Fuster appeared in awe of Paige's abilities (including his ability to draw a crowd), as many writers were. At one point he referred to him as a "prima donna" and said, "Some sports figures are built up through publicity. Not so with Satchel; he makes news."[43] Paige was popular with Fuster and the *Call and Post* until he got in the way of the paper's ideals regarding integration. In an August 1942 interview with the United Press, Paige said he was against the integration of white major league teams and instead thought it a better idea for a team comprised entirely of African American players to enter major league baseball. Paige feared that black players on primarily white major league teams would face great hardship in southern spring training locales. Paige was familiar with discrimination and racism and did not hold much optimism that it was a problem that could be solved overnight by the addition of a couple of African American players to white major league rosters. Also, he may have felt that an entire team of African American players would represent strength in numbers and produce a less volatile situation for black players. If these players performed well, then they would also exhibit black superiority every time they defeated an all-white team. The *Call and Post* likely rejected this separate team philosophy because it still represented segregation and was no different than the barnstorming tours of the 1930s and 1940s that featured white all-stars led by major league stars Dizzy Dean or Bob Feller playing black all-stars led by Paige and Jackie Robinson. The black team versus white team strategy had already been tried with few improvements to their social situation. Paige said he did not want a major league contract since he did not think that any white team would pay him the nearly $37,000 he made in 1941 while hiring himself out to black teams.

While Fuster conceded that Paige made a good point regarding white teams having spring training in southern locales, he suggested that teams did not need to train in the South. Even though a complete move of their spring training facilities might be costly, Fuster said that owners would see the money returned through increased gate attendance. The point of Paige's argument that Fuster hotly contested was the idea of a separate team of all African American players within the white major leagues. Fuster did not think this would solve the issues of segregation in American society. While a team like Paige suggested would at least provide some representation for African American players, the idea was basically an extension of segregation. Fuster thought that an all African American team would likely win multiple World Series championships against a team of white players. A mixed race team would show that whites and African Americans can successfully play alongside each other and it would demonstrate the equal democracy that blacks were fighting for in the war and at home. Fuster said that while Paige's observation was practical in the short term, he was likely unable to think of a long-term solution to the problem. Fuster added:

> The policy adopted years ago, the policy of accepting the white man's gratuities, humbly thanking him, and turning the other cheek when he cracked us, is mainly responsible for the white man's poor treatment of us today.
>   When you tackle this baseball situation, you will find that the main problem, is not an "athletic" problem ... it is a social and in this particular case a racial problem ... we hit it only as such.[44]

Satchel Paige raised Fuster's ire on several occasions, particularly when he spoke with reporters at the annual East-West All-Star Game in Chicago. Paige said he never wanted to play major league ball or accept a major league tryout until Jim Crow was eliminated nationally and he was offered a contract identical to an incoming white player. During his comments to white reporters (and a growing crowd of gathering fans), Paige said he would feel uncomfortable staying in a segregated hotel even if he played with a white team and did not like the idea of fans heckling him from the stands due to his race. Paige continued, "If the President hasn't made southern DEFENSE plants hire, and use Negro labor in government plants, how can Judge Landis, Connie Mack (owner of the Philadelphia Athletics) or anyone make the southern white folk accept the Negro as a ball player? His training camp life in the South would be miserable ... and the camps won't be moved for one or two Negroes." While it was a nice dream to think of African Americans in the major leagues, Paige thought that Jim Crow would keep it from happening.[45]

When one considered racial issues during the 1940s, it was apparent that activism increased among African Americans in many major northern cities, especially during World War II. When President Franklin D. Roosevelt signed the Selective Service Act in September 1940, the law was vague concerning the rights of African Americans and equality in the military. Walter White of the NAACP, Arnold Hill of the Urban League and A. Phillip Randolph of the Brotherhood of Sleeping Car Porters pushed Roosevelt to desegregate the military, but the president refused. This refusal caused leaders in the black community and the African American media to apply public pressure, even threatening a "Negro March on Washington." Rumors of the march were fueled by the black press, and eventually this threat led to negotiations and Executive Order 8802, which banned employment discrimination in the defense industries and in government departments. While the order did not cover military discrimination and included weak enforcement provisions, it was still seen as a victory through militant action for many in the African American community.[46]

As America became involved in World War II, national pride swelled as the United States portrayed itself as a model of democracy in the world, even though the model was flawed by the injustices African American citizens faced. Many black leaders saw the potential of drawing the attention of Americans to injustices in their own country as they followed the news of social injustices in other parts of the world. The *Pittsburgh Courier* even started the Double V campaign in 1942 in order to fight for military victories overseas and civil rights victories for African Americans at home. While desegregation in the military and the workplace were of the most importance to the African American community, baseball was a logical starting point for integration. Often referred to as "America's pastime," baseball was embraced by fans across the country, both white and black. As author Karen Ferguson mentioned in *Black Politics in New Deal Atlanta*, "Black reformers sought to find 'common ground on which to live as Americans with Americans of other racial and ethnic backgrounds.'" By proving they were respectable, blacks hoped to refute the implication from whites that they were a subordinate group, one not deserving of equal rights.[47] A popular sport where talented African American and white players could win games and championships together was the perfect opportunity to earn respectability and prove their equality.

Paige had seen opportunities for equality come and go and also experienced harsh racism throughout his lifetime. Born and raised in the South, it was likely Paige did not believe that Southerners were going to change at any point in the near future. He may have also felt that the government needed to take the first step in order to enact any kind of change and set an example that other organizations like major league baseball could follow. Fuster claimed that in his eyes Paige was saved only by his later denial of the comments he made and his contention that his words were misunderstood. "This column was ready to do all in its power to thwart the popularity of Satch Paige or anybody else dumb enough to insult the entire Negro race by advocating Jim Crow in baseball or in any form what-so-ever." Even though Fuster said he doubted that the reporters could have butchered his comments as much as Paige claimed, because of Paige's repentant attitude Fuster said, "Go Satchel Paige, and sin no more."[48] Fuster was probably angered that Paige chose such a public venue to make his claims, at the annual showpiece event for Negro League baseball, the East-West game. This was a game that Fuster knew white scouts were watching and the potential of integration could be riding on the players' performance. Fuster contemplated the damage as he said, "Whether or not it was good publicity for Satchel Paige when he apparently joined the ranks of the die-hard 'Uncle Tom's' and gave white newspapers an additional argument in the statement he is reported to have made against the induction of Negro baseball players into the ranks of organized baseball, remains to be seen."[49] Even though Fuster criticized Paige as a rather submissive "Uncle Tom," Paige probably did not make these comments in order to bow to the interests of whites. His frustration over the behavior of whites was a more likely cause for his lack of optimism that whites would allow integration to take place successfully in baseball, as well as his own economic situation.

Throughout much of the 1942 baseball season Fuster focused on the integration of major league baseball more than any other issue. Within the first month of the Buckeyes' official existence, Fuster was already pushing for integration in a portion of his column entitled "Let Us Into The Majors." Fuster had opened up discussion on integration with fans in Cleveland, not all of whom supported his ideas and goals. Like Paige, many people who wrote to Fuster, voiced concern about spring training for teams, since most traveled to southern states for their pre-season ritual. While Fuster did agree this posed a potential problem, he pointed out that there were warmer locales in a more accepting climate, such as California. Fuster thought America gave "its most backward citizens" from the South too much power. These "red-necks" were allowed to dictate racial policy in all aspects of American life, including the military and major league baseball.[50]

Even though he was the sports editor for the *Call and Post*, Fuster took on a greater role as he addressed integration in the military and tied it to baseball. It was possible that many, such as Fuster, knew that baseball was likely a good starting point for integration. Teams were run by businessmen who wanted to put fans in the seats and provide those fans with a winning product on the field. As more and more white players were called to duty through the war, there were now gaping holes on white major league teams in many cities. Black baseball was not as affected by the draft as the Selective Service Department maintained a ten percent and later only a five percent quota on the number of African Americans drafted for service.[51] Successful integration of a large institution such as baseball could easily fuel the argument that other aspects of life could do so as well. Fuster first tried to gain attention to his cause by pushing for an exhibition game between the Buckeyes and the Cleveland Indians.[52] At this point in time, the *Call and Post* did not offer coverage of the Indians games.

This push was aided during the summer of 1942 by major league baseball commissioner Kenesaw Mountain Landis, who publicly said there were no official bans on African American players in baseball and that it was up to individual teams to decide if they would sign black players. Cleveland Indians owner Alva Bradley told the *Call and Post* that he supported Landis in his stance that there was nothing officially preventing major league baseball from integrating and claimed he would consider signing African American players to the Indians. Indians manager Lou Boudreau said he did not object to African American players on the team, but believed the decision should be left to Bradley since he owned the team. Even though Bradley appeared willing to sign African American players, he did not rush to sign players or even offer tryouts. Bradley avoided questions asked of him about scouting Negro League games, including the East-West All-Star Game, when he directed all questions regarding scouting to head scout Bill Bradley. Bradley was conveniently out of town at the time, scouting players in Tennessee. Alva Bradley even went as far as to place responsibility back on African American players when he said, "No Negro players have contacted me in any way," implying that he would not offer a tryout until he was asked for one.[53] The *Call and*

Post specifically suggested that Bradley take a look at Buckeyes star pitcher Eugene Bremmer and star hitter and outfielder Sam Jethroe. Bradley offered no official response to the tryout request but said he would consider African American players in the future. When the paper suggested these two players from the Buckeyes, it admitted that the majority of players who might be selected for major league baseball would probably come from NNL Eastern teams, who had stars like Josh Gibson of the Homestead Grays. Players like Bremmer and Jethroe, while talented, lacked the star power and commercial draw of a Josh Gibson or a Satchel Paige. The Negro National League was also based in major East Coast population centers, which aided the visibility of these players.[54]

The *Call and Post* attempted to mobilize both white and black publications to battle for integration, struggling for the topic to be recognized by newspapers across the country. The writers took credit, as did several communist white publications such as the *New York Daily Worker*, for encouraging Landis to acknowledge that there were no official bars against integrating the major leagues. A story in the *Call and Post* claimed, "We have plugged and plugged, until at long last we have got the question out into the open, and into the news columns of the large white dailies, onto the air over important radio chains, into the minds of millions of white people who previously never had given it a thought either pro or con." The paper even hoped the major leagues could be integrated by the spring of 1943 and attempted to enlist the help of writer Ed Bang of the *Cleveland News*, one of the major white dailies in Cleveland, due to his "broadness of mind and a lack of racial prejudice." Bang later declined involvement in the situation as he gave the *Call and Post* permission to quote him as being in favor of integrating the major leagues, but he did not think the *News* should get involved in the dispute.

The *Call and Post* contacted other major Cleveland white papers, with mixed results. Franklin Lewis, sports editor of the *Cleveland Press*, refused to editorially support the integration of major league baseball as he said, "This move to put Negroes into baseball is untimely." By untimely, Lewis meant he thought the war would finally lead to a complete shutdown in major league baseball by the next season and to talk about integrating something that may not even exist was pointless. Lewis did concede the fact that even if the war caused major league baseball to go on hiatus in 1943, integration could set a precedent once the war was completed. Like many others, Lewis cited familiar concerns regarding integration, such as transportation, training and the housing of African American and white players across the country. Even though Lewis only compared Negro League baseball with white minor ball league at the Class AA level, he thought that if enough African American players were found "capable" that he would support their inclusion. Lewis did not agree with the idea of scattered tryouts and thought that every major league team should sign, at the same time, one or two African American players. The *Call and Post* was frustrated by Lewis' lack of commitment to the cause and said, "It is regrettable that the Press, one of the leading newspapers in this theoretically open-minded and democratic city, is passing up this opportunity to BOOST DEMOCRACY AT HOME by taking a stand beside the New York daily, PM, and other truly democratic white dailies, a stand for our boys in the major leagues and on the Cleveland team in particular." The *Call and Post* also lept on less-aggressive African American writers and said they needed to realize that it was a prime opportunity for change and should start to encourage it through their writing. The *Call and Post* never called anyone out by name, but did say that "black sports writers who are so 'old fogey' that they cant [*sic*] see a chance for this marvelous change, and who say 'It just ain't so' would do well to wake up and start plugging ... Now!"[55]

Baseball was not the only realm that the *Call and Post* sought to change, as the paper believed that the African American press should be on the front lines of any type of social change. The *Call and Post* was concerned with equality in the workplace as they advocated for a strong Fair Employment Practices Committee (FEPC) that would enforce improvements in housing for African Americans in Cleveland. They often encouraged readers to contact them about problems experienced in the community and tried to encourage city leaders to help enact incremental changes. One of the first issues it tackled was organizing with other African American publications. William O. Walker, editor of the *Call and Post*, also served as president of the Negro Newspapers Association during 1942 and said in a letter regarding the importance of the African American press in the war effort, "The importance of the Negro Press in developing and maintaining our nation's morale needs to be recognized."[56] Walker also advised the black press to remain militant and to help combat forces of intimidation against African American papers in the South, mainly with

Northern papers assisting the Southern papers. He advised solidarity, especially during the war, and said, "Because of the war, there are many problems facing our papers which no one editor can solve individually. All of
us will get more respect from all sources if we have an active trade association. We are not well enough established for any of our papers to remain
outside of the fold. The Negro papers are the front line in our fight for
complete equality of citizenship."[57] Walker later chose to use this alliance
to fight for equality as it pertained to baseball when he called on members
of the National Negro Newspaper Publisher's Association to assist in press-
ing for the integration of major league teams.

Walker advised members of the association in cities where there was
a major league team under the jurisdiction of Commissioner Landis to
form a committee comprised of leading citizens and sports figures in order
to press for the addition of African American players to these teams. In
Cleveland former baseball player and prominent attorney John Shackelford
was asked to serve on the local committee along with numerous others,
including Mayor Lausche, Wilbur Hayes, *Call and Post* city editor Charles
H. Loeb and sports editor John Fuster. The idea for these nationwide local
committees came from a conference with Walker and Shackelford. The
committee was supposed to gather information that showed the advantages
of integration for both African Americans and major league baseball
teams.[58] In addition to the integration of baseball, the *Call and Post* also
pushed the topic of employment and military equality for African Americans. This was very similar to the Double V campaign waged by the *Pittsburgh Courier* in February 1942 in which the *Courier* fought for victory
abroad and victory for African Americans at home in the battle against
segregation. By drawing on the image of oppression overseas that Americans were fighting, the paper could also draw attention to the oppression
that blacks faced in their own country every day.

> Americans all, are involved in a gigantic war effort to assure victory for the
> cause of freedom.... We, as colored Americans, are determined to protect our
> country, our form of government and the freedoms which we cherish for our-
> selves and for the rest of the world.... Thus in our fight for freedom we wage
> a two-pronged attack against our enslavers at home and those abroad who
> would enslave us. ... WE ARE AMERICANS TOO![59]

Another large campaign adopted by the *Call and Post* was fielding
complaints regarding job discrimination throughout Ohio. With the assis-

tance of Mayor Lausche, who promised a "showdown" with any employer in the city of Cleveland who refused to hire African American workers, the *Call and Post* began a campaign called "Jobs for Victory." The newspaper promised to assist any citizen that contacted the *Call and Post* about finding a war industry job in Ohio; they need only prove their skills and mail a printed form to the newspaper office. They also encouraged citizens to contact their local mayors for assistance if they lived outside the city of Cleveland. It was suggested that citizens form their own "Jobs for Victory" committees within their towns in order to provide support for citizens. The *Call and Post* promised to investigate every claim of discrimination they received.[60]

Despite the push by the black press in Cleveland, one of the most likely candidates to integrate following Landis' statement appeared to be the Pittsburgh Pirates, not the Indians. William Benswanger, president of the Pirates, agreed to offer tryouts to three African American players — Roy Campanella and Sam Hughes of the Baltimore Elite Giants and Dave Barnhill of the New York Cubans. (Campanella would eventually join the Brooklyn Dodgers with Jackie Robinson in 1948.) Bradley continued to dodge an official tryout, while Benswanger appeared much more open to integration through the tryout offer to Campanella, Hughes, and Barnhill. The *Call and Post* strongly encouraged the signing of one or more of these players but realized the likely impact to Negro League baseball: "The induction of Negro stars into the majors will probably ruin or seriously weaken the drawing power of teams in Negro circuits. It is true that with the elimination of Jim Crow in any phase of life, a few Negroes suffer, but the masses are benefited."[61] The *Call and Post* wanted to see African American fans pester major league owners to sign players since African Americans were among "the country's most rabid baseball fans." The paper asked how "rabid" would African American fans be if they had a chance to cheer for integrated major league teams. It encouraged fans to not only write Alva Bradley of the Indians but also Benswanger of the Pirates and Powel Crosley of the Cincinnati Reds.[62]

Owners of Negro League teams were cautiously optimistic about integration despite their potential financial losses if baseball integrated. These owners often expressed their hope that the first African Americans in the major leagues would exhibit respectable qualities that whites could easily accept. Several of the owners that spoke out to the *Call and Post* in favor

of integration included Hayes from the Buckeyes; Effa Manley, owner of
the Newark Eagles; Dr. J.B. Martin, president of the NAL and owner of
the Chicago American Giants; and J.L. Wilkinson, co-owner of the Kansas
City Monarchs. Even though Manley said she would not stand in the way
of any of her players who had a chance to join the major leagues, she urged
caution in the matter as she said, "Let's be careful from the beginning.
Let's do this thing right when we get the chance. If we just let anybody
go up for trial, we're leaving ourselves open for a set-back. The big leaguers
will look over what he has to offer, find him unsatisfactory, then turn him
down with a 'Well, there you are, we gave your star a chance and he failed.'"
Martin named several players whom he felt would be able to find success
in the major leagues and said, "If it did affect colorful baseball financially
… I want it known that I am against discrimination in any form, and
regardless of financial considerations or anything else, I want to see them
make the grade." Hayes believed that the Negro Leagues would actually
benefit from the signing of African American players and said, "We'll lose
some players, but the interest in baseball for young Negroes will be height-
ened. They will use our teams as builders for the majors and you'll see a
lot of Negro talent that otherwise would remain hidden." Hayes even envi-
sioned exhibition games throughout the season between the NAL, NNL
and white teams; exhibitions he believed were easier to arrange once there
were African American players in the major leagues. Once integration was
widely accepted, it would open doors for other integrated contests. Wilkinson said he believed Monarchs pitcher Paige and Homestead Grays catcher
Josh Gibson would attract the most attention and expressed a willingness
to let Paige out of his contract if he got the chance to pitch in the major
leagues.

Several white officials of major league teams seemed much more concerned about the harm to the Negro Leagues. Larry McPhail, president of
the Brooklyn Dodgers, said he was against signing African American players
due to the fact that Negro League teams would be upset that their talented
players were taken. McPhail also said since there were not that many talented players in the NNL and NAL, to take the most talented for the
white major leagues would basically destroy the Negro Leagues. Clark
Griffith, head of the major league Washington Senators, shared this view
as he said, "Negro leagues ought to build themselves up to where their
topnotch clubs could play the major league top clubs for the world cham-

pionship." Others from white baseball did not necessarily share this seg-regationist viewpoint, including former Chicago Cubs catcher and minor league manager Gabby Harnett: "If given permission I wouldn't hesitate one minute. I am not interested in a player's color, just his playing ability. There are any number of good Negro players around the country, and I'm sure that if we were given permission to use them, there'd be a mad scramble between managers to pick them up."[63]

Manley touched upon an idea that was definitely a concern among many supporters of integration — the player must be carefully chosen not only for his qualities as a baseball player but also his qualities as a man. This was important for proving respectability to whites and showing them blacks were not second-class citizens. In a column, Fuster addressed this issue and appeared more concerned about the behavior of African American fans than he was the behavior of the players. He believed the players were intelligent people that were able to ignore taunts from racist white fans. What concerned Fuster was the possibility of African American fans being unable to endure a race-baiting white fan that happened to sit near them in the crowd. He was also afraid that black fans might accuse white players of committing errors on purpose, especially if there was an African American pitcher on the mound. Fuster advised fans to "just take it as you've always taken it. Those guys draw big-time pay-checks, and they are not going to jeopardize their value to their teams by 'throwing' any ball games." Fuster admitted there would be challenges with transportation, training and housing if African American players were integrated into the major leagues but pointed out that problems such as these were not new. He claimed that African Americans were "hardened" to racist behavior from whites and were used to the denial of certain rights in their everyday lives. For Jim Crow to end whites needed to learn more about African Americans, which included increased contact between the races. Integrated baseball was the perfect opportunity to increase interaction between the races and to publicly display interracial cooperation.[64]

Fuster finally convinced the Indians to consider signing several Negro League players. He obtained permission from Wilbur Hayes to push for a tryout for three Buckeyes participants in the upcoming East-West All-Star Game: third baseman Parnell Woods, pitcher Eugene Bremmer and center fielder Sam Jethroe. The written request to Alva Bradley was signed by Parnell Woods, the only one of the three men who had a college degree

Eugene Bremmer was a star pitcher with the
Buckeyes throughout the 1940s. In 1942
John Fuster of the *Cleveland Call and Post*
pushed the owner of the Cleveland Indians,
Alva Bradley, to offer a tryout to Bremmer,
Sam Jethroe and Parnell Woods.

and about whom the *Call and Post* said, "Woods is generally accepted as one of the game's real gentlemen." Bradley said he would respond directly to Woods since the request was in his name.[65] Unfortunately, all three men performed poorly in the East-West All-Star Game three days later, the reason Bradley gave for refusing a tryout for any of them. "We have scouted these men ... we saw them play at the Stadium on the night of August 18th, and frankly, Mr. Fuster, they are not big league material. Why, not one of them got a hit ... and the pitcher, Bremmer, was knocked out of the box. They just don't stack up as material for the Indians." One will never know how serious Bradley was about integrating the Indians at this point in time. It is possible the East-West All-Star Game performance of the three players led him to believe they would not survive in the major leagues. It is also possible that the poor performance became a convenient excuse to exclude them.

Fuster was obviously frustrated with the players' performance and admitted he was shocked by how poorly the three performed. It was an exceptionally bad night for the three players. Bremmer only pitched for three innings, yet allowed at least two hits in every inning he pitched and was finally forced off the mound in the third inning after he allowed four walks, four hits and five runs to score, leaving the game with the bases loaded and two outs. Jethroe only got one hit, in the ninth inning with the bases empty, and dropped a routine fly ball earlier in the game in center field. Woods did not get a hit the entire game and let two balls past him at third base. Rather than point out that it was possibly just a bad night for the players, the *Call and Post* seemed to abandon its support of the three men and instead encouraged the Indians to consider other talented African American players. "If the Indians are sincere in their declaration that the color of a man's skin will not keep him off their team, they certainly have the opportunity to prove it.[66]

Even though the *Call and Post* never outwardly questioned Bradley's refusal to integrate the Indians at this point, the paper did publish a national story toward the end of the season that asked, "Are Big Leagues Fooling Us?" The author of the story, Mabray Kountze, was frustrated by the fact that African Americans had to form their own leagues while other ethnicities, such as German-Americans, Italian-Americans, or Polish-Americans were accepted into major league baseball. Even Germans, in the midst of World War II, were not forced to form their own league in order to get attention from the majors. Kountze added, "We are the only Americans who have to parade our boys around like a circus establishing them somewhat in the class of foreigners who just came over on the boat. The foreigners, however, have a better chance." Kountze criticized African American writers throughout the country for being so quick to support Commissioner Landis when he suggested the possibility of a separate black minor league system in order to serve as a feeder to white major league teams. "This is the time for colored editors to organize and to stand firm for the principles of which we have sacrificed these many years. I'm afraid some of our writers seek appeasement." It seemed that Kountze viewed anything other than a completely integrated major and minor league system as unsatisfactory. Kountze also was leery of estimates that the major leagues could be integrated as early as 1943 and said these were purely political promises. He would see how many major league teams actually signed African American players for the next season.[67]

Even though Fuster and the *Call and Post* were supportive of Cleveland's acquisition of a Negro League team in the Cleveland Buckeyes, to them it was just another reminder that African Americans were separate and unequal, unable to play a sport alongside white players to whom they were assuredly equal in terms of talent. So as the *Call and Post* encouraged fans to attend Buckeye games and criticized the lack of support for the team, even the newspaper itself could not offer unequivocal support of the Buckeyes. Writers did not necessarily want to see an end to the Negro

Leagues since they provided a great opportunity to showcase talented black players. They wanted to see whites and blacks playing together on the field and also see improved management and communication in the leadership and operation of the NNL and NAL. The press had a difficult time obtaining statistics and game scores from teams, and teams often ignored promotional strategy, a fact proven when the Buckeyes were still advertising catcher "Buster" Brown in promotional billboards in July of 1943, even though the player died the prior September in an automobile accident.[68]

The African American press, including the *Call and Post*, considered itself a major player in the civil rights movement and felt that through a unified front it could help bring about change in American society. The press more than likely realized the potential for integrating major league baseball, where owners were likely to be more concerned with making money than they were about racial prejudice. It was a perfect opportunity for the *Call and Post* to advocate change, even if it was at the expense of promoting the new Negro League team in town, the Buckeyes.

3

Building a Champion

Assembling a Winning Team in 1943 and 1944

As the Buckeyes began their second full season in the Negro American League, they faced a number of challenges and changes. Prior to the 1943 season the team ended its association with Cincinnati and announced that Cleveland would be their sole home city. World War II shortages in gasoline and rubber impacted the travel plans of all Negro League teams. This coupled with the fact that the Buckeyes probably earned more money from their Cleveland home games likely led to the switch. The Buckeyes were forced to deal with the losses the team suffered at the end of the 1942 season when multiple players were killed or injured in an automobile accident. Mexican baseball provided increased competition for Negro League players, as the circuit offered more money and less blatant prejudice south of the border. The Negro National and Negro American leagues continued to experience disorganization and inter-league squabbles created by a lack of centralized leadership. The *Call and Post* continued to examine its role in society, particularly its attempts to establish equality in society for African Americans. The paper continued to push major league baseball to integrate, particularly because of the player shortages brought on by the players' departures for military service. Many of these issues extended into the 1944 season as the Buckeyes played well yet fell short of the Birmingham Black Barons in both 1943 and 1944.

William O. Walker, editor of the *Call and Post*, expressed concern for the public behavior of new Cleveland residents as Southerners came to the North for jobs in the war industry. Walker thought that these migrants did not understand the proper etiquette of northern cities and factories and that their behavior might upset northern whites. In his opinion, the "zoot suiter" that worked in a defense plant had no respect for authority and was likely to cause fights in his factory. Because African Americans were "too new in these plants," they could not risk behavior that may make them look bad. It was the job of the good workers to let these bad apples know how they should act and to let them know that they were responsible for the entire race. According to Walker, "Condoning and pampering these bad actors is committing economic suicide for the whole race." He suggested that citizens also watch their behavior on buses and street cars so that it did not look like blacks behaved poorly in public. Even those that behaved well were not to be let off the hook, since it was their job to reign in the people who could not control themselves in public, according to Walker. Proper etiquette at sporting events was just as important as other aspects of daily life.[1]

In another column, Walker discussed the importance of the black press, specifically in the North. Within the ten years prior to Walker's 1943 column, he said the black press had many accomplishments throughout the country in the fight against racial inequality. According to Walker, the job of a black editor was "to blast the oppressors on the backs of their people." He said that the black press came under fire during World War I, and Walker now believed the government was again apprehensive of black newspapers. The government and other critics wanted to destroy the African American press because they knew its power. Walker said, "They don't mind Negroes killing and cutting each other, but they do mind Negroes intelligently and determinedly demanding their rights as American citizens." Even though he did not offer this type of commentary on the sports pages, this strategy came through in articles and columns from the sports writers. Even though Walker never specifically mentioned sports in this particular column, the theme coincides with that of the sports pages.[2]

Walker continued this theme in an editorial that was reminiscent of the Double V campaign waged by the *Pittsburgh Courier*. Walker wondered how African Americans could be asked to wholeheartedly support a war "for the four freedoms" while their freedoms were challenged in their own country.[3] Another editorial blatantly claimed that the black press was a major influence in the effort to improve rights for African Americans. The article claimed, "The Negro Press is first and last an advocate of freedom and democracy."[4] If industry took the same attitude as major league baseball, according to future sports editor Bob Williams, then America would lose the war. Williams also encouraged African Americans to boycott white baseball games since they could practically be considered an un–American activity due to segregation.[5]

In August Cleveland mayor Frank J. Lausche called both white and black city leaders to his office to discuss race relations. Called "The Mayor's Committee on Democratic Practices," it included clergy from churches, representatives from industry and labor as well as social institutions, newspapers and businesses. After recent riots in New York and Detroit, Lausche wanted to calm any surging feelings in the city of Cleveland and make sure that any similar riots would be averted in the city. Lausche hoped the committee would look at housing problems and instances of Jim Crow and segregation in Cleveland. They also wanted to make sure there were more recreation opportunities for African American children, whose parents were involved in war work in the city.[6]

The Negro Leagues and the major leagues both had major concerns related to World War II, particularly regarding transportation and manpower. The president of the Negro American League, Dr. J.B. Martin, assured fans that Negro League baseball would not see a work stoppage due to the war unless the government ordered such a stoppage. The Negro League teams still faced transportation problems due to war-time shortages and limitations but still planned to play games. Players that were called to duty through the military would be replaced by other players, and the possibility of a smaller baseball schedule was initially considered in 1943.[7] The league considered eliminating weekday games, but league officials ultimately decided that these games would boost the morale of war workers. In the end, the league confirmed that they planned to play a full schedule during the upcoming season.[8] Due to the uncertain transportation situation, the Buckeyes planned to train around Canton, Ohio, about 60 miles south of Cleveland, rather than at a southern locale. Even though the team did not specifically cite it as a reason, a move to Canton could stimulate interest for the Buckeyes in a community close to Cleveland. Third baseman Parnell Woods was named manager for the season, with Archie Ware at first base, "Little" Bill Horne at second, Johnny Lyles at shortstop, and Sam Jethroe, Emmett Wilson and Duke Cleveland in the outfield.[9]

As many major league teams faced player shortages due to military enlistments, they scrambled to find replacement players to fill their rosters. The Cleveland Indians, short on outfield talent, signed former New York Yankee Roy Cullengine, who was nursing a foot injury at the time of the signing. The *Call and Post* was disgusted by the fact that the Indians and other teams would rather sign an injured or untalented white player instead of a talented African American player. The paper joked that the Indians would probably re-sign Tris Speaker (star of the 1920 world championship team who retired as a player in 1928) before they gave a black player an opportunity. The *Call and Post* added, "It is doing as much to break down the morale of the Negro than it does to raise that of the white man." The author even suggested that if teams continued to refuse to sign or offer tryouts to black players, then perhaps it was time to contact the War Manpower Commission. The *Call and Post* said the commission could potentially get teams to stop their practices of racial exclusion or would prevent the major leagues from playing altogether.[10] Another editorial by Art Cohn claimed the fact that "the fans would rather see younger, more brilliant Negroes taking over for some of the ancients" was ignored by major league owners. All of these owners believed that "the 'National Pastime' is restricted to white players, war or no war." Cohn thought it was sad that if black players were considered for major league teams, it was only because there were not enough talented white players to fill team rosters. He did not think major league owners would integrate their teams on their own accord.[11]

In the midst of these integration debates, the Buckeyes prepared to start the season, despite the ban on bus travel, and planned to play their first home game at League Park. The team planned to do much of their travel by train, a much more expensive alternative than bus travel. With wartime rationing, the team was forbidden to use its bus. The *Call and Post* said that despite these challenges, the team still planned to make the season "one of the best in history."[12] Since they were considered the "surprise team" during the 1942 season, there were high hopes that the Buckeyes would have a strong season in 1943. In fact, many people thought that the 1943 team was more balanced than the strong 1942 squad.[13] The *Call and Post* did attempt to lower these high expectations for the Buckeyes before the season started when the newspaper said, "They will be hard-pressed to maintain the terrific pace they set when they finished second in the first half (of 1942)."[14]

The transportation limitations added to some of the other concerns about Negro League baseball. Since teams drew a great deal of attendance from their Sunday contests, a rainout could cause them to lose almost a week's worth of profits. If a team traveled to an out-of-town rainout, they had to pay for transportation with no profits to offset the costs. Teams were given the choice of riding in multiple cars or taking trains to the games. Bud Douglass of the *Call and Post* complained that more resources were used in the driving of multiple cars than a bus.[15] Douglass predicted a good season for Negro League baseball since they lost less talent than the white major leagues to the war effort. He added, "The fact remains that the majors or even the minors won't give them the chance so the best thing for us to do is to go to see the colored boys play as a team."[16]

Gordon Cobbledick of the *Cleveland Plain Dealer* also spoke out in favor of adding African American players to major league squads. He believed that teams could ease some of their wartime manpower shortages if they added black players. The *Call and Post* commended him for his stance and said they wished other daily writers would go public in support of this idea. Bob Williams, the new sports editor at the *Call and Post*, said that he thought the black press had a special duty, "a sort of guardianship whereby it must watch for, point out, and help eradicate such forces and influences as may injure the race, or retard it's [sic] progress in any way."[17]

In a *Call and Post* column, track and field star DeHart Hubbard compared baseball to industrial work during the World War II era. He argued that the major leagues were like a specialized industrial job — both were the pinnacle of their respective fields. Just like in industry, African Americans were kept from the highest paying industry jobs, as they are kept from the higher-paying major leagues. World War II provided blacks a chance to break some of these old prejudices. There were work shortages in factories, as well as in major league baseball. Hubbard said that if African Americans were just given an opportunity, they would be able to prove their skills. He even considered the possibility of Negro League teams competing with white minor league teams on a regular basis. This would represent a starting point in the path to full integration.[18]

Cleveland sports figures and *Call and Post* writers offered suggestions for appropriate behavior from African American fans and players. Harry Walker said, "We have passed the 'Uncle Tom' age and are now grown-up. We must show brilliance, intelligence, character and a lot of natural ability. (We have the latter.)" Bob Williams thought that when major league teams finally started to sign African American players, they would pick them based on "character and natural ability" and "of these two — character will come first." Williams believed that a team would not want to take a chance on a player just to have him "embarrass them" with inappropriate behavior. He was afraid that if even one owner thought he made a mistake in signing a black player, other teams would shy away from signing additional African American players. "My guess is they'd rather have a man batting .250 with good strong character than a sensational batter who might create a scandal," Williams said. He added there were always scouts watching Negro League games and that sometimes they were disappointed with the players' conduct on the field. "Our boys, apparently not realizing that there are other important points that make a great athlete besides excellence of performance have not always been at their best behavior before, during, and after the game."[19]

In early June there was a highly touted series between the Buckeyes and the Kansas City Monarchs, the type of series a scout would be likely to follow. What was of particular interest to fans and the media was the pitching duel between the Monarchs' Satchel Paige and the Buckeyes' Theolic "Fireball" Smith. The *Call and Post* anticipated the series would be "the most interesting colored baseball of the year." Writer Bud Douglass called Paige "legendary" and said he would have been considered one of the all-time greats if a major league team had signed him in his prime. On the positive side, Douglass said, "By playing colored ball he is able to pitch for what ever team he cares to. He pitches twelve months out of the year and makes thousands of dollars more than he would with a big league team." It was reported that Paige made $75,000 during the two previous years, and expected to add $40,000 more to that total in 1943. Douglass joked that Paige didn't have to worry about the draft since he pitched during the last war (a not-so-subtle dig at Paige's age). As he entered the series with the Monarchs, "Fireball" Smith had pitched 23 straight innings without giving up a run. By the time game day arrived, it was a bit of a disappointment. There was rain throughout the morning, which kept "hundreds, if not thousands" of fans away from the park. It turned out to be "Fireball" Smith's last game with the Buckeyes for nearly a month, as he was ordered to return to the St. Louis team after a contract dispute (St.

Louis claimed he was still rightfully their player). The dispute was settled and Smith returned to the team in July.[20]

Just a couple of weeks after the series with the Monarchs, Cleveland fans were treated to some fireworks in the midst of a Buckeyes game with the Chicago American Giants. The doubleheader between the two teams was interrupted by a 45-minute brawl that supposedly "interrupted the tranquility of Cleveland's baseball vista." The incident started with a disputed play and went downhill from there. Cleveland outfielder Duke Cleveland made a diving catch of a fly ball hit by Chicago player Art Pennington. Chicago fans claimed the Cleveland player trapped the ball rather than catching it; the umpires maintained the play was a fair catch. Two Chicago players were thrown out of the game for "offensive language" and for "placing their hands on" umpire Harry Walker. Chicago refused to continue the game after the men were thrown out, and claimed it did not have enough players to take the field after the ejections.[21]

At this point, the argument escalated and entered the realm of the bizarre when Cleveland supposedly learned that Chicago had fourteen players on its roster. Only two Chicago players were ejected by umpires, which meant there were more than enough players to complete the game. The Buckeyes claimed that the American Giants had eleven men on the field at times during the game, rather than the maximum nine. The *Call and Post* even accused Chicago of a cover up when the paper claimed that several of the team's players were ushered off of the field to keep the story straight. In an attempt to diffuse the tense situation, Wilbur Hayes asked that the umpires' decision be overruled and the Chicago players be allowed to remain in the game. He supposedly was also afraid of the crowd's reaction if the games were called off in the midst of the doubleheader. The 5,400 estimated fans in attendance did see the completion of the doubleheader; the Buckeyes lost both games and were knocked out of first place in the Negro American League.[22]

Bud Douglass feared the behavior of the Chicago players made all African American baseball players look bad and that such behavior might give major league teams more excuses not to sign black players. Douglass questioned who the umpires worked for — "the league or the ball team?" Umpires supposedly worked for the league but only worked in their "home cities" and had no set wage level within the Negro National and Negro American leagues. Douglass said, "If Negro baseball is to model itself after its white counterpart, they will have to stop being unorganized and give their officials some power. It's a sad commentary on the game of Doubleday when an umpire has to summon the armed forces from the stands to evict the undesirable players and then to have the players remain in the game and sneer through the rest of the afternoon." Douglass believed this game established bad feelings between the Buckeyes and the American Giants that could erupt in the future. Douglass added, "The players ran the game. The two Chicagoans were allowed to remain in the game which the Chicago team went on to win handily." "Baseball received a black eye in Cleveland last Sunday. When it hurt Cleveland it also hurt every other team that has to come here and play. They'll all suffer and unless the teams and league officers do something about it there won't be any Buckeye team. Clevelanders are funny that way." Douglass was convinced Cleveland fans had no interest in watching fights on the baseball field. To prevent future incidents, Douglass said that any player who physically touched an umpire should be fined and potentially suspended if his behavior could not be controlled.[23]

The fight was still a hot topic a week later, when the *Call and Post* offered umpire Harry Walker the opportunity to tell his side of the story. Walker, the home plate umpire during the Chicago games, said he intended to go to the heads of the league and inform them of the Chicago players conduct. They obviously were already familiar with the situation, as Dr. J.B. Martin, president of the Negro American League, sent a letter to the *Call and Post* commending Walker for his conduct during the difficult situation with the American Giants. Walker believed he was between a rock and a hard place during the doubleheader since a forfeit of the game would hurt baseball in Cleveland. Throughout the events with the Chicago American Giants, Walker said he was pleased with the support he received from Douglass and the *Call and Post*.[24]

Harry Walker was a respected figure in Cleveland sports and throughout Negro League baseball; he was even asked to umpire the East-West All-Star Game for 1943. He umpired the "majority" of black baseball games in Cleveland, dating to 1923, according to the *Call and Post*. Wilbur Hayes gave Walker a great deal of credit for advancing black baseball in Cleveland and for crusading against profanity in Negro League games. As head umpire, Walker saw attendance figures rise in Cleveland, from 1,000 to the recent figure of 8,000. The Buckeyes saw his appointment to the East-

West game as "a well-deserved" honor. Walker even wrote a column for the *Call and Post* where he discussed his experiences at the East-West game in 1943. He claimed that during his trip to Chicago he heard repeated compliments about Buckeyes owner Ernest Wright, who Walker considered one of the most popular owners in the game.[25]

The *Call and Post* worked to differentiate the Cleveland Buckeyes from the actions of the Chicago American Giants throughout the summer of 1943. The paper highlighted a disputed call in Chicago that involved player/manager Parnell Woods. Woods was thrown out of the game by umpires and did not return to the field following his ejection. Douglass said this was "not only because that was the rule of the game but also because the Giants didn't want him in the game, and they were running the whole show there just as they did here." He pointed out that J.S. Simmons, general manager of the American Giants, was also secretary of the Negro American League. Douglass did not believe this was something one would see in major league baseball, and said it would be like commissioner Kenesaw Mountain Landis also working as the New York Yankees traveling secretary.[26] This complaint about the American Giants "running the whole show" was reminiscent of complaints from Cleveland Negro League officials during the 1920s and 1930s. These people believed that cities like Cleveland were overlooked while the larger teams, like the Chicago American Giants, were given unfair consideration.

Bob Williams still felt the need to separate the Buckeyes from the American Giants in August. Even though he thought that any team but Chicago would be envious of the Buckeyes' second-place won-lost record (Chicago was currently in first place), Williams believed the Buckeyes were much more popular with their fans. "The Bucks have a clean record, with no stigma of any sort. For effort, they rate 100 percent. On the road, the Bucks have played cleanly and well, earning the admiration of their opponents as well as out of town fans." The Buckeyes, who came a long way in a short amount of time, played hard and did not start trouble, in Williams' opinion. He wanted to make sure that fans realized, and possibly even people within major league baseball, that Cleveland players were not involved in actions like the ones displayed by the American Giants.[27]

The Buckeyes did not escape criticism from the media in Cleveland as Douglass questioned the Buckeyes' decision to travel to away games via multiple cars instead of the train. Even though the *Call and Post* seemed to argue against the high costs of train travel early in the season, Douglass now said that other teams survived financially traveling by train. He also thought that teams that traveled by train seemed more rested and prepared for their away baseball games.[28] By August the Buckeyes opted for bus travel after regulations limiting gasoline and rubber consumption by teams were relaxed. The bus did not necessarily make travel simpler for the Buckeyes, especially when it broke down between Memphis, Tennessee, and Cairo, Illinois, as they traveled to Wrigley Field for a series against the Kansas City Monarchs. Because there were no seats left on the train, the Buckeyes players had to stand for the ride from Cairo to Chicago and arrived about an hour before the game was due to start. The Buckeyes, tired and late, supposedly "fell easy victims" to Satchel Paige and the Monarchs when they finally reached Chicago for their series.[29]

In July *Call and Post* writer Bob Williams moved to the sports desk at the paper. As sports editor he continued many of Douglass's critiques of the Negro Leagues and also compared black professional baseball to the major leagues. Williams seemed to view the majors and Negro Leagues almost as apples and oranges; they were difficult to compare because they were ultimately too different from each other. Williams also criticized some of the Buckeyes' poor attempts at promotion in Cleveland, and mentioned the failed promotional material that included posters with the deceased Buster Brown. This poster also included Johnny Lyles, a utility man that left the Buckeyes by July, and Livingstone James, a shortstop that never actually appeared with the Buckeyes in 1943. Two of the Buckeyes' top pitchers, "Fireball" Smith and Willie Jefferson, were not listed on the poster, nor was Cleveland native Alonzo Boone. The posters were further evidence that the team was marketed poorly to fans.[30]

William Brisker, in a *Call and Post* article, offered more evidence of the differences between the Negro Leagues and the major leagues, especially when it came to scouting, promotion, and business methods. He noted the tight organization among major league teams, specifically when it came to scouting and organizing talent. Brisker believed that the major leagues had superior "propaganda" skills, "as good as that of any nation at war." The majors had a promotional advantage because of specialized baseball writers in the white media; these writers became experts of the game and formed various associations. Brisker thought Negro League teams needed to work on scouting as well as preparing players for professional play, which should start at the high school and collegiate level. Negro League teams also needed to keep a tighter leash on their profits and establish a solid relationship with the black press "by giving the writers and the papers a tangible reason for wanting to keep colored baseball alive." This was a logical suggestion since the black press provided free, in-depth coverage for Negro League contests. Even though the major leagues had a proven record of success, Brisker said that the Negro Leagues did little to copy the major leagues's model.[31]

While the Negro Leagues did not need to worry at this point about losing players to the major leagues, they did have to be concerned about players defecting to Mexican teams. The Buckeyes decided to fight back when the team learned that officials from Mexico were in the stands scouting their players during an away game in 1943. Wilbur Hayes and Rufus "Sonnyman" Jackson from the Homestead Grays physically removed the Consul of Mexico from Forbes Field in Pittsburgh before the man could convince any players to join a team south of the border. Hayes was furious and said, "Well I'm not letting anybody come along to fool with my efforts after we begin to enjoy a little success. What would you do, let somebody come along and tear down what you had built up the hard way? We don't care who he was, he wasn't coming into that park after the game was over and do that it us, it isn't right!" Hayes already lost future catcher/manager Quincy Trouppe prior to the season when he jumped his Buckeyes contract and went to play in Mexico. "Fireball" Smith also pitched in Mexico before he came to the Buckeyes.[32] Mexico was a constant lure to many Negro League players since the circuit usually offered higher wages than most league teams. Many players admitted they felt more comfortable in Mexico and that they experienced less racism than they did in the United States.

Bob Williams and others within the Negro Leagues thought the Buckeyes had a lot of potential, even if they did struggle at times throughout the season. Williams interviewed "Candy" Jim Taylor when he visited town in July as manager of the Homestead Grays. Taylor thought the Buckeyes were a good team but added, "You have no right to expect a championship club out of them in the first year or so — it takes time and all things considered they're doing very well." Williams considered this high praise because Taylor was well respected in Negro League baseball. As manager of the powerful Grays, Taylor had come a long way since he managed some of the hapless Cleveland clubs in the 1920s. If anyone would know that a new club needed to be given a chance to survive, it was Taylor.[33] When the Buckeyes began to slip in September, Bob Williams was somewhat critical and complained that no one never really knew what to expect from the team. At times they played like champions but then "the next time you look at them, they're scrambling all over the park like a bunch of amateurs." It was during these "amateur" times that Williams thought a high-ranking sandlot team might be able to beat the Buckeyes. He did add that the Buckeyes don't play bad very often, but when they did they lost respect from the fans. Despite these bumps in the road, Williams said, "Cleveland still has a good ball club — all things considered, but doggone it, we'd like to stop using that expression!"[34]

The *Call and Post* even received a letter from a local fan named Leo Ransfer, who was supportive yet critical of the Buckeyes and the Negro Leagues. Ransfer offered several suggestions for improving Negro League games, which included the interactions between umpires, fans and players between innings. He thought that friendly chatter between these groups looked unprofessional and slowed the pace of the game. Ransfer claimed that during the last Buckeyes game he witnessed, there was a seven-minute delay while the crowd waited for the umpires to return to the field. Scorecards posted around the park that included the game's batting lineups were often inaccurate and did not represent what took place on the field. Ransfer also took issue with the way plays and players were announced over the public address system, and thought there should be fewer announcements throughout the game. He said, "If Negro baseball is to be expected to ever participate in white major league clubs, promoters, players and everyone connected with the game must give respect to the game as a great American sport by putting color and not too much ballyhoo in it."[35]

In early August the Buckeyes maintained their second-place position in the league standings as Eugene Bremmer pitched a one-hit shutout of the Memphis Red Sox at League Park. Even though they did not reach the Negro League World Series at the end of 1943, the Buckeyes enjoyed a solid season and increased attendance. Bob Williams claimed the Buckeyes often outdrew the Indians during the season. When the team honored Wilbur Hayes at a game in September, Hayes announced that team attendance for the season cleared 40,000. Season attendance figures for 1942 were estimated at 8,000, while they were later estimated at about 39,000, nearly three times the 1942 totals. While Hayes said he believed the Buckeyes were off to a good start, he would not be happy until he built a championship team in Cleveland. The Buckeyes were named the outstanding team of the year by the Negro American League, in part because of their increase in attendance over the past two years. The Buckeyes were also commended for their second-place finish in both 1942 and 1943. Sam Jethroe was named runner-up to the Negro American League's most valuable player for 1943, Ted "Double Duty" Radcliffe, of the Chicago American Giants. Many of the Buckeyes planned to spend the winter working; some players accepted jobs in Cleveland, while others returned to their hometowns to look for work.[36]

The Negro Leagues hoped to establish a statistics bureau for 1944 that would help the leagues compile and disseminate statistics to fans through the media. This initiative immediately turned controversial when the Negro Leagues selected a white agency to handle the job. Wendell Smith, a sportswriter with the *Pittsburgh Courier*, was initially under consideration for the statistician position before the league selected the white Monroe Elias Agency. Writer Don Deleighbur of the *Baltimore Afro-American* said, "To go out of their way to hire a white man to do a Negro's job (is) an insult no matter how one looks at it." Deleighbur thought the move was a slap in the face of African American sportswriters and the black press in general. He added that the league lacked a strong leader since the death of Rube Foster, who was known for his close ties with the black press.[37]

Bob Williams emphasized the importance of the black press to the Negro Leagues in one of his columns. He said the press was in an awkward position to support Negro League baseball while they tried to move these same players to the major leagues through integration. Williams insisted the African American press was not alone in determining talent as he said, "The American way has usually recognized real talent and insisted upon exploiting it to its fullest possibilities." The black press pushed for integration during World War II because they realized the war offered a prime opportunity: major league teams had roster holes due to military enlistments. If the most talented players were pulled from the Negro Leagues and placed in the major leagues, only the Negro League owners would be disappointed, according to Williams. He thought, along with Don Deleighbur, that when the Negro Leagues hired the Elias Bureau, it was a "slap in the face of the Negro Press." Williams added, "The Negro Press has stuck it's [*sic*] neck out for Negro baseball and provided countless columns of space as it's [*sic*] chief spark of life," especially since the white press tended to ignore the Negro Leagues. The black press provided free publicity to the Negro Leagues, in Williams' opinion, and when the leagues had the chance to pay the papers back with the statistician position, they chose Elias instead. League officials claimed they saved a great deal of money by contracting with Elias, although Williams claimed that African American newspapers were likely to lose money in the deal. Smith planned to share the information for free if he were chosen, while each paper had to pay the Elias Bureau for information. Williams argued that the Elias bid was lower because it planned to make up the difference by charging the African American papers to run the information.[38]

Cum Posey, owner of the Homestead Grays, attempted to defend the league's decision to select the Elias Bureau. He argued that race did not factor into the owners' decision since there were four teams that had at least some white representation in ownership: the Kansas City Monarchs, the Birmingham Black Barons, the Indianapolis Clowns, and the Philadelphia Stars. Posey commended these men for their financial investment in the league and said they should not be "constantly faced by racial antagonism by some members of the Negro Press." Posey also seemed somewhat critical of the African American press for their constant attempts to integrate the major leagues. He posed this question to writers: What if Negro League team owners continually tried to convince white papers to hire a few black writers? With white papers integrated, Posey said that circulation would probably drop at weekly African American papers. Despite this critique, Posey did add that if any major league team wanted to sign one of his players, he would gladly allow the player to have the opportunity.[39]

Prior to the 1944 season Bob Williams continued to pressure the Indians to integrate when he phoned owner Alva Bradley and asked him point blank why the team continually refused to sign African American players. Intercepted by Bradley's secretary, the woman tried to convince Williams to call major league Commissioner Landis with his request. He reminded the secretary that Landis gave a public statement that claimed the matter of integration was left to individual teams. Expecting a brush-off, Williams was surprised when Bradley returned his call. Bradley acted rushed during the phone conversation and told him that he didn't have time to thoroughly discuss the matter. Bradley suggested that he and Williams discuss the matter again in a month or so, but told the writer, "It would appear as if the Negro is still a long way from playing on major league ball teams."[40] Bradley thought that any player from the Negro Leagues must first pass through the minor league system before he could be considered eligible for the majors. When he claimed there were no players in the major leagues who did not play in the minors first, Williams immediately countered with Indians ace pitcher Bob Feller. Forced to concede Williams' point, Bradley reminded Williams that he scouted Jethroe, Woods and Bremmer in 1942 but that none of them played well enough to warrant an official tryout.[41] Even though Bradley was evasive and somewhat negative during the conversation, he did say, "Ten years ago nobody would have thought that Cuban players would be in the majors. Now it is accepted."[42]

In 1944 the Buckeyes were not concerned about losing players to the major leagues but were afraid they would suffer on the field due to player losses to the military and to Mexican teams. The team already lost second baseman Marshall Riddles and new pitcher Herbert Bracken, and there was some concern that the team would lose pitchers "Fireball" Smith and Eugene Bremmer to the military. In the end both were rejected for service; Smith because of a broken left shoulder he suffered playing college football, and Bremmer due to injuries he sustained in the 1942 automobile accident. Parnell Woods was called away from the Buckeyes' spring training camp in Clarksdale, Mississippi, and the team named Archie Ware acting manager in his absence. In the end, Woods was rejected for military service and returned to the team before the regular season matches began.[43] Even though Mexico attempted to lure some of the Buckeyes players south of the border, Ernest Wright said he was willing to match any offers they received in order to keep the men in Cleveland.[44]

Despite this comment from Wright, pitchers "Fireball" Smith and Willie Jefferson defected for Mexico just prior to the start of the 1944 season. Jefferson actually returned in time to win the first game of a doubleheader against the Indianapolis Clowns in the home opener. The team was still set to have a number of youngsters, which Bob Williams viewed as positive when he said, "They give you something to work with. You can neither reform nor improve those old birds, most of whom are still playing 1926 baseball."[45] The Buckeyes claimed that they broke attendance records for a Negro League game at League Park with 10,000 fans present for their home opener with the Clowns. Williams seemed irritated by the Clowns and referred to them as a "circus team." He added that he "will rate them otherwise only when they call their brand of baseball their only claim to fame." Williams thought the Clowns were not necessarily good enough to qualify for league membership based on their talent alone; the added attraction of clowning secured their spot in professional black baseball.[46] Despite these criticisms, the Clowns remained a popular team. It was probably not a coincidence the Buckeyes set their attendance record against this particular team.

The Buckeyes managed to draw close to 10,000 fans when they played the Birmingham Black Barons the next weekend. The Buckeyes won both games of the doubleheader, 3–1 and 2–1, and took the lead in the Negro American League pennant race. Bob Williams thought they had a chance to win the pennant in 1944, in part because of the Buckeyes' solid play against the talented Barons. Jack Cressen, announcer for the Cleveland Indians, claimed that the games against the Barons were some of the best he ever saw played in Cleveland. There was a bit of controversy during the Birmingham series as Wingfield Welch, manager of the Black Barons, pushed umpire Harry Walker when the skipper disagreed with one of the arbiter's calls. Williams admitted that Walker made a bad call, and eventually it was reversed in the Barons' favor. Williams accused Welch of having a childish temper tantrum to get his way, and added, "His actions were no credit to himself, nor did they improve the attitude of the many persons present who have come to regard Negro baseball as a picnic or holiday attraction."[47]

The umpires in Cleveland were named to their positions by Wilbur Hayes prior to the 1944 season. Walker, Finis Braneham and Jimmy Thompson were the umpires Hayes selected for the Buckeyes' home games, and Hayes claimed the men had complete authority for the 1944 season. Even though Williams criticized Welch for his behavior over the disputed call, it seemed as if Walker was in control throughout the outburst. The umpires also had the support of league president J.B. Martin, who threatened to suspend and/or fine any player who got out of line during a game. This was seen as a positive development because it would show that "they mean business, from now on, and that they will not tolerate the kind of disgrace that featured in the Cleveland-Chicago mix-up last season." This is the type of authority that Walker requested from Martin in his letter last year; the league obviously listened to his complaints.[48]

When the Buckeyes squared off against the Chicago American Giants in late June, Bob Williams claimed there were again disruptions from the teams during the games. While he declined to elaborate on the details, Williams said the games were marred by bad behavior from the players. These disruptive bad seeds "run the teams, the umpires and the fans." Even though he admitted that some disputes in sporting events were natural, Williams said, "But when ten thousand people must sit and wait, after paying their money, while a bunch of rude uncouth rednecks leer and threaten, and fuss and fume with everybody from the managers and officials to innocent bystanders, it seems like taking a thing too far. What are umpires for? What are managers for? And what are rule books for? Maybe some of the arguing players can tell me."[49]

Williams continued to complain about the players' on-field conduct in a July column, and claimed that bad behavior possibly harmed attendance figures. Even though attendance was steady in 1944 as most Sunday games attracted roughly 10,000 people to League Park, Williams thought it could be even higher. He honestly believed that poor player conduct kept fans away because they didn't want to spend their hard-earned money "to come to a ball game and watch a bunch of bozos squabble over everything in the sun except why they fail to catch so many balls, or why they stood stupidly at the plate while the third strike was being called." Williams said that the quality of Negro League baseball improved during the war years, which should translate to increased attendance. Fans supposedly booed players during a recent series with the Memphis Red Sox every time they started to argue with an umpire or exhibited "unsportsmanlike" conduct. Williams was not surprised by this development; in fact, he was surprised that it took this long for fans to rebel against bad conduct. If this poor behavior continued, Williams feared an African American would never make it to the major leagues.[50] When the American Giants were set to return to League Park in August, the *Call and Post* said, "Here's hoping the Chicago boys who are so good they tell everybody how to run the game will be in Chicago helping the West to win. Maybe then, we can have a clean, lively baseball game at League Park."[51]

DeHart Hubbard continued to suggest ways that Negro League baseball could improve, and harped on the standard issues of umpiring, organization and publicity. He thought the Negro Leagues could improve by allowing all owners to have a degree of power as opposed to just a handful of powerful teams and promoters. The problems with the players' on-field behavior could be averted with a written code of conduct and incentives for good behavior. Umpires should be appointed by and paid for by the league, which would eliminate some of the problems Harry Walker faced. The leagues and owners should team up for better and more efficient publicity throughout the Negro Leagues. NAL teams should stay in the West and the NNL teams in the East in order to save on transportation costs and improve fan interest. The season also should be expanded to include at least 100 league contests. Hubbard thought players should be signed to notarized contracts to avoid players jumping teams to sign with competitors or Mexican outfits. Hubbard wanted the public to realize that black baseball was "an outstanding and progressive enterprise reflecting credit on the Negro people." He added, "Opportunity is knocking loudly. Either we take advantage of it now or lose it, probably forever."[52]

As he did during the 1942 East-West All-Star Game, Satchel Paige attracted controversy over his involvement in the 1944 all-star matchup. Satchel Paige threatened to sit out that year's game if he wasn't paid more. When that plan appeared to backfire, he assured the league that he planned to donate his increased salary to an army or navy relief organization. Writer Billy Young supported Paige in a *Call and Post* column and claimed that league officials never made any kind of charitable donation from East-West game proceeds. As for Paige asking for more money, Young said, "We believe in free enterprise, don't we? We advocate Negroes demanding what is theirs on the basis of merit, talent and ability? If so, the Negro businessman must pay off just the same as the white business man." The public just wanted to see Paige, according to Young, and the leadership of the Negro Leagues should not deprive fans of that experience. Owners claimed they took losses for many years before they were finally able to make money. Young still believed that if someone looked at many of the owners' financial records, he or she would still see a big difference between what the owners earn and what the players earn.[53]

Paige told Bob Williams that his holdout was not about money, but simply represented his belief that the money should be donated to a military relief fund. Paige told Williams that he made $800 for his 1943 appearance in the East-West game and anticipated he would net $2,500 in the 1944 game. Williams said that most sports writers across the country were not sympathetic with Paige's revolt and claimed he suggested the money be donated to charity only after he did not get the wage he wanted. Williams expressed his belief that Paige was sincere when he said, "This year, Satch was merely interested in being patriotic — and was willing to sacrifice himself to possible martyrdom on behalf of his country." Williams accused many writers (specifically eastern writers) of siding with the Negro National League on most occasions rather than individual players. Reportedly, Paige's absence did not do much to diminish attendance at the game.[54]

At the end of the season, the *Call and Post* celebrated the Buckeyes' season, even though they did not make it to the Negro League World Series. Bob Williams commended the team for its solid play throughout the season and said the Buckeyes drew about 65,000 fans to League Park during the season. Another estimate put that figure at 75,000, but that total included an estimated 10,000 fans that came to League Park for an exhibition series between the Buckeyes and the Homestead Grays after the regular season concluded.[55] Multiple Buckeyes were honored after the season by the Negro American League. Sam Jethroe earned the batting title for the NAL with a .353 batting average and also had the most runs (55), hits (97), total bases (121), doubles (14), and stolen bases (18) in the league. The Buckeyes led the NAL in team batting for 1944 with an average of .271 and in team fielding with a .958 mark. The entire Buckeyes infield — Archie Ware, John Cowan, William Horne and Parnell Woods — led the league in fielding percentage at their respective positions. Even though Satchel Paige technically had the best earned run average in the league during 1944, he only pitched 48 innings and did not qualify for the ERA title. Instead, the honor went to two Buckeyes pitchers, George Jefferson and Lowell Hardin, who tied with a 1.00 ERA. During the season several of the Buckeyes players, Parnell Woods, Willie Grace, Sam Jethroe, Archie Ware, Buddy Armour, Johnny Cowan and Jefferson Guiwn, earned the nickname "Murderer's Row" because of their hitting proficiency.[56]

The Buckeyes barnstormed throughout the South during the fall with a new player added to their roster: a catcher named Quincy Trouppe who "could hit and throw like nobody's business," according to the *Call and Post*. Wilbur Hayes tried to sign Trouppe for the previous three years and finally succeeded after the 1944 season.[57] In order to obtain Quincy Trouppe, Wilbur Hayes traded "Fireball" Smith (who returned to Cleveland during the 1944 season) to Kansas City. The Buckeyes named Trouppe manager for 1945, while Parnell Woods remained with the team as captain with no drop in salary from the previous year. Hayes said that he discussed this shift with Woods before the trade took place and both agreed that it gave them the best chance of obtaining Trouppe since he wanted to manage. The Trouppe signing represented a huge upgrade for the Buckeyes, as catcher was their weakest position during the 1944 season. Hayes complimented the city of Cleveland for its support of the Buckeyes and noted "the splendid spirit of cooperation the Buckeyes were given by fans and press of Cleveland, which has become one of the best cities for baseball."[58]

In 1943 and 1944 the *Call and Post* continued to push for integration as the newspaper likely realized that World War II provided unique advantages to African American players. As major league players were increasingly called to duty by the military, their absence left large holes on the team rosters. To keep bodies in the dugout, the major leagues were often forced to sign retired, injured or mediocre players. The Negro Leagues offered an untapped, talented group of players that could potentially help a number of struggling white teams. As America fought for freedom around the world, it became painfully obvious that many of its citizens lacked rights in their own country. Many writers in the African American press pointed to this hypocrisy and argued that the integration of baseball was a great step toward eliminating some of these inequalities. The Negro Leagues faced challenges during this two-year period, as they lost players to military enlistment and the Mexican leagues. The black press remained vigilant when it came to the on-field behavior of the Negro League players because they knew that major league teams would be reluctant to sign a player who was viewed as a troublemaker or a hothead. While the press campaigned for integration, Wilbur Hayes and Ernest Wright assembled a talented group of black ballplayers that would shock the nation in 1945.

4

When the Underdog Ruled

The Buckeyes Win the 1945 World Series

The 1945 Cleveland Buckeyes were the perfect Cinderella story; their World Series victory that season was scripted like a storybook Hollywood ending. While the African American press continued to push for integration in baseball, the writers paused to acknowledge one of Cleveland's great baseball teams and one of the largest upsets in the history of the Negro League World Series. When the Buckeyes accomplished a resounding four games-to-zero defeat of the powerful Homestead Grays, it was shocking, yet not unfathomable. While sports writers tossed around the "Cinderella" and the "Hollywood ending" lines and touted the power of the Grays, they admitted the Buckeyes were a talented and underrated team. Did fans and the media realize that the 1945 squad was a special team early in the season, or did the World Series victory come completely out of left field? This season was a great moment in the history of Negro League baseball in Cleveland, but the Buckeyes' victory was bittersweet. After the World Series Branch Rickey and the Brooklyn Dodgers signed Jackie Robinson and announced that he would start the 1946 season in the team's minor league system. After integration the Buckeyes were forced to fight for their survival. The integration of major league baseball in Cleveland was just two years away.

Bob Williams continued to criticize segregation in the major leagues and wondered how far teams would go before they accepted African American players. Teams still suffered from war-era manpower shortages, and Williams thought the next move was to include women on teams or cut the number of players on active rosters. He added, "It's surprising how far you can go off-side to avoid doing the only obvious thing to do — if the brain is sufficiently agile — and the mind is sufficiently clogged with the venom of race prejudice."[1] Williams continued to push the 61-year-old Alva Bradley, whom he referred to as "old man Bradley," and said that he was likely too set in his ways to change his mind at this point. If Bradley reversed his stance on integrating the Indians, Williams said that "all will be forgiven."[2]

The passage of an anti-discrimination bill in New York pushed some teams to consider African American players for their teams in 1945. Bob Williams was critical of Branch Rickey and the Brooklyn Dodgers, and said that teams approached integration "half-heartedly" and only went far enough to avoid violation of the anti-discrimination law. (Little did Williams know, Rickey was serious about integration.) In order for these tryouts to be considered successful, Bob Williams said that players actually had to sign contracts with these teams. Harry Walker even weighed in on the subject of integration and said that if major league teams were serious about adding African American players, they should sign them and train them in the minors, as they did promising young white players. Williams seemed guardedly optimistic about the chances of integration when he said, "Although the gateway seems ajar, victory is not really in sight. It seems near — and at the same time it seems so far away. But who can tell how much farther open the door will be shoved by this new anti-discrimination law of New York City. (And someone said you couldn't legislate liberality and fair play, as if EVERY law on the books were not an example of it!) All we can do is keep fighting to the very end."[3] The issue even reached the national level when Congress opened an investigation into the hiring practices of major league baseball in May of 1945.[4]

During this same time period, the Buckeyes prepared for the 1945 season. The team spent much of spring training that year in Muskogee, Oklahoma, and played games throughout Texas and in New Orleans. After one particular match-up in New Orleans, the *Call and Post* (likely sports editor Bob Williams) gushed about new manager/catcher Quincy Trouppe. He called Trouppe "sensational" and said that Hayes' belief that a quality catcher would balance the team was accurate. The article continued to say that the "giant" 6'2", 228-pound catcher "hits the ball hard, and is a fine receiver, with a true, fast-throwing arm, and the ability to catch and throw with lightning-like speed." Trouppe alone was fun to watch, according to the article.[5] Hayes had high hopes for the season and talked about two early games against the Chicago American Giants, where the Buckeyes won, 9–8 and 14–2. Hayes believed the team looked strong during this pair of games — particularly Sam Jethroe and Avelino Canizares, who each homered, and pitcher George Jefferson. Hayes hoped to increase attendance for the 1945 season and wanted to involve more fans from regional Ohio cities like Youngstown, Akron, Warren, Canton and Lorain.[6]

During April of spring training one Buckeyes player, star outfielder Sam Jethroe gathered national attention. The Boston Red Sox offered Jethroe, Jackie Robinson of the Kansas City Monarchs, and Marvin Williams of the Philadelphia Stars a tryout at the team's Fenway Park in Boston. The *Call and Post* said it was the first time a Cleveland player was offered a major league tryout, and neglected to mention the paper's earlier efforts to convince the Indians to sign Jethroe.[7] Cum Posey called the tryout a sham and said it was "the most humiliating experience Negro baseball has yet suffered from white organized baseball. It was humiliating to the writers who took these players to the campus." This comment was in reference to the African American media figures that accompanied the players, a group that included Wendell Smith of the *Pittsburgh Courier*. None of the players was asked to run or throw, which Posey said were two of the primary skills that scouts wanted to see from young players. Posey continued, "Any white rookie one-half as good as any of these players would have been kept for at least a week and sent to some minor league club."[8]

When Jethroe recalled the event in 1993, he claimed that his most dominant memory from the tryout was the three players' discussion of President Franklin D. Roosevelt, who died within days of the audition. The men were instructed to wear their team's uniforms for the tryout, even though it was often standard practice for the auditioning team to provide the uniforms. While the motives of the Red Sox ownership were called into question, Jethroe still believed that if he was given the opportunity, he could succeed in the major leagues. When Jethroe, Robinson and Williams were turned away from the tryout, Jethroe recalled thinking, "I can still have my fun in the Negro Leagues."[9] In 1945 Jethroe had the thrill of a primary role in the Buckeyes' World Series championship. In 1950 he made it to the major leagues with the Boston Braves and was named the oldest Rookie of the Year at the age of 33.

The *Call and Post* predicted that Jethroe and the 1945 Buckeyes squad would be fun to watch, and hyped the team after the season opener. Bob Williams said the Buckeyes were a "classy" bunch of ballplayers and were considered strong in every area. New catcher and manager Quincy Trouppe was considered a major addition to the team, and Williams also touted the "superb pitching" and the "murderers row" of the lineup. He was also excited about the team's new shortstop, "classy Cuban" and "home run king" Avelino Canizares. Reportedly, Canizares endeared himself to Cleveland fans during a doubleheader sweep of the Memphis Red Sox at the end of May when he hit an inside-the-park home run. Williams said that the excellent hitting, running and fielding by the young shortstop, who could not speak English, made him "the first player to capture the fans' attention without the aid of ballyhoo."[10] While exact figures were unclear, reportedly the Buckeyes had the second-highest payroll in the Negro Leagues, just after the Homestead Grays. For Bob Williams, this fact proved Ernest Wright wanted a championship team bad enough to pay for it.[11]

The Buckeyes jumped out to an early lead in the Negro American League and by mid–June the *Call and Post* claimed they were "drunk with recent successes" and bragged that they led the AL by a comfortable margin. They also led the league in team batting (.316) and fielding (.996). The Buckeyes won the first-half title as Bob Williams declared, "It looks like Ernie Wright and Wilbur Hayes have picked a winner." The team won the first half despite the fact that Trouppe missed about two weeks with a dislocated shoulder and Buddy Armour sat out two weeks after the removal of a tumor from his neck.[12] The team was compared to the Indians, who Williams bragged could not play as well as the Buckeyes at the moment.[13] In July, Williams admitted that while anything could happen in the second half of the season, there was a "tremendous" chance that the Buckeyes would be the league champions for 1945.

The summer did not pass without a bit of controversy and excitement in Cleveland, specifically more incidents that involved umpires' decisions. During a game in June the Buckeyes were locked in a 2–2 tie with the Chicago American Giants in the bottom of the 13th inning. Avelino Canizares crossed home and was called safe by umpire Harry Walker for the game-winning run. The call was immediately disputed by the Chicago American Giants, and three of their players physically grabbed Walker, forcing police at the park to intervene. The *Call and Post* was forced to admit that Canizares was likely out and that Walker did make an inaccurate call. He was the victim of catcalls and yelling when he came out to umpire the second game of the doubleheader. Supposedly even the home crowd yelled at Walker, or at least the fans that were not there for the Buckeyes.[14] As the *Call and Post* acknowledged the umpiring mistake, Bob Williams defended Walker and emphasized that he was only human. In fact, Williams claimed to have had a brief discussion with Walker in between innings right before the botched call. Walker said that this was a stressful part of the game, but that the winner would get no help from him. Williams said he was a friendly, fair and courageous umpire who did a lot for sports in his 20 years in the profession. In fact, Walker even gave a letter to all players on Opening Day at League Park, reminding them to behave themselves and hold themselves to high standards. Walker said that umpires in Cleveland would not tolerate profanity from players since fans were so put off by it. Perhaps Williams tried to remove any suspicion that the call was made on purpose, rather than on accident.[15]

The second umpiring incident was a bit more disturbing and sent reverberations throughout the league. Less than a month after Walker's inaccurate call, the Future Outlook League of Cleveland, a group the *Pittsburgh Courier* referred to as "a militant civic organization," sponsored a game against the Birmingham Black Barons to raise money for the organization at Cleveland Municipal Stadium.[16] With more than 10,000 people in the stands, a figure that included two major league scouts, Birmingham Baron second baseman Lorenzo "Piper" Davis became angered at a call during the third inning and "brutally attacked" umpire Jimmy Thompson. The disputed play was actually similar to the June play with the Chicago American Giants. Once again the Buckeye player in question was Canizares, only this time he was called safe at first when the opposing team (the Barons) believed he was out. Davis began to argue with Thompson, and Thompson ordered him off the field for swearing at him. The *Call and Post* claimed that as Thompson tried to walk away from the argument, the Barons first baseman attempted to trip him. Seconds later Davis punched Thompson in the face, knocking him over and leading him to receive treatment at Charity Hospital in Cleveland. The *Call and Post* also made a point of mentioning that Thompson had two sons in the armed services overseas, and that no Buckeye player would ever do such a terrible thing.[17] Fans were said to be outraged. NAL president Dr. J.B. Martin fined Davis $50 and suspended him indefinitely; Davis was also criminally charged with assault and battery and held overnight on $1,000 bail.[18]

The Barons apologized for Davis's conduct and defended him, saying that he was "not evil by nature" and was actually a mild-mannered man. Abe Saperstein, owner of the Barons, vouched for Davis, who also played on Saperstein's Harlem Globetrotters basketball team. This incident would be mentioned sporadically for the rest of the season, with reminders of how awful Davis's conduct was and how that type of behavior would not be tolerated in Cleveland.[19] Bob Williams thought the NAL showed "extreme reluctance" to punish Davis for the incident with Thompson. He was only suspended while the case was pending in court. It was not clear who, but someone convinced Thompson to withdraw the assault and battery charges. Williams said, "League officials were more interested in 'ironing out' the affair with a minimum of public reaction than they were in setting an example that might have improved the quality of player conduct at whatever cost to the particular player or club affected."[20]

John O. Holly, president of the Future Outlook League, publicly denounced the attack on Thompson. He said, "Why, never in the history of the FOL — at no kind of affair we have ever given or taken any part in — have we faced so shameful an issue." Holly hoped to establish a group of citizens that would warn visiting teams that such conduct was unacceptable in Cleveland.[21] Holly demanded an apology for the injury to the "little five-foot, two-inch unwary umpire weighing a scant 120 pounds."[22] The FOL was an organization that supported working-class African Americans in Cleveland. They backed boycotts in the city of Cleveland when stores would not hire African American workers and assisted blacks in finding employment.[23] They were involved with several Buckeyes games as recipients of a portion of the proceeds.

Not every disputed call turned into an incident like the ones with the Chicago American Giants and the Birmingham Black Barons. When the Kansas City Monarchs and Satchel Paige came to town in July, the Monarchs took issue with a close call at first base during the ninth inning. Some of the Monarch players began to "swarm" onto the field to protest the call but returned "obediently" to the dugout at manager Frank Duncan's orders. (This was the same Frank Duncan that managed some of Cleveland's early entries in the Negro National League.) The *Call and Post* claimed that Duncan chose to "properly" protest the umpire's call and conducted himself "according to regulations." Ironically, this game was Thompson's first contest back in uniform after his injury during the Barons game.[24]

The Buckeyes continued to win throughout the summer, and in anticipation of a Negro American League pennant, the Buckeyes held a Wilbur Hayes Day on September 1 in order to thank the general manager for the strong team he assembled. Fans were encouraged to attend in order to have a portion of their ticket payment go toward a present for Hayes — a new Chevrolet automobile. The *Call and Post* said that Hayes was honored for his contributions to the sports world and also for turning the Buckeyes into a championship club in just three years. Hayes said he did not search for individual stars, but instead looked to build an all-around solid team. Even though there were a few standout players, the goal was for a strong

In 1945 the Cleveland Buckeyes shocked the Homestead Grays when they defeated them 4 games to 0 in the Negro League World Series. Top row, left to right: John Brown, Johnny Cowan, Avelino Canizares, George Jefferson, Quincy Trouppe, Parnell Woods, Ernie Wright, Willie Grace, Wilbur Hayes. Bottom row: Earl Ashby, Buddy Armour, Gene Bremmer, Willie Jefferson, unidentified child, Ernie Wright, Jr., Frank Carswell, Archie Ware.

team. Hayes was credited with work in the community and for always thinking about everyone but himself.[25] Hayes and Wright obviously knew what they were doing when they built the Buckeyes squad. Even though the economic climate was much more favorable during World War II, no other Negro League team in Cleveland came close to what this team accomplished.

At the end of the season, it looked like the Buckeyes might need to hold a playoff against the Chicago American Giants, the second-place team in the standings. The NAL initially thought the Buckeyes did not play in enough league contests, which, if true, left them ineligible for the second-half title. That meant the Buckeyes, the first-half champs, would play the American Giants, the second-half champs, in a one-game playoff. However, at the last minute extra league games were "discovered" and the playoff was deemed unnecessary as the Buckeyes were named second-half champions.[26] Bob Williams mused at how far the Buckeyes had come since the 1941, 1942, and 1943 seasons. During those years, he thought the Buckeyes looked "like a team of scrub sandlotters, ready for the ash can." Williams asked how a team could play so poorly so consistently, and added that the team was "supposedly too mediocre, even for the most tolerant or race-conscious individual."[27]

The *Call and Post* believed that the championship series would draw record crowds, both white and black fans, to the games in Cleveland. The contest was the first World Series appearance by a Cleveland baseball team since the Indians beat the Brooklyn Robins (later the Dodgers) in 1920. The strong 1945 team was given an even chance to beat the Grays by the *Call and Post* since the Grays were "steadily declining in the power and flaws which highlighted some of their earlier title triumphs." The Buckeyes were both young and strong and "have the thrill of early success behind them," according to the newspaper. However, the *Call and Post* pointed out that as Wright and Hayes gathered this group of talented players, the Grays were "steamrolling" everyone else. They had more "top-flight" hitters on the Grays, even though the Buckeyes supposedly feared no team. The Buckeyes hoped to make the Grays fear them in 1945.[28] The Buckeyes had their share of dangerous hitting: Jethroe finished first in the league in batting average for the second year in a row with an average of .393, which prompted the *Call and Post* to refer to him as "king Jethroe."[29]

In game one of the World Series at Cleveland Stadium, the two teams went "toe to toe" for seven innings as Buckeyes pitcher Willie Jefferson and Grays pitcher Leroy (Lefty) Welmaker battled. The game was scoreless in the bottom of the seventh inning when Quincy Trouppe tripled. Buddy Armour struck out before second baseman Johnny Cowan hit a sacrifice fly to left to make it 1–0. In the eighth inning, Archie Ware singled, Parnell Woods walked and Willie Grace hit a looping single to right that scored Ware. According to the *Call and Post*, despite the streak of scoreless innings, Jefferson spent much of the game in trouble. One example was during the seventh inning when he gave up a lead-off double to Dave Hoskins but never allowed him to score. Hoskins eventually scored the Grays' only run in the ninth inning off a Josh Gibson single to make the final score 2–1.[30]

The Buckeyes' win in game two prompted the media's "story-book thriller" comments. The *Call and Post* called the end of the game a "made to order movie baseball thriller" as starting pitcher Eugene Bremmer drove in the winning run and effectively "won his own game." Down 2–0 in the seventh inning at League Park, Willie Grace opened the Buckeyes' half of the frame with a home run over the Gem Safety Razor advertisement on the right field wall. Next, Buddy Armour doubled to right and scored the tying run on a Jelly Jackson error at second off a ball hit by Eugene Bremmer. Bremmer held the Grays scoreless the next two innings, and in the bottom of the ninth Trouppe doubled to right. As a pitched ball got past Grays catcher Josh Gibson, Trouppe moved to third. The next two batters, Buddy Armour and Johnny Cowan, were intentionally walked by Grays pitcher John Wright. Trouppe actually left third briefly to coach the next batter, Bremmer, in his at-bat. Whatever Trouppe said must have worked; Bremmer hit a deep fly ball to right field that allowed the catcher/manager to score from third.[31]

The *Courier* claimed that game two of the series had a story book ending for a "Cinderella team." The paper added that the Buckeyes carried Bremmer off the field after the team won the game. Willie Grace was supposedly showered with more than admiration after a seventh-inning home run; the *Courier* claimed that fans threw money at Grace, the Buckeyes' outfielder, as he crossed home plate. The *Courier*, specifically writer Wendell Smith, thought the Grays would wake up and still manage to win the 1945 World Series. Despite his confidence in the Grays, Smith had to admit that the Buckeyes were no fluke and that they "used the skills of a great artist." After they lost the first two games of the series, the *Courier* claimed the Grays were "grief stricken" and did not have the "fire and dash" they once had. Wilbur Hayes supposedly did a little dance on the field after game two, while Wright was "all smiles" according to the *Courier*. Grays owner Cum Posey was "glum" and left immediately after the second game for Pittsburgh. The Buckeyes were still very cautious of the Grays' heavy hitters, as Willie Jefferson admitted he feared that if one started to hit, it would open the floodgates.[32]

In the end, the Buckeyes never had to worry about a sudden barrage of hitting since the team totally shut down the Grays powerful offense in the next two games, 4–0 and 5–0. George Jefferson earned the victory in the 4–0 shutout in Washington, D.C. Both papers seemed to downplay the events of games three and four, and provided fewer blow-by-blow details (particularly the third game). The first two games of the World Series were both close and relatively exciting, whereas two shutouts likely decreased the tension in the last two contests. In fact, the *Call and Post* claimed that the only time the Buckeyes showed signs of trouble in the fourth game was when pitcher Frank Carswell found himself in a bases-loaded jam in the third inning. The Buckeyes scored after Canizares got an infield single, Ware walked and Jethroe singled to load the bases. Parnell Woods was safe at first on an error by the Grays' second baseman, which allowed Canizares and Ware to score. In the fourth inning Grace singled to center, and Trouppe followed with a single. Grace went to third on a wild pitch and scored on a sacrifice fly to left by Cowan to make it 3–0. Cowan and Carswell scored the last two runs in the seventh inning on a hit by Jethroe to center.[33]

The *Call and Post* said the 1945 Buckeyes were one of the greatest teams of all time, and umpire Harry Walker even said the Buckeyes reminded him of powerful New York Yankee teams from the last two decades. Walker complimented the individual Buckeye players and said they were the nicest men he ever umpired, a team of gentlemen.[34] The *Call and Post* claimed that Wilbur Hayes always predicted the Buckeyes would win the series in four games, although this prediction came conveniently after the completion of the World Series. Despite this claim, the *Call and Post* writers admitted they were surprised by the Buckeyes and said they did not initially expect that they would be a championship team. The paper lamented, "They were great and we never really knew them." Bob Williams even admitted that he thought the Grays would manage to conquer the Buckeyes, even after they won the first two games of the series. The fact that the Grays were set to return to more familiar eastern cities was part of Williams' reasoning, although he added, "Darned if the Buckeyes didn't run 'em right off the field!"[35]

After their World Series victory, the Buckeyes played in a couple of exhibition games and celebrated their victory at the Majestic Hotel in Cleveland. The city council also passed a resolution congratulating the team for its win. At the Majestic party, Ernest Wright spoke to the crowd and became so overwhelmed by emotion he could not speak. Quincy Trouppe also shared a portion of his management strategy for 1945 with the crowd at the Majestic. Trouppe said he decided during spring training that every player must focus on fundamentals and "master them before we can hope to march towards a championship." He admitted that winning a championship was his lifelong ambition, and Trouppe said he realized by the end of spring training the team may accomplish this goal. Trouppe said the Buckeyes' players mastered fundamentals before they even left spring training to travel north for the season.[36] The *Call and Post* also received from a Cleveland citizen a letter congratulating the team on its success. Specifically, the fan said that "Wilbur Hayes, manager of the championship team, should be the happiest man in the world having accomplished in four short years, a job which managers of the Cleveland Indians had been attempting for the last twenty years — to bring Cleveland a real baseball team."[37]

About a month after the victory, Bob Williams placed most of the credit on Quincy Trouppe as the "man behind the scenes" in the Buckeyes' World Series victory. Trouppe guided a team who "within one season, romped through the Grays as if they were a sandlot team." Since there were only two additions — Trouppe and Canizares — to the roster in the offseason, and since the former shortstop, Billy Horne, was also good, it showed that Trouppe made a difference. Williams believed that Trouppe improved the fundamentals of the current players, which was his stated goal before the season started. When Trouppe discussed the team, he said, "I knew I didn't have power hitters, with the exception of myself, so I had to utilize the speed, hit-and-run, bunt, and other batting techniques to the greatest possible advantage over my opponent." After he chose the appropriate strategy, Trouppe's next task was to teach the players when and how to implement the plan during a game. Trouppe and the Buckeyes

Quincy Trouppe was a star catcher with the Buckeyes and was manager for their 1945 World Series victory and their 1947 World Series appearance.

successfully implemented his strategy against the Grays in all aspects of the game: pitching, fielding and hitting. While some of these comments from Trouppe seem somewhat self congratulatory, Bob Williams claimed it was difficult to convince Trouppe to admit to his successes, and that "he looks and seems to act like a big boy in his teens, but his men will attest to his forcefulness, intelligence, and sincerity." Williams thought that Trouppe stood out as unique among Negro League managers.[38]

In his autobiography, Trouppe said he received important advice from "Candy" Jim Taylor that he carried with him through his managing career. This advice included "try to know your men ... know their abilities, and know when to change pitchers." Another important lesson that Trouppe learned from Taylor was to keep his own business private so that it did not interfere with the morale of the team.[39] He also realized how good the 1945 Buckeyes were. Even though Trouppe admitted that the Buckeyes were young and may have been a bit star struck by the Grays, they "were not a fluke."

The team also had a great deal of speed. According to Trouppe, "We could run the tongue out of anybody's head." He said that the Grays participated in a great deal of good-natured heckling towards the Buckeyes that continued even after they lost the first game of the series to the Cleveland club. Trouppe said that the more the Grays heckled, the more the Buckeyes hustled. After the Buckeyes won game two, the Grays stopped joking. They were in shock after the series, although Trouppe admitted that many Buckeyes also found it difficult to fully realize what they accomplished.[40]

Soon after the end of the Negro League World Series, Jackie Robinson made history when he signed a major league contract with Branch Rickey and the Brooklyn Dodgers on October 22, 1945. The Dodgers planned to send Robinson to one of the club's minor league teams, the Montreal Royals of the International League, for the 1946 season. Even though Robinson would not reach the majors until 1947, and there was no guarantee of his success in the Dodgers' system, some Negro League owners still rebelled against the development. Writer Don Deleighbur was angered by the Negro League owners protests, since the press and the public fought for baseball integration for many years. Monarchs officials claimed they planned to fight the Dodgers' acquisition of Robinson, and other Negro League owners were expected to join the fight. Deleighbur admitted that integration of the major leagues would likely kill the Negro Leagues but did not seem too concerned about that possibility. Dr. J.B. Martin, president of the Negro American League, later claimed that the NAL had no objections to the Robinson signing but believed that Rickey should compensate the Monarchs for Robinson.[41]

In hindsight the Buckeyes' world championship seems somewhat bittersweet; with integration on the horizon in Cleveland, the 1945 title was one of the last great moments for Negro League baseball in the city. Even though the Buckeyes made it back to the World Series in 1947, they lost to the New York Cubans, four games to one. Even though the *Call and Post* still encouraged integration throughout the 1945 season, the newspaper paused to acknowledge the accomplishments of a special Buckeyes team. Over the years, Negro League baseball in Cleveland struggled and the city failed to offer a team with a winning record. In just a few short years the Buckeyes took themselves from "just another attempt at a Negro League team" to world champions. The 1945 Homestead Grays were the type of team that used to travel to Cleveland to embarrass the home team. This time, the Cleveland team shut them down with a four games-to-zero shutout in the World Series.

5

The Buckeyes on the Brink
of Integration

After their World Series title in 1945, the Buckeyes hoped to maintain their success for several years. Unfortunately, there were a number of events in 1946 and 1947 that harmed the Buckeyes in the short term and impeded their success for the long term. Several players from the 1945 squad chose to play in Latin America, which left several gaps on the Buckeyes' roster. At the end of 1945 the Brooklyn Dodgers signed Jackie Robinson and announced that he would spend the 1946 season with their Montreal farm club. Even though this was a positive development in baseball and American society, it was a sign that things were changing for the Negro Leagues. Once other African American stars left the league to play for major league baseball, it caused damage from which the Negro Leagues could not recover. The Buckeyes returned to the Negro League World Series in 1947 but lost by a four games-to-one margin to the New York Cubans; one of the last shining moments for a team that would cease to exist just three years later. When Larry Doby joined the Cleveland Indians in 1947 and Jackie Robinson and the Brooklyn Dodgers reached the World Series in the same year, the accomplishments of the Buckeyes were forgotten by fans and media alike.

Despite the changes on the horizon for Negro League baseball, there were efforts to improve and strengthen the leagues in 1946. Cleveland Jackson of the *Call and Post* offered a number of suggestions and critiques to improve the league and help it survive a potential loss of players to the major leagues. Jackson said, "Negro baseball is at the crossroads of its existence as a race enterprise, despite the loyalty of its faithful fans and the sage advice of the Negro Press." He added that there was "dissension and mistrust" in both the Negro National League and the Negro American League that threatened to destroy both institutions. Jackson was encouraged by the fact that at their winter meetings the leagues decided to institute a contract system that was similar to the major leagues. As it was previously, Negro League players could move around at the end of each season rather than adhering to a contract with a specific team. While this couldn't stop the major leagues from signing players, as they did with Jackie Robinson of the Kansas City Monarchs and Johnny Wright of the Homestead Grays, they hoped it would lead to a fairer exchange, with compensation paid to the teams.[1]

Jackson also found it bothersome that almost no Negro League team owned their fields; they all relied on the rental of major league parks. Even though Pittsburgh Crawfords owner Gus Greenlee had his own field in the 1930s, Greenlee Field, the park was torn down in 1938 in favor of public housing in Pittsburgh's Hill District. Jackson was afraid that major league clubs might "put the pinch on" the Negro League teams and refuse them the opportunity to play in their parks. Despite the challenges teams faced with playing venues, Jackson said that Negro League teams did well financially during World War II. He hoped that teams could survive financially after the integration of the major leagues since not all African Americans were Jackie Robinson or Johnny Wright, the other black player signed by the Dodgers. For 1946 the Buckeyes continued to rent League Park and Cleveland Municipal Stadium from the Indians, with the majority of their games played at League Park. A fan paid $1.30 for a grandstand ticket and $1 for a pavilion ticket at League Park, while at Cleveland Stadium it was $1.80 for a grandstand ticket and $1 for a pavilion seat. The Buckeyes claimed that the higher prices for Municipal Stadium games were to cover the cost of using the lights.[2]

Negro League teams, including the Buckeyes, faced increased competition from teams in Mexico and Latin America when it came to signing players. A number of Buckeye players from the 1945 world championship team spent the winter of 1945–46 playing baseball outside of the United States, many in Venezuela. Ernest Wright and Wilbur Hayes actually traveled to Havana, Cuba, in the offseason to scout players and to "contact the wandering members of their 1945 Negro baseball champions."[3] Hayes signed Perez Larrinago, a right-handed hitter who was supposedly "the sensation of the strong Havana League." In February of 1946, Hayes learned that he was likely to lose the Buckeyes' shortstop from 1945, Avelino Canizares, to Laredo in the Mexican Baseball League. The "lucrative" contract that Canizares signed was supposedly for less money than the Buckeyes offered; the Buckeyes were unable to match the $3,000 bonus that came with the Mexican contract.[4]

Cleveland Jackson was confident that the rest of the Buckeyes would avoid the temptation of Latin American baseball and return to Cleveland for the 1946 season. George and Willie Jefferson, Quincy Trouppe, Parnell Woods and Sam Jethroe all left the United States to play during the off-season; their absence would severely hamper the Buckeyes. Jackson was concerned that the Laredo club might draw other Negro League players south of the border since they already signed several American players. In addition to Canizares, Lloyd "Ducky" Davenport left the Buckeyes to play for Laredo. There was a rumor that Roberto Estalella, a former outfielder for the Philadelphia Athletics, signed with Laredo for $11,000. Due to a new Negro League regulation, any player that left the league to play outside of the United States was supposed to receive a five-year ban from the Negro Leagues. Players were allowed to leave for winter baseball leagues without penalty, as long as they returned for the regular season.[5]

Sam Jethroe reportedly was offered $15,000 over three years by two brothers, Jorge and Bernardo Pasqual, to play in Mexico. The brothers first made an offer to Jethroe while he played winter ball in Venezuela; the $15,000 contract was the second such offer the Pasquals made Jethroe. During the 1945–46 offseason, Jethroe played for Caracas in Venezuela; the team offered Jethroe $800 to stay through May and a $400 bonus if the team won the pennant. Jethroe did not stay and take the extra money since he was already committed to the Buckeyes for the 1946 season. Jethroe played well for Caracas with a .322 average over the 22-game season and also hit three home runs in a single game.[6]

The *Call and Post* published reports from a Mexican League correspondent throughout the season and the stories painted the league in a very positive light. The correspondent, Michael Singer, said that an African American player and a white man who formerly played for the New York Giants walked across the field "with their arms around each other," a scene indicative of baseball "below the border." Former Brooklyn Dodger Mickey Owen praised the African Americans in the league and said that racial discrimination did not exist in the Mexican League. Owen said, "They don't know a color bar down here, not in this league. A man plays ball, white or Negro, and does the best he can. That's all the clubs want, and that's all the fans ask. And that's the way it should be." This quote shows one of the reasons that many African American players went to Mexico to play; the fact that they felt less discrimination outside of the United States. While larger salaries likely enticed many players, their comfort on the Mexican teams probably kept them in Mexico. Fans followed both white and black players and Singer called them the "strongest diamond zealot in the world."[7]

John Lee, a nationally syndicated writer whose columns appeared in the *Call and Post*, was complimentary of the Pasqual brothers and Mexican baseball as a whole. Lee said that the Mexican League was evidence that one is more likely to see the "American way" in a locale that was outside the United States, as a reference to the level of equality that African American players found in Mexico. Lee said that as the Pasqual brothers assembled teams in Mexico, they "didn't handicap their efforts by asking the color of a man's skin, but they did show anyone who was interested the color of their money." Lee credited the pair with sharing a great percentage of their profits with their players, rather than hording the money as he claimed many American team owners did. He also believed that there were at least a dozen black players in the Mexican League that could immediately find success in major league baseball in the United States. Lee even predicted that Jackie Robinson might end up playing in Mexico for the Pasqual brothers since the pair made several attempts to sign him.[8]

There were some concerns about the Buckeyes prior to the season in 1946 since many players had not yet returned from Latin America. The Buckeyes had Billy Horne back from the military, and several new players were signed by Hayes; they hoped these moves would fill any holes on the team. The Buckeyes met in Birmingham, Alabama, for spring training under the direction of team captain Archie Ware and Eugene Bremmer because manager Quincy Trouppe had not returned from the Panama Canal Zone at the start of spring training.[9] There were three new players who earned starting positions with the team after spring training: Tommy Harris, Horne, and Perez Larrinago. There were some concerns in the media about the Buckeyes' pitching, as some writers believed it was not up to regular-season form. These concerns were excused by claims that one can't expect too much from pitchers in spring training. Harris came to the team from Canton, Ohio, where he was a 1942 graduate of Canton McKinley High School. In high school Harris played baseball and football, wrestled and competed with the track team; he also played for the Canton City Merchants after high school. He was set to work as a backup catcher to Trouppe. Larrinago was a shortstop who was reportedly just 5'1" tall and 155 pounds. Jimmie Jones of the *Call and Post* thought that with Horne at second and Larrinago at short, the Buckeyes could expect strong defense up the middle for the 1946 season.[10]

Despite high hopes from the *Call and Post* that the Buckeyes would repeat as world champions, there were ominous signs that the 1946 season would be difficult for the team. Larrinago had to leave spring training early and travel to Cleveland with Hayes to see team physician Dr. H.F. Harris for a sore arm. Despite the rather negative prognosis, the Buckeyes still believed Larrinago would be healthy enough for Opening Day on May 5. As of the last week in April, three players had not returned to the team from Latin America — Sam Jethroe, Parnell Woods and Willie Jefferson. All three players were participating in the Central American title series in Caracas, Venezuela. They were scheduled to return to the United States on April 29, but some feared they would not be ready to start the season by May 5. The Buckeyes also announced that umpire Harry Walker resigned from the Negro American League staff and that umpiring duties in Cleveland would be handled instead by Johnny James, Jimmy Thompson and Finis Branahan.[11]

The Buckeyes opened the season with a doubleheader against the Birmingham Black Barons in Cleveland in front of 8,364 fans. The Buckeyes split the doubleheader, as they won the first game, 2–1, and lost the second game, 7–1. Larrinago was not fully healed and the other half of their double-play combination, Billy Horne, was out of the series with tonsillitis. Buddy Armour played third base while "raw rookie" John Oliver played shortstop. In the first game of the doubleheader the infield committed five errors, but a solid pitching effort from Walter "Lefty" Calhoun held the Barons to four hits.[12]

The Buckeyes continued to play inconsistently as the season progressed and lost a doubleheader to the Indianapolis Clowns, 11–8 and 7–3, in early June. Trouppe named Curtis Jones the starter for one of the games, a Cleveland native who played on the *Call and Post*'s local sandlot team. Several Buckeyes were off to good starts offensively, including Billy

Horne, who led the league in batting average with a .433 mark, and Quincy Trouppe, who was fourth in the league at .394. In front of nearly 7,000 fans at the doubleheader with the Clowns, second baseman Johnny Cowan made four consecutive errors in the fourth inning, which led to two unearned runs. The Buckeyes' new highly touted white pitcher, Eddie Klepp, made his Cleveland debut in the ninth inning as he entered the game with the bases loaded and one out and the Buckeyes up 8–7 with Clowns star Reece "Goose" Tatum coming to the plate. Tatum hit a line drive up the middle that got away from Klepp, allowing two runs to score. Two more runs scored on a long single later in the evening that gave the Clowns the victory, 11–8.[13]

Problems seemed to plague the Buckeyes throughout the summer of 1946, from poor play on the field to disputes with other teams and umpires. During the May home opener with the Birmingham Black Barons, Cleveland Jackson said that "game officials were subjected to rude, ungentlemanly conduct by players from both teams." The Barons objected to a call at home plate where Sam Jethroe was called safe. Jackson said that umpire Jimmy Johnson was surrounded by a "rowdy crowd of threatening Birmingham players" after he called Jethroe safe at home. Reportedly the game was delayed about 30 minutes, and the fans had to sit and wait as the teams finished arguing. Jackson claimed the delay was so long that the second game was cut to seven innings in order to finish before it was too dark. There was another disputed call in the second game as Trouppe took issue with Johnny James' strike call on a pitch from Birmingham. Jackson said, "The giant Buckeye catcher-manager voiced his views loudly and lengthily; in a manner that was not appreciated by the spectators." Several Buckeyes ran onto the field to take a copy of the rulebook to the umpire, a move Jackson criticized since those players had no place on the field at that point in time.[14]

There was another incident during the Birmingham-Cleveland doubleheader that caused Jackson to propose league-wide solutions to limit umpire-player disputes and reign in player behavior within the league. Lorenzo "Piper" Davis of the Barons hit a home run to left field. On his way to the dugout after he crossed home plate, fans along the third base line offered Davis dollar bills in appreciation of his big hit. Jackson claimed that Davis "practically stopped the game" as he walked along the seats collecting the money. A short time later, two of Davis' Birmingham teammates passed a hat along the left field boxes to collect more money. Jackson was infuriated as he said, "There it was ... out on a big league diamond, big league Negro players soliciting nickels, dimes and quarters from a crowd of 8,364 spectators who had paid $1.40 apiece [*sic*] for admission." Jackson argued that the act "cheapened" the Barons and made it seem like black players made little money when they actually made good salaries. He believed that if Negro League baseball had a commissioner, this figure could stop many of these in-game issues. The idea was that players would be less likely to misbehave if they knew there were potential sanctions from a commissioner. Since umpires were hired locally by each home team, there were often disputes from players who believed the umpire unfairly favored the hosts. Players were less likely to react poorly to an umpire's decision if they knew they may face punishment for their actions.[15]

Later that summer there was another contentious issue with an umpire that actually led to the forfeit of a game in Cleveland. During a double-header with the Newark Eagles in July, the Buckeyes lost the first game, 6–5, and then won the second game by virtue of forfeit in front of 3,500 fans at League Park. Newark and Cleveland were tied 1–1 in the eighth inning of the second game when umpire Jimmy Johnson called Newark's substitute runner out because he failed to "report to a game official before taking the base." Angered over the call, the Newark players left the field in protest and refused to return until the call was reversed. Johnson eventually awarded the victory to the Buckeyes since the Eagles players never returned to the field. A review of the official major league baseball rules showed that Johnson's initial call was wrong, and that the Newark player should not have been called out. Fans were reportedly angered by the situation, even though the decision went in favor of the Buckeyes.[16]

Cleveland Jackson was very critical of the situation during his weekly column and wanted to inform Johnson (in case the umpire did not already realize it) that "many a baseball fan is asking for his umpire's cap after last Sunday's unpopular performance." Jackson said the fan outrage over the call showed that fans will not tolerate "second rate performances by players or officials." Buckeyes pitcher Chet Brewer initially brought the situation to Johnson's attention — he was the one who noticed the substitute runner had not reported to an official. Jackson commended Brewer for his readiness "to exploit any opening," but said that "it is apparent that Jimmy Johnson is not a first class baseball umpire." Jackson added, "His indecisiveness and slow decisions have brought frequent violent squabbles and protests from visiting and home town players during the past two seasons." Jackson pushed Johnson to accept retirement since he had lost the respect of both players and fans and "is on the verge of ruining Negro baseball in Cleveland." Wilbur Hayes did not ignore the controversy; shortly after the incident he announced that he planned to replace Johnson with an umpire from the Cleveland Baseball Federation. This particular umpire called a game between the Buckeyes and the Memphis Red Sox in the past and reportedly did a good job. This incident was a rare occurrence when a reporter with the *Call and Post* sided with the players rather than the umpire involved with the disputed call. It may be due to the fact that the umpire violated a stated rule rather than made an error in judgment during an on-field play.[17]

The Buckeyes struggled for much of the season in 1946 as the team and the *Call and Post* tried to determine what went wrong and how the team could improve. The team lost several players to injury and to Latin America, and its defense and pitching often suffered. Jimmie Jones once said, "There seems to be no end of the fielding 'Jitters' that have taken hold of the World Champion Cleveland Buckeyes who for some unknown reason have failed to show anything like championship form." The Buckeyes were unable to stop the Kansas City Monarchs, who led the Negro American League throughout much of the summer. Eugene Bremmer was hit hard in his first appearance of the season in mid–June, against the Monarchs in Toledo. At one point Sam Jethroe was forced to play second base because of an injury-racked infield; he committed an error as he made a wild throw to Archie Ware at first base.[18]

The poor defense did not help a pitching staff that already struggled for victories. Bremmer still wasn't back to full strength from the arm injury he sustained in spring training. George Jefferson struggled upon his return from South America and complained of a sore arm for much of the season, while John Brown fought throat problems. Veteran Walter "Lefty" Calhoun had to be relieved in all but one of his six starts through June, and Frank Carswell only won one game in six starts. Sam Woods and Curtis Jones both had no wins, which left Vibert Clarke as the only reliable starter through the first half of the season. Jimmie Jones predicted the team would soon undergo a shake-up if they were unable to improve in the near future.[19]

In fact, within a week of this prediction, the Buckeyes announced they planned major changes and would rebuild for the second half of the season. They released white pitcher Eddie Klepp and signed two new pitchers and a shortstop from Puerto Rico.[20] Cleveland Jackson figured that the losses the team sustained to injuries and Latin American baseball were just too difficult to overcome. Willie Jefferson, Parnell Woods, Avelino Canizares and Lloyd "Ducky" Davenport never rejoined the team and chose instead to play in Latin America. The injury problems that plagued Bremmer and George Jefferson also harmed the team. Defense on the left side of the infield was so poor that Jackson said, "Base hits trickled through with the regularity of water dripping through a well worn faucet." Trouppe tried to use Johnny Cowan at third base but later moved him back to his natural position at second base. Obviously the experiment of using Jethroe in the infield did not work well, so Trouppe eventually began to use Leon Kellman, a utility infielder from Panama. Buddy Armour's .276 average was solid, but Jackson noted that it did not compare to Davenport's .340 average from the 1945 season. Rookie pitchers Curtis Jones and Sam "Buddy" Woods, who initially showed promise with the team, were not expected to finish the season. Jones reportedly quit the team due to a sore arm after a July doubleheader with the Indianapolis Clowns. Jackson said that Jones left his uniform on the team bus and walked away without saying a word to the other players. When the team bus was ready to depart, Jones was nowhere to be seen. Woods also complained of a sore arm, which did not respond to treatment. Despite this multitude of problems, Wilbur Hayes believed that he plugged many of the team's glaring holes midway through the season and the Buckeyes were poised to make a run at the second-half title.[21]

One of the brighter points of the season for the Buckeyes came in a July 4 doubleheader against the "hapless" Chicago American Giants, the last-place team in the Negro American League. The Buckeyes won games, 5–4 and 7–2, in front of about 6,500 fans at League Park. In the first game the Buckeyes trailed, 4–0, as they entered the bottom of the ninth, where they proceeded to score five runs on no hits to beat the American Giants, 5–4. Chicago pitcher Walter McCoy allowed only six scattered hits before the ninth inning, which started with Willie Grace grounding out to second. The next batter, Johnny Cowan, was safe at first on an error by the right fielder. McCoy then walked the next three batters, Tommy

Harris, Quincy Trouppe and Vibert Clarke, which forced in the first run. Harris was able to score from third on a fielder's choice by Sam Jethroe. McCoy then walked Archie Ware and Buddy Armour, forcing Trouppe home to make the score 4–3. Herman Howard relieved McCoy and entered the game with the bases loaded. After Trouppe substituted Elijah Chism to run for Ware, Leon Kellman hit a sharp line drive that was fumbled by the American Giants' second baseman. A wild throw to first pulled the first baseman off the bag, allowing Kellman to be safe at first. Clarke and Chism scored the winning and tying runs on the play. In the second game, Eugene Bremmer's strong pitching performance helped the Buckeyes glide to the 7–2 victory.[22]

The Buckeyes offered a number of promotions in 1946 that attempted to draw more attention and fans to the team. Because the team struggled on the field, it was possible that Wright and Hayes needed another way to attract fans to the ballpark. Harry Walker, who went to work for the Buckeyes in a public relations capacity after he left his umpiring position, scheduled a "bathing beauty contest" for the Fourth of July. The team hoped to draw women from across the state to compete for the $100 prize.[23] Boxing legend Joe Louis was also scheduled to be a personal guest of the Buckeyes at the July 4 doubleheader.[24] The Indians even hoped to cash in on the success of African American athletes as they arranged for a foot race at Municipal Stadium between track legend Jesse Owens and Indians outfielder George Case, who led major league baseball in steals. Owens ran the hundred-yard course in 9.9 seconds and defeated Case, who was timed at ten seconds flat. Owens, who wore a Cleveland Indians uniform for the race, was awarded $1,000 for his victory.[25]

It was hard for the *Call and Post* to focus on the Buckeyes at times, in part because the integration of major league baseball appeared on the horizon. Jackie Robinson played with Montreal in 1946 and drew national attention as he won the International League batting title. Cleveland Jackson knew that Robinson faced many challenges at the beginning of the 1946 season as he said that Robinson and fellow African American teammate John Wright should "place their trust in a brand of ball playing that is no less than twice as good as that of their position competitors." Jackson said that Robinson "valiantly" endured taunts and harassment from the crowds but managed to play well in spite of those negative instances. He added, "His examplary [sic] action and play have paved the way for many more to follow." Jackson claimed that Robinson's popularity affected fans in Cleveland, and that more people in Cleveland took an interest in baseball because of Robinson. During 1946 there were seven African American semi-pro teams organized in Cleveland, which Jackson saw as a direct result of Robinson's popularity. He claimed that they struggled to assemble sandlot semi-pro teams in previous years. The *Call and Post* even considered the sponsorship of a "Jackie Robinson Special Train" to Buffalo when the Montreal club was visiting. Jackson thought that entire African American church congregations would arrange trips to see Robinson as he passed through their towns.[26]

The Robinson signing encouraged the *Call and Post* to contact the Indians' ownership throughout 1946 to push for integration. The ownership of the Indians changed hands during the 1946 season, from Alva Bradley to Bill Veeck. When discussions with Bradley went nowhere, writers then approached Veeck in hope of a different outcome. Jackson approached Bradley after he returned from spring training and was told that the Indians had no plans to sign an African American player. In fact, Bradley hinted that there were no black players who were good enough to play on the Indians. Jackson argued that Bradley probably never scouted African American players and had no idea of the talent that was available to the major leagues. Several white reporters in Cleveland lauded the Indians for their diversity since they had players from many different ethnic backgrounds. Jackson was critical of this opinion and pointed out the fact that none of the ethnicities included African Americans. He suggested that the roughly 100,000 African American fans in the Cleveland area should not patronize Indians games if the team still refused to sign an African American player.[27]

By the time Jackson approached Bill Veeck in July of 1946, he appeared more receptive to the idea of integration than Bradley. Veeck said he had no problem signing an African American player for the Indians, but believed that player must have "the highest possible all-around qualifications." Veeck added, "The pressure is too great to take a chance on a fellow who couldn't take it." This was a fear expressed by many African American writers during the 1940s, as they believed if a black player performed poorly in the major leagues, white owners would use it as an excuse to continue policies of segregation. Veeck wanted the Indians to win a championship, and if an African American player could help them reach that goal, Veeck planned to sign him. Veeck said he wanted to purchase a player from the Negro Leagues, not obtain one "by means of raids" like Branch Rickey did. Rickey did not offer compensation to the Kansas City Monarchs for Robinson, which meant that many teams stood to suffer if they lost a number of players without compensation. Jackson thought that Veeck "spoke without reservation and was very frank in his opinions" and that he was very knowledgeable when it came to Negro League teams and players. Even though Veeck also claimed there were currently no African American players in the Negro Leagues good enough for the major leagues, he appeared to escape the level of criticism that Jackson directed toward Bradley. It was possible that this was due to Veeck's knowledge of the Negro Leagues.[28]

Veeck spoke highly of Jackie Robinson and claimed he wanted a similar player for the Cleveland Indians. Veeck said his first choice was Negro League slugger Josh Gibson, but there's no way to know if he truly planned to sign him. Gibson died in January of 1947, seven months before Veeck signed Larry Doby to integrate the American League. Gordon Cobbledick, a writer with the *Cleveland Plain Dealer*, traveled to Mexico in 1946 and observed the integrated Mexican Leagues. After the experience, Cobbledick said he saw no reason why African Americans could not play in the major leagues. Cobbledick expressed concerns that fans could create a disturbance at an integrated major league game, but Jackson disagreed with this statement. Since there were mixed-race crowds at football games each year with no reported problems, Jackson thought this was proof that baseball fans would get along with each other. Jackson predicted, "It is apparent that the picture of Negroes entering the major leagues in numbers is not a remote possibility." He added, "Although they may not arrive in droves, they are sure to be among the big league ranks within the next few years."[29]

A highly publicized barnstorming event between Bob Feller and Satchel Paige brought more attention to the issue of integration in 1946. Feller and a team of white major league players joined Paige and his team of Negro League players and traveled the country entertaining fans. Jackie Robinson also established a traveling team of African American players after the season, but that team didn't gain the attention in Cleveland that the Paige-Feller series did. The *Call and Post* believed Feller was under pressure since he was expected to easily defeat the Negro League stars.[30] Paige's team, which included Sam Jethroe and Quincy Trouppe from the

Buckeyes, lost to Feller's team, 5–0, when they played at Cleveland Stadium on October 1. There were nearly 10,000 fans in attendance, which the *Call and Post* estimated at two-thirds African American. In other regional games Paige's team won, 3–1, in front of 4,000 fans in Pittsburgh, while the Feller all-stars took a game, 11–2, in Youngstown, Ohio. Jimmie Jones thought Robinson's experiences in 1946 and the Paige/Feller series were victories for African Americans. The Paige/Feller games showed that whites and blacks could play and travel together, as Jones said, "It was the conduct and comradeship on the part of both teams that again amazed the fans." The players from both teams got along well together and were often seen complimenting each other after their games. Even though Feller's team won the majority of the games, the series showed that African Americans could compete successfully against white players.[31]

Imagine Cleveland Jackson and the *Call and Post*'s surprise when Feller came forward after their 17-game barnstorming tour and said that no African American players were good enough for the major leagues. Feller admitted that Paige had the skills if he were younger, but added he saw "none who can combine the qualities of a big league player." Feller even went so far as to say that Jackie Robinson was not good enough to last in the major leagues. Jackson was floored by the comments and surprised to see an athlete pass judgment upon so many of his peers. Jackson thought that Feller should worry about his pitching skills and focus on leading the Indians to a pennant in 1947, adding, "It is regrettable that the former Iowa farm boy's philosophy of life is far below his sterling pitching qualities." Jackson saw Feller as a potential Hall of Fame candidate (Feller was admitted to the Cooperstown shrine in 1962), but thought that his critical comments could harm his chances of entry. As far as Jackson was concerned, "Brains and intelligence are primary pre-requisites and Feller has demonstrated a lack of both."[32]

Despite Jackson's criticisms of Feller, he attempted to find an explanation for the great pitcher's attitude. Jackson considered the possibility that Feller's statements were just an act to protect his image since a number of major leaguers were openly against integration. Jackson feared that Feller's comments, despite their intent, could be used by major league owners as an excuse to not integrate their teams. With Feller one of the Cleveland Indians superstar players, there was probably a great deal of concern that his statements could influence the Indians ownership. Nobody could ignore the popularity of the Paige/Feller all-star teams, especially among African American fans. Jackson estimated that 20 out of every 25 fans that attended the games were black, which showed "that Negro fans will support a sport wholeheartedly, if some attempt is made to attract their attention." An estimated 230,000 fans saw the barnstorming tour across the country, and in New York and Los Angeles the crowds topped 20,000. It was the tour's popularity that led Jackson to ultimately believe that Feller's comments did not inflict long-term damage. Jackson said, "It will take more than the hasty words of an Iowa farm boy to stop one of the greatest athletic movements in the history of sports."[33]

That movement was in full force at the beginning of 1947. As Jackie Robinson prepared to join the Brooklyn Dodgers, Cleveland Jackson contemplated the resistance he could face from white major league players. Jackson said that white players were "touchy" when it came to African Americans playing with them as equals. The white players likely felt this way because "the further thought of countless Negro stars entering competition for their jobs is a horifying [sic] one for the many mediocre players in the majors." Jackson believed that financial concerns could aid African Americans in terms of integration. Owners might ignore racial controversy if they made more money through an integrated team. In fact, many southern cities initially threatened to block the integrated Dodgers from playing in their towns during spring training. They eventually allowed the team because of the fears of lost revenue. Jackson said that prejudice disappeared when people were afraid of losing money.[34]

In the first months of 1947, Hayes worked to prepare the Buckeyes for the upcoming season. The team hoped to bounce back from its disappointing 1946 season but still faced competition from Mexico and Latin America. Hayes signed five rookie players prior to the 1947 season, and considered a trade with the Birmingham Black Barons that would send Buddy Armour, Archie Ware, and Johnny Cowan for two of the team's star players — shortstop Arthur Wilson and pitcher Alvin Gipson.[35] Sam Jethroe actually turned down a lucrative offer to play winter ball in Venezuela and instead chose to stay at his home in Cleveland. Hayes claimed Jethroe wanted to be in top shape for the 1947 season; the *Call and Post* agreed as they said his play in 1946 was "dull and colorless" compared to his performance during the 1945 championship season. Quincy Trouppe, Willie Jefferson, and Parnell Woods spent the winter playing baseball in Venezuela, while Willie Grace and Frank Carswell played in Puerto Rico.[36]

The Buckeyes hoped three players that stayed in Latin America for the 1946 season, Avelino Canizares, Parnell Woods, and Willie Jefferson, would return to Cleveland for the 1947 campaign. Unfortunately, the Buckeyes needed approval from the league hierarchy for this to happen; in the spring of 1946 the league instituted a five-year ban for players that left the Negro Leagues for Latin America. According to Cleveland Jackson, without these three players the Buckeyes "were just a mediocre nine." Wilbur Hayes believed that Woods, Jefferson and Canizares should be allowed to return because the situation was not entirely their fault — they were "innocent victims of a vicious international chicanery." Hayes claimed that Woods and Jefferson planned to return to the United States in the spring of 1946 but found their passports delayed by Venezuelan officials. Since the two found it impossible to make it home in time for the Negro League season, they instead decided to sign with a team in Caracas. While there may be some truth to the claim, it seemed as if it was a rather convenient excuse to try to influence the league's ruling on the matter. Hayes said that Canizares should not be classified as a "jumper" since he was a Cuban citizen. When Canizares left the Buckeyes, he did not return to Cuba; he went to play for the Pasqual brothers in Mexico for double his Buckeyes salary. If the Buckeyes were able to sign the three, the only player missing from their 1945 squad would be Lloyd "Ducky" Davenport.[37] Canizares decided to stay in Mexico for 1947 when he signed a contract worth more than $10,000 after bonuses were added. Jackson thought the move put a damper on the Buckeyes' pennant hopes for 1947.[38]

The Buckeyes announced that no veteran was safe at the team's 1947 spring training in Tampa, Florida. Manager Quincy Trouppe said the Buckeyes wanted to place the best team on the field, even if it meant that rookies displaced veterans.[39] The Buckeyes won 14 of their 17 spring training games and had high hopes for the 1947 season. When the Buckeyes opened the season against the Birmingham Black Barons, Cleveland Jackson said the team resembled the 1945 squad as it beat the Barons, 9–4. He thought the Buckeyes "demonstrated a brand of play that caught the fancy of their many enthusiastic followers." The Buckeyes showed a lot of hustle and got base hits "with the confident abandon of a winning ball team." Even though the Buckeyes hoped to draw 20,000 fans to their home opener, they had only 6,683 fans in attendance. Jackson blamed the disappointing total on the cool, dreary weather and the fact that the Indians were playing a doubleheader across town at Cleveland Municipal Stadium against the Washington Senators.[40]

Throughout May of 1947, the Buckeyes struggled to find their footing on the field and drew a series of disappointing crowds to League Park. The team anticipated 10,000 fans for a May 18 doubleheader against the Memphis Red Sox but ended up with only 3,200 as they beat the Red Sox, 11–7 and 4–3. By the end of May the Buckeyes were at .500 and in third place in the Negro American League; the *Call and Post* blamed their mediocre play on the great number of rainouts the team endured during the first month of the season.[41] A winning streak in early June put the Buckeyes at 10–5 as they took five of six games from the Chicago American Giants. The Birmingham Black Barons, the team the Buckeyes were battling for the league lead, were due in town the next week. The *Call and Post* anxiously awaited the series because the "bitter rivalry between the two teams has always resulted in some of the greatest competition in the league." The Buckeyes hoped the series would finally bring a large crowd to League Park.[42]

Even though the integration of the major leagues hurt teams like the Buckeyes in the long run, in the short run it actually proved beneficial. Shortly after the Cleveland Indians added Larry Doby to their roster on July 5, the St. Louis Browns signed second baseman Henry Thompson and outfielder Willard Brown from the Kansas City Monarchs. Lorenzo "Piper" Davis of the Birmingham Black Barons was signed by the Browns later in July. The fact that two of the Buckeyes' greatest competitors in the Negro American League, the Monarchs and the Black Barons, lost star players meant that the Buckeyes now had the advantage. Jimmie Jones said the Buckeyes "may take an extra breath while realizing their strongest opponents have lost valuable performers just when the competition meant the most."[43]

The Buckeyes had yet to lose players to the major leagues, but there were constant rumors involving Sam Jethroe and both of the Boston teams — the Red Sox and the Braves. Jethroe, along with Jackie Robinson, tried out for the Red Sox in 1945. He denied any contact with the Red Sox since that tryout, and several Boston reporters claimed it was the Braves that were interested in signing Jethroe. Wilbur Hayes and Ernest

Wright admitted the departure of Jethroe would be a severe blow to the pennant hopes in 1947 but vowed they would not stand in his way if he were offered a contract by a major league team. Cleveland Jackson tried to put a positive spin on the situation and said that the Buckeyes could benefit from the loss of Jethroe if the major league team provided compensation. He claimed that if the Buckeyes were able to sell Jethroe for about $40,000, it would enable the team to pay off some of its debts. The Buckeyes carried two extra outfielders throughout much of the summer in 1947, and Jackson mentioned that fact could help the team if Jethroe was lost.[44] Jethroe was eventually signed by the Boston Braves, but not during the 1947 season.

Even though Hayes seemed to accept the fact that he could lose players to the major leagues, he refused to lose them to Latin American teams. There were rumors that the Mexican League had its eyes on Archie Ware and that the Pasqual brothers were interested in signing several Cleveland sandlot stars. Several of these rumors were fueled by the *Call and Post*, which claimed that a "distinguished Mexican" was staying in town at the Olmstead Hotel. Even though the *Call and Post* claimed to have confirmed this fact after they placed a call to the hotel, nobody was able to contact this mysterious individual for an interview. Just in case the rumors were true, Hayes positioned himself outside of the League Park entrances "in order to watch the movements of anyone who smacked of Mexican appearances."[45]

Hayes was primarily concerned about the loss of Archie Ware because he was batting .352 and dazzling fans with his fielding. If the Buckeyes lost the 29-year-old Ware, it would be a severe blow to their playoff chances. Ware said he was unaware of any interest from Mexican teams and claimed that nobody contacted him about playing south of the border. Nobody spotted either Pasqual around League Park, and Cleveland Jackson joked that if the men were there, they wore excellent disguises. Jackson was so determined to discover a covert operative from the Mexican League that he called the Mexican consulate to see if any Mexican citizens contacted them. The secretary at the consulate told Jackson she knew of no Mexicans in Cleveland and assured him that they were likely to register with the consulate if they were in the United States. Jackson said, "The shadowy actions of the mysterious Mexican visitor, the undercurrent atmosphere that bespeaks feverish winter plans, the anxiety of local baseball owners, and the frantic antics of rabid baseball fans, all demonstrate that the great American game has, once again, gained a hold in the sports public."[46]

Despite Hayes' paranoia over the potential loss of Archie Ware, he had no trouble taking a player from another team if he thought they could help the Buckeyes. Hayes found a 21-year-old pitcher named Sam "Red" Jones (also nicknamed the "strikeout king") who played in the Florida State League. Jones played for the Orlando All-Stars and supposedly struck out 70 batters in just seven games to start the team's season. Cleveland Jackson said that "inside reports" claimed Hayes "took his life in his hands" as he tried to pry Jones away from the Florida team. Orlando manager Charles Pelham tried to stop Hayes from taking Jones and suggested that he and Hayes go outside to settle the situation "man-to-man." Hayes attempted to diffuse the situation and told Pelham that they did not need to go outside; they could just discuss the matter inside. Jackson said that maybe Hayes' straightforward attitude was too much for Pelham since Hayes brought Jones to Cleveland in the end.[47]

Parnell Woods never returned to Cleveland for the 1947 season, although he maintained his home in the city. He found a great deal of success playing for a team in Venezuela, where he played third base and won the 1947 batting title with a .354 average. Woods also led the league in steals with 21 in the 36-game season, was named to the league's all star team, and was awarded medals and an $800 custom ring for his stellar play throughout the season. Woods said he chose to stay in South America because of the proposed ban on Negro League players that left the United States, and because he found there was no color line in Venezuela. He claimed that the Venezuelan natives loved baseball and paid no attention to the color of the player's skin. Woods was even invited to speak on a panel sponsored by Venezuelan newspaper *Ultimas Noticias* on discrimination in American baseball and Jackie Robinson. He said, "One only realizes the extent of prejudice when experiencing the fair treatment there." Woods said that he had no intention in the near future of playing baseball in the United States again, although he returned to the Buckeyes in 1949. He planned to play winter ball in either Cuba or South America and hoped to return to Venezuela for the summer seasons.[48]

Throughout the summer of 1947, the Buckeyes continued to win despite the fact the team was fifth out of six teams in the league in batting and fielding. The *Call and Post* said the team maintained its hold on first place because of its "hustle and fighting spirit."[49] On the Fourth of July the team had a 27–13 record; Quincy Trouppe's solid leadership was listed as one of the causes of their success. Hayes was also credited with assembling a "well rounded pitching staff" led by Panamanian Vibert Clarke and Chet Brewer.[50] The Buckeyes clinched the pennant by early September and had a 54–23 record in league play for a .701 winning percentage. They were ahead of their next-closest competitor by 8½ games. Sam Jethroe led the league in five different offensive categories: runs scored (90), total bases (162 on 98 hits), doubles (31), triples (9), and stolen bases (50). Jethroe achieved these feats in just 70 games; Bob Dillinger of the St. Louis Browns won the major league stolen base title in 1947 with 34. One must consider that the major league season consisted of 154 games at this point in time, far more than the Negro League season.[51]

Quincy Trouppe was honored by Louis Seltzer, editor of the *Cleveland Press*, as best manager in the Negro Leagues. Trouppe was presented with the award at a doubleheader against the Baltimore Elite Giants and experienced some stage fright as he approached the microphone to speak. The Buckeyes lost the first game against the Elite Giants, 10–5, while the second game was called for darkness at the end of the fifth inning with the two teams tied, 7–7. During the first game the two teams were actually tied, 5–5, in the ninth inning when the Elite Giants scored five runs, aided by two errors from second baseman Leon Kellman.[52] This doubleheader was viewed by some as the beginning of the end for the Buckeyes. Reportedly the team looked sloppy and tired against the Elite Giants and never seemed to reach mid-season form once it met the New York Cubans in the Negro League World Series later in September.

A.S. "Doc" Young replaced Cleveland Jackson as sports editor at the *Call and Post* just in time for the start of the World Series between the Cleveland Buckeyes and the New York Cubans. The *Call and Post*'s coverage of the 1947 World Series was far different from its coverage of the Buckeyes' 1945 World Series appearance. This could be a result of the new sports editor or the fact that the Buckeyes were lost in the Larry Doby and Jackie Robinson hype. Since the *Call and Post* published weekly, its writers already knew the Buckeyes lost the 1947 World Series before they had a chance to print a synopsis of the games. It's possible that they saw no need to hype a Buckeyes loss. When the Brooklyn Dodgers reached the

1947 World Series against the New York Yankees, the event received far more attention than the Buckeyes-Cubans series despite the fact that the Dodgers lost to the Yankees.

The Buckeyes were slight favorites in their series with the New York Cubans, although many believed the two teams were a relatively even match. The Cubans were the first New York team to win a pennant in the Negro National League as they topped the Newark Eagles for the title. Young believed the Eagles, who were world champions in 1946, would have won the title again if the team still had Larry Doby on its roster. The Cubans had several stars on their roster, including Luis Tiant Sr. and Orestes "Minnie" Minoso, who would eventually play in major league baseball for the Cleveland Indians and the Chicago White Sox. The series was scheduled to start on September 19 at the Polo Grounds in New York City, with other games in Yankee Stadium, Philadelphia, and Cleveland.[53]

The schedule for the World Series was uprooted because of rain; in fact, the weather changed the dates and locales for the games throughout the series. The first game at the Polo Grounds was called due to rain with the score tied, 5–5. The two teams met for the first official complete game at Yankee Stadium on Sunday, September 21, as the Buckeyes defeated the Cubans, 10–7. Cleveland was supposed to host two games in the series, on Tuesday, September 23, and Thursday, September 25, with both games at Municipal Stadium. On Tuesday, for game two of the series, the Cubans beat the Buckeyes in front of just 3,000 fans to tie the series at 1–1. Barney Morris held the Buckeyes to just five hits; they recorded multiple hits in just one inning, the second. The only time the Buckeyes came close to scoring was when their shortstop, Al Smith, doubled in the fifth inning (the only extra-base hit of the game). Two consecutive walks following the double left the bases loaded, although the Buckeyes were unable to make the Cubans pay. Gene Smith pitched a shutout for the Buckeyes through the seventh inning, but Doc Young believed he looked unsteady throughout much of the game. Quincy Trouppe lifted him in the eighth inning with two on, two out, and the count 2–2 on Barney Morris. Red Jones, the pitcher Hayes found in Florida, relieved Smith and allowed two runs before he was pulled with one out and the bases loaded in the ninth inning. The Cubans added four more runs in the ninth as ten men went to the plate.[54]

Even though the next game in the series was scheduled for Municipal Stadium on Thursday, September 25, the two teams instead decided to play the next Cleveland game on Sunday, September 28, at League Park. This meant that instead of hosting games two and three, Cleveland would host games two and five. The reported reason for the change in venue was that "the lake-front night air is a bit too chilly for fans [sic] comfort." It was also possible that the measly crowd of 3,000 fans that came to Municipal Stadium was a huge disappointment for the Buckeyes and Cubans. Perhaps they hoped that more fans would come if it was held at League Park; if nothing else, 3,000 fans seemed like more people at League Park compared to the cavernous, 80,000-seat Cleveland Stadium.[55]

The Cubans won game three, played in Philadelphia, 9–4, and game four, played in Chicago, 9–2. This brought the two teams back to Cleveland, where the Buckeyes hoped to stay alive in the series with a win on their turf at League Park. Even though the Buckeyes thought that moving the game to Sunday afternoon at League Park would improve attendance, they still managed to draw only 4,500 to what would be the final game of the 1947 Negro League World Series. The Buckeyes went from series favorites to the underdogs as they now trailed the Cubans, 3–1, in the best-of-seven series. Game five looked promising for the Buckeyes; they led the Cubans, 5–0, as late as the fifth inning. Right-hander Gene Smith held the Cubans to no runs on just three hits until the Buckeyes "came apart at the seams" in the sixth inning. The Cubans scored three runs on two hits, a hit batsman, and two consecutive errors by second baseman Johnny Cowan. The Cubans added another run in the seventh inning and two in the eighth to pull ahead of the Buckeyes, 6–5. The Cubans completed the victory without their shortstop, Silvio Garcia, who was ejected in the fourth inning by umpire William Warren for arguing a call. The World Series loss was disappointing for Buckeyes fans, who thought the team's large margin of victory over the rest of the Negro American League would translate to a World Series victory. The *Call and Post* said the Buckeyes "gave the impression that they weren't too much interested in winning either the Series or the late-season 'exhibitions' with National League clubs." The newspaper seemed to believe the Buckeyes lost because of laziness or apathetic play rather than a match-up with a better team.[56]

Quincy Trouppe received much of the credit throughout the season for the Buckeyes' solid play. Since the Cleveland defense and team hitting statistics were poor for much of 1947, the *Call and Post* decided that Trouppe was the reason for their success. After the disappointing World

Series loss, Ernest Wright said he wanted a "new look" on the team for the 1948 season. He hoped for more "showmanship" during games, and also wanted to offer promotions for fans, like prizes and band performances at home games. Wright thought their late-season slide and World Series struggles were caused by "fatigue and lack of depth at certain positions."[57] A lack of team depth seemed to imply a failure on Hayes' part to secure enough talent at certain positions. Instead, the first move for the "new look" Buckeyes was to fire Quincy Trouppe and replace him with veteran Buckeye pitcher Alonzo Boone. Boone, a member of the team since 1942, also played for the Cleveland Cubs and the Cleveland Bears after he started his career with the Memphis Red Sox in 1929. Hayes said that he and Wright "always held Boone in the very highest esteem" and decided he should get the management job after they became dissatisfied with Trouppe.[58] Even though Trouppe won a World Series with the team and helped the Buckeyes reach a second World Series, it was not enough to save his job in the end. It's possible that Wright and Hayes hoped a dramatic shake-up would help revive the fans' interest in the Buckeyes, especially with an integrated Indians team playing across town.

When Boone was named the new manager in December of 1947, the *Call and Post* never mentioned an article the newspaper published attempting to shame the Buckeyes' pitcher. The paper often attempted to improve the housing conditions for many African Americans in Cleveland, and would publish stories on bad landlords in an attempt to shame them into upgrading their properties. One of the people the *Call and Post* targeted in April of 1947 was Boone and his wife, who owned a property in the city of Cleveland. The story said, "Alonzo Boone might be one of the Cleveland Buckeye's top hurlers but for some thirty persons who live at a reconverted slum dwelling at 5807 Central Avenue, the baseball sensation is a landlord who fails to keep his firetrap property in a livable condition." Tenants claimed the home was haphazardly partitioned into unsafe and overcrowded apartments. The second floor of the building lacked sinks, which forced those families to travel downstairs to fetch water. The upper floors of the building also reportedly lacked adequate fire escapes.[59]

The *Call and Post* claimed that Boone charged about $30 per month in rent, a figure that was higher than the government Office of Price Administration allowed. Boone reportedly made about $275 in rent from the tenants in the converted house. Even though Boone was not available for comment on the situation, his wife defended their position and said that when they purchased the house, it was already haphazardly divided into apartments. She also blamed the tenants for many of the problems in the building, saying they did not maintain their apartments properly. From her perspective, the tenants were destructive to the property and broke the sink on the second floor. Even though there were obviously two perspectives on the incident, city and building inspectors said they would handle the situation. The incident was never mentioned again by the newspaper.[60]

It seemed like fans and the *Call and Post* were already pulling away from the Buckeyes. Every time the team anticipated a high attendance total throughout the season, the Buckeyes were disappointed when only half or even a third of the expected crowd came to League Park. The *Call and Post* dedicated much of its space on the sports page to discussions of Robinson and Doby, or they looked for ways to involve more African Americans in major league baseball. Since Doby spent much of his time on the bench in 1947, there were concerns about his future with the Indians. Rumors were rampant that Bill Veeck planned to "unload" Doby and sell his contract to the Pacific Coast League.[61] In a post-season interview with Doc Young, Veeck confirmed that Doby would still be with the Indians organization in 1948, although he'd yet to determine if it would be in the minors or with the parent club in Cleveland. Veeck still believed that Doby had a promising future in major league baseball despite his disappointing season. He admitted that he handled Doby poorly and said that the young player probably should have spent a year in the minors, as Jackie Robinson did in Montreal.[62]

Veeck escaped much of Young's criticism, as the writer instead chose to focus his ire on Lou Boudreau, the manager of the Indians. There were rumors that Veeck wanted to replace Boudreau, also the Indians' shortstop, as manager of the team. When Young questioned Veeck about Boudreau's handling of Doby, the owner avoided a set opinion on the subject. Veeck claimed that he purchased the players for the Indians and after that it was Boudreau's call on how to use them. Young thought that Boudreau did not talk to Doby enough and that he and his coaches did not attempt to help Doby improve on the field. Young was also afraid that Boudreau was not a good enough manager to help the Indians contend for the pennant.[63] Even though he appeared impartial towards Boudreau during his interview with Young, Veeck had reservations about Boudreau's management skills and considered replacing him. In his autobiography *Veeck — As in Wreck*, Veeck said his main objection to Boudreau was that "he managed by hunch and desperation." Veeck also claimed he wanted to oust Boudreau since he had Casey Stengel "waiting in the wings, ready to sign."[64]

Even though Veeck questioned Boudreau's managerial skills, he believed that Boudreau was the best shortstop in baseball. Because of this, Veeck had to tread lightly while he dealt with Boudreau over the management job. He considered trading Boudreau but was concerned that fans would riot if the popular shortstop left the team. Veeck also considered asking Boudreau to step down as manager but was afraid that Boudreau would refuse since he "was holding all the cards and he knew it."[65] In the end Veeck realized that he was backed into a corner by the situation and offered Boudreau a new two-year contract. One of Young's main concerns at the end of 1947 was Doby's lack of playing time; he believed if Doby were able to play full time, the Indians could have a chance to win the pennant. Doby received more playing time in 1948 and helped lead the Indians to the World Series; Boudreau was just 31 years old when the Indians won.

Young believed Doby's struggles in the major leagues were part of a larger issue — African American youth were not taught to play the game of baseball properly. Young pointed to Sam Jethroe, who despite his high batting average had "about as much follow through as a drunk playing jai alai." Young did not blame Jethroe for this, and argued that nobody ever taught the speedy outfielder a proper swing. According to Young, even Brooklyn Dodgers catcher Roy Campanella claimed he did not learn to properly throw to second until he reached the major leagues. Despite his criticisms, Young said it was not his intent to slam the Negro Leagues but to point out these issues could be improved "if our baseball men would get together and study the game, work to improve it, forget a few cute didoes and play fundamental, scientific baseball." He quoted Cool Papa Bell, who said, "The major leaguers play brain ball — we play brawn ball!" Young wanted someone to form a group in Cleveland that would promote better baseball fundamentals and work with African American players.[66] Young saw the differences between the Negro League and major league styles of play as a problem; he worried that African American players might not be able to succeed in the majors. He wrote this column after the 1947 season, so it's obvious that Doby's struggles the prior season weighed on him during the offseason.

Young expressed concern about the image of African American players in his very first column with the *Call and Post* in September of 1947. He was concerned with conduct but also with the wardrobe choices of black players in the major leagues. Young claimed that when Henry Thompson and W.J. Brown signed with the St. Louis Browns in 1947, they were photographed wearing t-shirts as they signed their Browns contracts. As a comparison, Larry Doby "arrived in Chicago dressed in a style immaculate" and was photographed signing his Indians contract in more formal clothing. Young said, "A good future is breaking for our athletes and there's no reason to louse it up" when he talked about the importance of player conduct and dress. Young said that image probably had no bearing on the players' careers, which means he was probably more concerned about what the general public thought of the new African American players.[67]

The 1946 and 1947 seasons were somewhat bittersweet for the Cleveland Buckeyes. In 1946 they basked in the glow of their 1945 Negro League World Series win as they tried to maintain their core group of players. Latin American baseball and injuries kept the team from contention as the Newark Eagles, with future Cleveland Indian Larry Doby, won the 1946 World Series. When Jackie Robinson played the 1946 season with the Brooklyn Dodgers' minor league club in Montreal, it was an incredible step forward for major league baseball and race relations in America. Unfortunately, it was an ominous sign for Negro League baseball, which now had to worry about major league teams as well as Latin American teams taking players away from them. The only difference is that most Negro League team owners supported the loss of players to the major leagues because of the larger goal of racial equality. Wilbur Hayes stood at the gates of League Park to block Mexican officials from signing Archie Ware, but he made no effort to stop either of the Boston major league teams when rumors circulated about their interest in Sam Jethroe.

The 1947 Negro League World Series was truly the Buckeyes' last moment in the spotlight in Cleveland. Their 1947 season was overshadowed by Jackie Robinson's first season with the Brooklyn Dodgers and the Cleveland Indians' addition of Larry Doby on July 5 of that year. Crowds, which averaged about 10,000–15,000 at their peak during World War II, now dwindled to less than 5,000 for most games. Even the World Series games played in Cleveland, which included future major league stars like Sam Jethroe and Minnie Minoso, only drew about 3,000 and 4,500 fans. The *Call and Post*, which pushed for the integration of baseball throughout much of the 1940s, started to shift its attention from the Buckeyes to the Cleveland Indians. With smaller crowds and less media coverage, it would be increasingly difficult for the Buckeyes to survive for much longer, especially as the rest of the Negro Leagues started to collapse around them.

6

The Integration of
the Indians

In Cleveland during the 1940s, the African American weekly *Call and Post* covered the exploits of the Negro American League Cleveland Buckeyes, as well as the introduction of African American players Larry Doby and Satchel Paige to the Cleveland Indians in 1947 and 1948. Black fans of the Negro Leagues had long viewed baseball as a form of entertainment. Talented athletes, such as Satchel Paige, had often become larger-than-life figures whose exaggerated antics played to the crowd's desire for amusement and release from everyday concerns.

With the integration of professional teams, however, the *Call and Post* and many of its readers linked their hopes for black social and economic progress to the success of Doby, Paige, and other black players in the major leagues. Black achievements on the baseball diamond and the behavior of baseball players in the public realm had the potential to help break additional racial barriers in the worlds of business, government, and education. After 1947, the *Call and Post* increasingly turned its attention from the Buckeyes to the Indians. The newspaper and its readers recognized that Doby's and Paige's achievements on the field and their behavior off it would play a crucial role in defining the public meanings of black manhood and respectability. Doby came to embody the masculine qualities that many hoped would win white support for integration, while some African Americans feared that Paige's character and reputation might confirm and reinforce white stereotypes of black inferiority. With the Negro Leagues already struggling with publicity and financial problems, the major leagues were possibly a welcome change for many African American fans.

Lawrence Eugene Doby had the natural athletic talent of a baseball star and the maturity and patience to handle the curveballs that integration threw at him. Born in South Carolina, Doby moved to Paterson, New Jersey, when he was a teenager to join his mother, who had moved there searching for work. During high school, Doby played several sports, including baseball, football and basketball. He attended Long Island University when he completed high school, but World War II interrupted his education. Doby was drafted into the navy in 1942 and was sent to the South Pacific, where he served until 1945.[1] After he returned from his service in World War II in 1946, Doby began playing for the Newark Eagles, a Negro League team based close to Doby's hometown of Paterson. It was not long before he grabbed the attention of major league baseball executives. Many teams started to scout the Negro Leagues in search of talent that could help their teams make it to the World Series. Bill Veeck, general manager and part owner of the Cleveland Indians at the time, started to take notice of several Negro League players, with Doby at the top of his list. At the time of his signing, the 22-year-old Doby led the Negro Leagues with a batting average of .458, 13 home runs and 16 doubles; it would have been hard for Veeck not to take notice of someone with statistics such as those.[2]

Throughout his lengthy career in the Negro Leagues, Paige often hoped he would one day cross the barrier into major league baseball. During the 1930s and early 1940s, Paige bounced between Negro League teams in the United States and teams in Mexico and the Caribbean, which earned him a reputation as an unreliable contract jumper. Whichever team would give Paige the best deal at that time was the team that would earn his services. He spent a good portion of his career with two Negro League teams, Gus Greenlee's Pittsburgh Crawfords and J.L. Wilkinson's Kansas City Monarchs, and also earned money barnstorming across the country. By the time Jackie Robinson, Paige's former teammate on the Monarchs, was signed by the Brooklyn Dodgers in late 1945, Paige felt insulted and thought that maybe he missed his chance at playing major league baseball.

Signing Jackie like they did still hurt me deep down. I'd been the guy who'd started all that big talk about letting us in the big time. I'd been the one who'd opened up the major league parks to the colored teams. I'd been the one who the white boys wanted to barnstorm against. I'd been the one who everybody'd said should be in the majors. But Jackie'd been the first one signed by the white boys and he'd probably be the first one in the majors.[3]

The white major leagues seemed more interested in signing young African American players who lacked lengthy service time in the Negro Leagues. Paige had a reputation built for him by the end of the 1940s as a Negro League institution and entertainer, which meant it would be hard to change his image with the American public. It was much easier to create an image for a young player like Doby, who had a clean slate compared to Paige. A year after the Cleveland Indians signed Doby as the first African American in the American League, they also added Paige to the team. The contrast between the two men was great. Aside from the nearly twenty-year age difference, the men also had different educational backgrounds, upbringings and personalities. Doby served in the Pacific while in the navy; Paige had no military service to his credit. However, Paige claimed in his autobiography that he wanted to serve and even lied about his age during World War II to increase his likelihood of being drafted. Doby had a serious relationship with a woman he later married, while Paige had a reputation as a playboy. He was married and divorced once by the time he married Lahoma in 1947 at the age of 41.[4] Paige traveled the country for more than 20 years playing in Negro League games and barnstorming, while Doby only spent one year in the Negro Leagues before the Indians signed him in 1947.

Integrating the major leagues had been on Veeck's mind for about ten years but his motives for doing so are unclear. In his autobiography, *Veeck — As in Wreck,* he discussed failed plans to purchase the Philadelphia Phillies and replace the inherited players with a team of African American players. It was likely that Veeck felt badly about the discrimination against African Americans and felt so strongly about his opinions on equality that he wanted to become involved in integration. It was also likely that Veeck wanted to draw attention to him and ruffle the feathers of fellow owners in baseball. It was no secret that Veeck liked to agitate other owners, something he openly bragged about throughout his autobiography. It was also no secret that Veeck liked attention and making a splash. This was the same man who once sent Eddie Gaedel, a midget, to bat in a major league game wearing the number ⅛ on his jersey with the theory that a man who was not full-sized did not need a whole number. He also pioneered the idea of fireworks after baseball games and came up with an idea for an exploding scoreboard at Comiskey Park in Chicago. His son, Mike, was credited with the ill-fated idea of Disco Demolition Night in the late 1970s at Comiskey, where fans were invited to bring disco records to be destroyed before the game. The scenario turned into a riot and forced the Chicago White Sox to forfeit the game. It was tough to say whether or not the signing of the first African American in the American League was another notch in his promotional belt or if he had an honest desire to help African Americans receive equality. His autobiography leaned toward an emphasis on altruistic motives, but at the same time, the autobiography was self-congratulatory on some issues; it was difficult to take Veeck's word as gospel on the matter.[5] It was also quite possible that Veeck simply wanted the most talented players for the Indians in the hopes of the team winning its first World Series championship since 1920. Doby would be relatively inexpensive to acquire, and his statistics were probably as good as or better than the majority of players available at the time. Paige was considered too old by many yet was still as sharp as pitchers half his age. It was also entirely possible that a combination of these factors led to Veeck's signing of Paige.

Veeck set his plans for integration into motion not long after his arrival in Cleveland. He even hired an African American public relations man, Lou Jones, to mediate between the team and the community. Before he signed Doby, Veeck said he spoke to African American leaders in the city "and told them I was going to hold them responsible for policing their own people in case of trouble. (There was nothing for them to be responsible for, of course. We never had one fight in Cleveland in which a Negro was involved)." Veeck was obviously fearful that African Americans in Cleveland would react violently if there was excessive prejudice directed at Doby. Veeck does not mention in his autobiography if he spoke to any white leaders in the city to try to curb any violence from that portion of the population. It is almost as if Veeck did not hold white Cleveland residents accountable for their actions, while black residents had to stay calm and peaceful, no matter how much abuse they or Doby took. The other Cleveland-related issue Veeck mentioned was that "if Jackie Robinson was the ideal man to break the color line, Brooklyn was also the ideal place. I wasn't that sure about Cleveland."[6] Veeck's doubts are interesting because he probably did not know much about Cleveland. He was born and raised in Chicago, lived in Arizona prior to his purchase of the Indians, and did not spend a great amount of time in Cleveland until he bought the team a year before he signed Doby. While Veeck may have expressed doubts

Bill Veeck signed Newark Eagle Larry Doby in 1947, making him the first African American player in the American League.

about Cleveland's ability to accept an African American player, he was not necessarily an expert on the racial climate in the city in the 1940s due to his limited time there prior to his purchase of the Indians. Fears such as these were probably commonplace and show why the *Call and Post* and African American residents in the city were concerned about how Cleveland appeared to the rest of the country. While Veeck was more actively involved in the acquisition of Doby, he left the signing of Paige up to talent scout and promoter Abe Saperstein, creator of the Harlem Globetrotters.

Veeck knew that Doby and Paige had different personalities, but may have misinterpreted the thoughts and feelings of the two men. Veeck made Doby out to be a hard-working, dedicated integrator, while Paige was portrayed as a fun-loving player with no desire to serve as a racial pioneer. Veeck said:

> Satchel Paige could not have been more different than Larry Doby. Satchel is above race and beyond prejudice. It has been interesting to me to notice that when the great Negro players are listed, Satch is sometimes completely forgotten. He's interracial and universal. Larry and Satch represent different eras of American history. Satch never appeared to be interested in fighting battles, changing social patterns or winning acceptance beyond what seems to come to him naturally as a legendary American folk hero. Satch wouldn't have been at all upset at not being allowed to stay in our hotel in Tucson that first year. He would not only have expected to stay across town, he would have preferred it. He doesn't want to go to white restaurants with you and he doesn't want you to go to Negro restaurants with him.[7]

While Veeck held this perception of Paige, it may not be entirely accurate. In his autobiography, Paige mentioned an occasion where he was angry when told he was not allowed to stay with the white players on the team. When Paige traveled with the St. Louis Browns, his team from 1951–1953, they stopped in Charleston, West Virginia, for an exhibition game. The Browns told Paige that he would be allowed to stay in the hotel with the white players, but upon his arrival, the clerk refused to check him in. Paige was angry and said:

> "I'm with the Browns. They said I could stay here." I was trying to sound quiet and not cause troubles, but I couldn't. I was getting louder. "They said you'd have a room here for me." That clerk just looked right through me. Something exploded right in my head. I grabbed the edge of the desk and squeezed. I had to squeeze like that to keep my hands down, to keep from hitting that man. I didn't hit him. I just turned around and walked out of that hotel. I went down to the airport. They had a plane leaving for Washington. I bought me a ticket.[8]

Paige also discussed the time he was not able to eat in a white restaurant with fellow players while barnstorming in Indiana. Paige was told to eat in the kitchen of the restaurant, standing up. Paige said, "That really shook me up." He added, "When I got out to the ball park, all these folks who wouldn't let me have a room or some food came up and asked for my autograph. 'Go to hell,' I told them. Ned Garver, who was a top pitcher with the Browns, was standing there by me. He looked kind of surprised when I turned down those autograph-hunters. He didn't know how I was eating up my insides over the way they'd treated me like an animal. I swung around and faced Ned. 'They won't let me eat here,' I snapped, 'but they want my autograph. To hell with 'em.' Ned just nodded."[9] By this passage, it does not sound like Paige did not care to eat with whites and preferred segregation. When one also took into account the fact that Paige was truly offended by the fact that major league baseball signed Jackie Robinson as the first African American rather than him, it looks as if Veeck really misinterpreted Paige's feelings on the subject. Veeck was not the only one to portray the two men differently.

The *Call and Post* tended to portray Doby as a shy, serious man and deemphasized Paige's personality except to mention his comic tendencies. Veeck and the *Call and Post* both agreed on the fact that Doby was a quiet and shy man. Where the newspaper differed, however, was when it chose to assign more of a moral role to Doby, citing his religious beliefs and moral qualities. Veeck portrayed Paige as an independent comic who was proud to be an African American and lacked interest in white society. The *Call and Post* did note Paige's comic tendencies, but more often portrayed him as an average ballplayer with average talents rather than a savior for the race. It was possible that the paper also wanted to deemphasize the aspects of Paige's personality that would reinforce the whites' stereotypical view of blacks.

The first issue of the weekly *Call and Post* that followed the signing of Doby exemplified the importance of the event through a collage of Doby photographs over the top half of the front page. The bottom half of the page almost seemed to be an attempt to temper the enthusiasm the African American community was sure to feel with the signing of Doby. Reprinted was a full press release from player/manager Lou Boudreau on Indians letterhead that called the signing of Doby a "routine purchase" and said, "Doby will be given every chance, as will any other deserving recruit, to prove that he has the ability to make good with us."[10] Throughout the story about Doby's first game in Chicago, author Cleveland Jackson described him as nervous and also noted that Doby had a "mild mannered personality" and "a soft spoken tone (that) lent a dignity rarely attained by a 22 year old athlete." Jackson also claimed that African American churches in the Chicago area dismissed their congregations early (even though he added that this possibly was not intentional) and that whole congregations headed straight to the park to see Doby.[11] It was nearly a year later when Paige signed with the Indians, and there was considerable less fanfare than the signing of Doby. Paige's signing broke no barriers in the American League, but the pitcher was a Negro League legend and was also known by white fans, in part due to his barnstorming tours with white major league pitchers, such as Dizzy Dean and Cleveland Indian teammate Bob Feller. The signing of Paige was buried on page 6B in the sports section, in sports editor A.S. "Doc" Young's "Sportivanting" column. Young discussed the historic event, and how pitcher Bob Lemon was removed from the game by manager Lou Boudreau after he was tagged by the opposing team's offense. Young described Paige's first major league appearance on the mound:

> They tell me that there was a flicker or nervousness; but you couldn't see it from the press box. Here was one of the most fabulous pitchers of any age, one of the greatest that has ever done it, a man that has become a legend all over the western world ... getting his chance in what would normally be the twilight of a guy's career.[12]

While there was a slight mention of nerves, overall he was portrayed as more confident and more relaxed than Doby. Part of that could be due to the fact that Paige was so much older than Doby, a point that Young mentioned when he said Paige was getting a chance in what would normally be the twilight of a career. Young mentioned that some people accused Veeck of signing Paige strictly for attention and not to help the team. Young said, "The performance of Paige proved to one and all that Bill Veeck brought him to help win games and not as another sidelight. That would be no kind of deal for so magnificent a pitcher as Satchel Paige." There was one reference to the fact that Paige felt tired after his debut and said, "I need about 10 days of running." There was also a comment from Doby about how if Paige could pitch that well out of shape, he would love to see him pitch in shape.[13] These comments were more negative toward Paige's age than ability or personality.

Through references to Doby's meticulous, soft-spoken or shy personality, it was like the newspaper was more interested in discussing the type of person he was rather than the type of player he was. There was even one column about a week after Doby was signed that cited his strong faith in God. Cleveland Jackson, in his "Headline Action" column, said that Doby would find success in the major leagues due to his strong faith. Jackson mentioned a conversation he had with Doby after his first at-bat with the Indians. "Solemnly Larry remarked, 'I was tight and tense when I walked up there to the plate, this afternoon. However I am in the best possible physical condition and feel certain that I can hit big league pitching. I'm not worried about making good for the Cleveland Indians because I know that God is with me.' Those words, spoken in a quiet, solemn tone and with a dignity and depth of feeling seldom found in a 22 year old athlete, were startling revelations of the man's solid foundation." Jackson also mentioned the fact that Doby was raised in a good home and also had a good wife and good friends.[14] Once again, words like "quiet" and "solemn" were used, and there was yet another reference to Doby's young age. So even though there are no comments in reference to religion or the solid foundation of a good family when Paige was signed a year later, it may also have been due to age rather than personality differences.

Doby often overshadowed Paige in *Call and Post* stories; many articles about the aging pitcher lacked the emotion of those about Doby. For example, an article would express how both men performed in games the prior week and how they contributed to an Indians victory. There was one case, however, in which Paige was credited with a pitching victory and the article said he won the game because of Doby. A good portion of the Paige stories tended to be factual and lacked the emotion of the Doby stories that used many complimentary adjectives to describe the young outfielder. One story followed the basic factual structure until the last couple of lines, which said, "It is worthy to note that Doby has been directly responsible for two of Paige's wins and has not failed to hit in a Paige-started game."[15] Even though the writer makes it seem as if Paige is unable to win games without Doby's assistance, Paige was winning ballgames for more than twenty years, a span that nearly equaled Doby's age.

Paige was often associated with clowning and comedy more than he was recognized for his talents as a pitcher. In one of his "Sportivanting" columns, A.S. "Doc" Young discussed the fact that a theatrical agent followed Paige for a time with "fabulous-sounding offers for him to go a-clowning."[16] This was an issue that confronted many Negro League players and teams throughout the years. There were teams such as the Indianapolis Clowns that in addition to playing actual baseball would pull more theatrical stunts, such as wearing grass skirts on the field to play or juggling baseballs for show before the game. Images such as these played into negative stereotypical images of African Americans from minstrel shows and the theater, where primary roles were secondary or served as comic relief. Some players shied away from association with these types of stunts. Larry Doby once commented in a 2001 interview that black players had to get away from the ideal of that comical mold and said, "I would be the world's worst actor if I have to act that way."[17]

Apprehensions about appearing comical exhibit the concerns some African Americans had at this time about how they were viewed regarding baseball and the white community. Doby, painted more as an integrator with an assigned role to break down barriers in baseball, did not want to be portrayed as a comic player. Paige, who by many accounts was witty and had a lighthearted and jovial personality, often was painted with the image that he was more of a comical player even though he was an extremely talented pitcher. This is an example of how the newspaper emphasized that Doby embodied more of the masculine qualities that could win support for integration among whites. Young also said in his column that he thought Paige could make a profitable career in the theater while Jackie Robinson could not. Young never said why he did not think Robinson was a good candidate for the theater, but he did elaborate on why Paige would perform well in the theater. "He has talent; plays the guitar, sings in Spanish, plays the harmonica, and, most important, he has a great talent for saying the funny thing.... This writer believes that Paige could be our top comedian within a period of five years." Young continued, "But, Satch should be warned that we want none of the Stepin Fetchit stuff.... Just as a lot of us didn't like the Step-n-Pitchit take-off that was fostered when he began to work for the Indians."[18]

Young, a prominent sportswriter, often addressed the black community as a whole through his columns in the *Call and Post*. Through his position, he reached African Americans across Ohio, as the *Call and Post* was distributed in most major cities throughout the state. Young probably was concerned with how African Americans were viewed at large in the white community and wanted to make sure they were taken seriously as ballplayers and not just seen as entertainers. Integration in baseball was potentially the first step to integration in other realms of society, such as business, government and education. The controversy that Young may have referred to regarding Paige was the fact that there was a slight issue about one type of pitch Paige threw that he called his "hesitation pitch." While there was nothing in baseball rules against the rather choppy motion in which Paige would almost complete his pitching follow-through before he released the ball, managers and players complained after Paige first used it against the St. Louis Browns in July of 1948.[19] By the end of the month, Will Harridge, president of the American League, ruled the delivery illegal with a man on base and considered it a balk.[20] A balk is when a pitcher does not follow through with a legal baseball delivery.

Young's concern about Paige's image was connected to a larger issue — the image of African Americans as comics versus their image as serious men. This stretched beyond the baseball diamond and encompassed many aspects of society. Author Melvin Ely in *The Adventures of Amos 'n' Andy: A Social History of an American Phenomenon* notes how whites often developed their views of African Americans from comic exploits like Amos 'n' Andy. Whites expected blacks to act like the characters from the popular radio and television program in everyday life, as if all blacks were actually like the characters.[21] While the show was popular with both white and black fans, it did gather criticism, especially from the black community. Ely cited a letter to the *Afro-American* of Baltimore from Clarence LeRoy Mitchell of Howard University, in which Mitchell asked if "his own people really cared how whites saw them." Mitchell was critical of blacks who helped perpetuate this stereotype, such as "free clowning by bell boys, porters and waiters, for their white spectators." He believed if whites only saw African Americans in this comical setting, then they would never be taken seriously in the white community.[22] This same reasoning probably also influenced the opinion of Young.

These issues were also tied to Abe Saperstein, the man who founded the Harlem Globetrotters basketball team and scouted Paige for the Indians. This was a potentially sore subject to both the *Call and Post* and Young since they worked to eliminate this image of a comic player in favor of a serious player that could also be respected in the white community. Here was the creator of the comical Harlem Globetrotters, who signed a man (Paige) that already had a reputation as a comic. The *Call and Post* was critical of Saperstein at times but dropped much of that criticism once the promoter was placed on the Indians' payroll. The writers did not turn their criticism to praise but instead left Saperstein alone in columns and articles. At one point prior to the signing of Paige, A.S. "Doc" Young called Saperstein a "parasite" in his column and warned the Indians against associating with him. Young accused Saperstein of exploiting African American players, and said that he took too much credit for the Indians' signing of Larry Doby. The credit for the Doby signing, according to Young, should go to Cleveland Jackson, the former sports editor of the *Call and Post*. It was Jackson that brought Doby to Veeck's attention, not the "athletic pimp" Saperstein, Young said. He was afraid that if African Americans were forced to make gains in society through men like Saperstein, then all accomplishments by blacks in sports like baseball will be nullified. Young concluded by calling Saperstein "Brer Abe," a reference to Brer Rabbit, someone who was not to be trusted.[23]

While Saperstein was vilified by the *Call and Post*, the paper never questioned the intentions of Veeck. This was despite the fact that some believed Veek signed Paige as a promotional event rather than to help the Indians win the American League pennant. The *Call and Post* defended Veeck in its "3 Cheers" column and said that Veeck had "vision," "imagination," and "courage." The column mentioned that the Indians needed better pitching in order to win the pennant and Paige could help fill this need. The column also said, "Sure thing, Satch will draw the fans and he will give them a show. But, it will not be any clowning! The man just exudes color from every pore, that's all. All the guys who sit back with gags about his age and tell the Stepin Fetchit jokes can well pause for a moment and reflect."[24] This is again an example that clowning and comical play would not be tolerated, that Paige was to play respectfully in order to appear serious to the white community. Paige also may have used the clowning to lure opponents into believing he was not a serious pitcher prior to overpowering them with solid pitching. The point made about the age gags referred to the fact that many joked that Paige was older than 42 when he signed with the Indians. The *Call and Post* even fell into this trap of speculation when the newspaper ran a story entitled "Here's Another Guess At Paige's Age!" just a week after the "3 Cheers" column.[25] Also in the "3 Cheers" column was another mention of Paige and clowning in the same breath, even though overall the column offered a defense of Paige.

As critical of Saperstein as the *Call and Post* was, it was likely that

Veeck realized upon signing him how popular Paige was and that he could boost the Indians' attendance. Throughout World War II, the Kansas City Monarchs, Paige's Negro League team at the time, drew better crowds than most other Negro League teams, with an average of 6,000 to 7,000 fans per game. When Paige pitched there were sometimes as many as 30,000 to 40,000 fans in attendance, with a relatively equal number of whites and blacks in the stands.[26] Throughout Paige's autobiography, he bragged about how many more fans came to games that he pitched. Veeck's gimmicks, such as fireworks and exploding scoreboards, were not only for personal gratification but also to increase attendance at games. He was a shrewd businessman who paid attention to what fans wanted when they attended a baseball game. It was also very possible that Veeck needed an extra pitcher to help the Indians in the pennant race and that the talented Paige could help win decisive ballgames down the stretch. By mid-summer, teams always look for those extra pieces to the puzzle that will give them a lift into the October playoffs. In his autobiography, Veeck said, "In 1948, after I bought [pitcher Sam] Zoldak, the time had come. [Pitcher Bob] Feller wasn't going well. [Pitcher Russ] Christopher was beginning to weaken. We were desperately in need of a pitcher who could make an occasional start and go a few innings in relief. I had already discussed Satch with Boudreau. Lou wasn't interested. He had heard somewhere that Satch had very little left."[27] Paige made Boudreau a believer after he pitched batting practice to him and the player/manager could not get a hit off Paige. "Don't let him get away, Will. We can use him," Boudreau said. Veeck had some comments about the signing:

> I had foolishly believed that nobody could possibly accuse me of signing Paige for a gag. Not when we were in the middle of a four-way pennant fight. But my talent for underestimating the Old Guard's resistance to reason and logic remained unimpaired. The cry went out that I was — yes — making a travesty of the game and — yes — cruelly exploiting an old man's reputation in his declining years.
>
> We were, at that moment, sitting in first place. We had already drawn over a million people and our advance sale alone assured us of reaching two million. In the face of all that, an astonishing number of presumably intelligent and literate writers saw the signing of Paige not only as a — yes — "cheap and tawdry" box-office stunt but as an admission that I was writing off our pennant chances.[28]

While Veeck took a slight chance on Paige, he really did not have much to lose when he signed the famous pitcher. In the worst-case scenario,

Paige joined the Indians and was not successful. Even if he was not successful, there was the chance that his presence on the team would boost attendance at some games the way he did in the Negro Leagues. If that were the case, then the team would not really take a loss from Paige's contract. In a best-case scenario, Paige would help out as a spot starting pitcher and a reliever for tired Indians starting pitchers like Bob Feller and Bob Lemon. Due to his ability to keep a team from scoring runs once he entered the game and his ability to start whenever necessary, the Indians would be able to win enough games to clinch the American League pennant and head to the World Series. The best-case scenario was basically what happened; Paige went 6–1 with an earned run average (ERA) of 2.48, including three complete games.[29] The Indians not only won the American League pennant but also defeated the National League Boston Braves to win their second World Series, the first since 1920.

The Buckeyes, who already took a back seat to the Indians post-integration in the *Call and Post*, were almost completely forgotten after the Indians' 1948 World Series win. Prior to integration the Indians were rarely, if ever, mentioned in the *Call and Post*. The popularity of the Buckeyes peaked in Cleveland when in 1945 they won the Negro League World Series against the perennial champs, the Homestead Grays. Sprinkled throughout the *Call and Post*, there was praise as well as criticism for the Buckeyes and the Negro Leagues in general, as well as criticism and praise for the African American community, depending on how well attended Buckeyes games were at that point in time. The *Call and Post* thanked fans for attending games and bragged about high attendance totals yet had scathing comments for African American fans when they stayed away from games and chose to attend Indians games instead.

Even though the Buckeyes were quite popular in 1945 as they defeated the Grays in the Negro League World Series, fans still showed more interest in an integrated Indians team. The Negro League World Series itself was not as popular as the annual East-West All-Star game, primarily because the series itself was played like a barnstorming tour instead of in the cities of the two championship teams, a la the major leagues. During the 1945 Grays/Buckeyes series, the schedule for the first five games called for games played in Cleveland, both at League Park and at Cleveland Municipal Stadium, a game in Washington, D.C., and a game in Philadelphia. (A game in New York City was unnecessary when the Buckeyes won in four

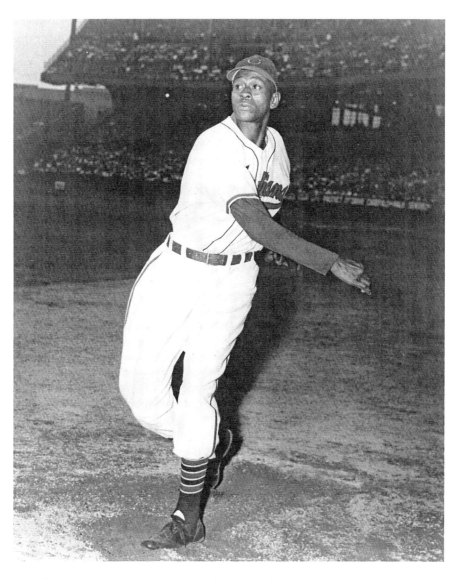

Satchel Paige was a Negro League pitching legend when he joined the Cleveland Indians in July of 1948. He finished the season with a 6–1 record and a 2.48 ERA, and helped the Indians win their first World Series since 1920.

games.[30]) It was likely difficult for fans to really follow the series with games played in three or four different cities, two of which had nothing to do with the teams in competition. Throughout the 1940s, the Grays played some of their home games in Washington, D.C., as well as Homestead. None of the first five games were even scheduled for Pittsburgh, the primary home of the Grays, even though it is only a few hours from Cleveland and a natural geographic rival for sports. While the Buckeyes did not have their own stadium in Cleveland, the team played many games at League Park, the old home of the Cleveland Indians in the east end neighborhood of Hough. The Indians did not use the cavernous Cleveland Municipal Stadium that seated roughly 78,000 until Bill Veeck purchased the team in the late 1940s. Prior to that, the team split its time between Municipal Stadium and League Park. The Buckeyes almost never used the cavernous Municipal Stadium, primarily because the team usually did not have a need for such a large facility. Usually their fans could fit easily within the confines of the smaller League Park, plus they were near to the fans' homes in the middle of a residential neighborhood.

The achievements of an integrated Indians team were far more important to the *Call and Post* than the accomplishments of the Buckeyes ever were. In 1948 when the Indians won the World Series, the entire front page of the newspaper was dedicated to stories about the team. In contrast, during the Negro League World Series in 1945, there were stories in the *Call and Post* about the Buckeyes, but the front page paled in comparison to the Indians in 1948. During the Indians' World Series, along the top of the front page with the *Call and Post* banner was the story "They're Really Our Indians," which was flanked on either side by large pictures of Larry Doby and Satchel Paige. In contrast, during the Buckeyes' 1945 World Series appearance, there was a small picture and caption on the bottom half of the front page.[31] The difference between these front pages shows the *Call and Post* was more interested in celebrating the integrated Indians than the Negro League Buckeyes. Following the Indians' victory, the front page of the *Call and Post* had a picture of Larry Doby and pitcher Steve Gromek hugging each other. The caption mentioned that Doby hit a game-winning home run in game four, the game that Gromek pitched in, and also mentioned that Doby was from Paterson, New Jersey, and Gromek was from Hamtramck, Michigan, and also said, "Happy, aren't they?"[32] One can imagine what the author of the caption tried to get across with such a minimal description, but it seems obvious that he wanted to point out that both men were from the North. The picture was also on the front page of the *Cleveland Plain Dealer* the day after the home run.[33] This picture is actually still discussed because of the prominent display of a white man and a black man embracing, thinking of nothing but the recent vic-

Larry Doby (shown with two unidentified young fans) became a fan favorite in Cleveland, where he played from 1947 through 1955, and again in 1958.

tory. As Veeck said in his autobiography, "Some of the players who had not seemed overjoyed at having Larry on the team became increasingly fond of him as it became apparent that he was going to help them slice a cut of that World Series money. The economics of prejudice, as I have discovered many times, cuts both ways."[34] Some white players were probably concerned that African American players would take their positions from them, and in turn take money from their pockets. Yet these same players were quick to welcome an African American player if he helped them gain notoriety and a World Series bonus.

The popularity of the Indians was in direct correlation to the fact that African Americans were tired of watching segregated baseball and wanted to see black players on the same stage as white players. Bob Williams, sports editor for the *Call and Post* in 1945, wrote in a column, "The people are tired of paying first class money for second class baseball. They are tired of this foolish ban on the Negro in this one sport when he has added color and excellence to every other sport in which he has participated."[35] Here Williams was extremely open about the fact that he preferred to watch African Americans play in the major leagues and was critical of the fact that white baseball ignored talented black players.

While the Buckeyes would struggle to draw fans in 1947 and 1948 following integration, the team posted decent attendance numbers immediately following World War II, according to *Call and Post* figures. For a four-game series at League Park in June of 1945 against the Memphis Red Sox, the Buckeyes drew 20,000 fans. With this statistic was the comment, "The Cleveland Indians could not have played a better ball game any day in the week. Neither could any other league club, for you can't beat the standard of perfect, gentlemanly ball playing, with thrills every inning, such as was exhibited at League Park during the Buckeyes' series with the Red Sox."[36] This was one of the rare occasions the Indians received mention in the *Call and Post* prior to integration and it was to say that the Buckeyes played just as well. This was also a month after the same author, Bob Williams, referred to the Negro Leagues as second-class baseball. It just serves as an example that the *Call and Post* appreciated the Buckeyes and the Negro Leagues in general, but an integrated team was far more important. The *Call and Post* was critical of the Negro Leagues' leadership and of the fans when they stopped attending the games. At the same time, they chose to heap praise upon individual Negro League players and cited their talents and style of play.

Prior to the integration of the Indians, the *Call and Post* encouraged fans to attend Buckeye games and support the institution of Negro League baseball. While these talented Negro League players often did not receive the pay that major league players did, they were still paid more than the average African American citizen in the 1940s. In fact, the Buckeyes were possibly one of the highest-paid Negro League teams, or at least the *Call and Post* had that perception. The paper said the only team paid higher was the Homestead Grays. The reasoning they gave for the high salaries was that team owner and Erie, Pennsylvania, native Ernest Wright wanted a championship team "bad enough to pay for it." Even though the *Call and Post* column applauded Wright for his willingness to spend on player salaries, author Bob Williams reminded Cleveland fans that they needed to play a part and attend the games and support the Buckeyes.[37]

In 1945 the *Call and Post* focused on fan and financial support of the Buckeyes as well as the behavior of the fans who attended their games. Wilbur Hayes, general manager of the Buckeyes, was used as an attendance ploy as the *Call and Post* called on fans to come to the game and let a portion of their ticket money go toward the purchase of a car for Hayes. The paper believed Hayes should be rewarded and lauded the Buckeyes for building a quality team not based on a few flashy star players, but instead by building a strong team that was solid in all areas. Hayes was given some of the credit for this and for bringing the team to Cleveland, and the *Call and Post* wanted to show appreciation by helping to purchase him a new car.[38] During the FOL-sponsored Birmingham Barons series in 1945, the attack on the game's umpire led Bob Williams and the *Call and Post* to criticize the act. Williams even encouraged fans to write to the league and complain about the conduct of the visiting Barons player.[39] It was possible that since it was an out-of-town player that caused the disturbance, Williams and others in Cleveland were afraid the event would paint the city in a bad light since it happened during a Buckeyes game at League Park. He also wanted to make sure that African Americans in Cleveland and other northern cities were not stereotyped as rowdy fighters.

The Negro Leagues often earned the *Call and Post*'s criticism, in general because of their disorganization and lack of leadership within the leagues. Exhibition games were often wedged into the schedule with meaningful regular-season games and at times there was basic disorganization and confusion. For example, there was the confusion over whether or not the Buckeyes actually qualified for the second-half championship in 1945 that would have forced a playoff with the Chicago American Giants.[40] How were fans expected to faithfully follow a team if they had no idea if their team was close to winning the league title? Fans probably needed personal scorecards to keep track of which games were meaningful to their team and which ones were simply exhibition. How was a fan supposed to know if their team was close to approaching the playoffs if the league itself did not know? With such confusion and lack of structure, fans were probably more than willing to jump ship to the major leagues as soon as they integrated, which would be one of the final nails in the coffin for Negro League baseball.

Author Neil Lanctot theorized in *Negro League Baseball: The Rise and Ruin of a Black Institution* that African Americans tended to gravitate toward the major leagues because they offered better publicity than the Negro Leagues and because the white leagues had the benefit of radio and television coverage.[41] By the time major league baseball began to integrate, Lanctot claimed that blacks wanted more than just a segregated version of those leagues. However, poor publicity and poor organization kept the Negro Leagues from offering fans an alternative to the newly segregated major leagues. Fans brought radios to Negro League games in New York City in order to listen to the progress of Jackie Robinson, while the Buckeyes offered fans updates on Larry Doby throughout their games in the hopes of holding the interest of Doby and Indians fans.[42]

Another obstacle to Negro League teams that were losing fans to the white major leagues was the fact that almost no teams owned their own ballparks. Due to scheduling conflicts in the stadiums they rented, there were few home games for Negro League teams. A rainout or other unexpexted cancellation could mean financial devastation for a team. While it was a common theory that the Negro League World Series moved from city to city in order to reach more fans, it is possible the shifts occurred due to lack of availability at the hometown team's stadium. According to Lanctot, Negro League owners never looked to the future to consider what would happen if the major leagues integrated. For example, when Chicago American Giants catcher John Ritchey left the team to sign with the San Diego Padres of the white Pacific Coast League, owner J.B. Martin demanded compensation for the player. However, Martin was forced to admit that through an "oversight" he had neglected to actually tender Ritchey an official contract. Since there was no way to prove the league had an established tie with the player, it was impossible for anyone to order the Padres to compensate the American Giants.[43]

The Negro Leagues were harmed by poor publicity and by an overall lack of media coverage, both before and after integration. When fans could turn on a television or a radio and watch or listen to the exploits of players like Larry Doby, Jackie Robinson, Roy Campanella and Satchel Paige, why would they attend a Negro League game? Even though one Buckeyes game was televised in Cleveland, overall media coverage for the Negro Leagues as a whole was spotty and uneven.[44] The outspoken owner of the Newark Eagles, Effa Manley, claimed that the black press had abandoned Negro League baseball. She was critical of the fact that they paid so much attention to African American players in major league baseball and focused almost no attention to Negro League players. Manley was involved in a publicized spat with Jackie Robinson in the media during 1948. Robinson said, "Negro baseball needs a housecleaning from bottom to top," and openly criticized the Negro Leagues in a 1948 *Ebony* article. Even though Robinson played in the Negro Leagues for only one season with the Kansas City Monarchs, he lambasted the Negro Leagues for poor governance of the leagues and an overall poor lifestyle for its players.[45] While it is difficult to know Robinson's exact motive for the comments, it is possible that he wanted to change the image of black baseball and how the white community viewed it. Manley lashed out at Robinson for his critique, called him "ungrateful" and said, "He is where he is today because of organized baseball. I believe that he never would have been noticed if it were not for the people and the teams he derides."[46] Ernest Wright, the owner and president of the Cleveland Buckeyes, leapt to Manley's defense in a letter he wrote to the Eagles' owner dated May 29, 1948. Wright said he felt compelled to react to Robinson and defend the Negro Leagues but that Manley expressed exactly what he felt. Wright continued, "So my hat is off to you for undertaking the job that we all felt it was our duty to do. With people like you on the side of right, it can never go astray. Again I say, 'bravo.'"[47] Even though other owners probably agreed with Manley, she was one of the few owners to lash out publicly against Robinson's statements. So while Manley may have claimed that the black press abandoned the Negro Leagues, they certainly did not take part in organized publicity, as there seemed to be no set response to the Robinson comments. Teams failed to promote their players and their game schedules, as exemplified by the 1945 Buckeyes debacle where the press did not know at the end of the season if the Buckeyes were the Negro American League champs.

Because of confusion over issues such as scheduling and promotion,

Cleveland Jackson of the *Call and Post* called on the Negro Leagues to step up to the challenges posed by integration. Jackson warned that major league owners were going after African American customers because "Negro buying power is one of the greatest undeveloped purchasing blocks in the country." Jackson's suggestions for the Negro Leagues included working to come under the jurisdiction of major league baseball and its commissioner, Albert "Happy" Chandler, and establish strong ties with major league baseball. Also, he advised them to "discard their old fly-by-night methods of operating, introduce modern procedures that will not only develop new players but will stimulate players toward maintaining the high type of competition so vital to healthy fan interest."[48] Within a few weeks of Jackson's column, the *Call and Post* announced that a recent Buckeyes game failed to draw 5,000 fans, even though the Buckeyes led their league at that point in time.[49] While Jackson's support showed a desire to save Negro League baseball, his plan was basically to save it by allowing white major league baseball to take it under its wing.

By 1948 the *Call and Post* had shifted focus to the Indians and the exploits of Larry Doby and Satchel Paige. However, when the Buckeyes truly began to struggle, the paper continued to encourage fans to attend their games. At the beginning of the season in April, the *Call and Post* asked what type of team do "we" have in a preview of the upcoming Indians season.[50] A month later the author of that story, A.S. "Doc" Young, dedicated his column to "A Batch of Reasons Why You Should Support Negro Baseball." Young recounted a recent conversation where he was accused of bashing the Negro Leagues in an earlier column. He called his comments "constructive criticism" and that despite the Negro Leagues' shortcomings, it needed the support of fans. He was critical of the fact that announcers at Buckeyes games interrupted at times to provide Indians updates and said the games needed to move along quicker to keep fans interested. Young said, "The Negro majors constitute the acme of the sport in our group. It's Negro business. It needs support from us the same as our laundries, groceries, insurance companies. It's an economic factor: it pays salaries — and not bad dough, either — to about 150 players in the American League alone and to countless officials, umpires, statisticians and the like, including hot dog salesmen. That's important!" Young addressed the quandary of watching the Buckeyes versus watching Doby by telling fans to simply watch both.[51] Within a month the *Call and Post* ran an editorial entitled, "What's Wrong With the Buckeye Fans?" The editorial asked why Buckeye fans stayed away from the game in "droves" despite the good play in their game with the Memphis Red Sox, the fact that two bands played during the game and that there was ample police protection. An official from the Indians is cited as saying that most African American fans chose to see the major league team play rather than the Buckeyes. The editorial said, "This writer does not pretend to tell you what to do with YOUR MONEY. Fact is, he sees the Indians too. But, he sees both. May it be repeated? He sees BOTH!" With approximately 130,000 African Americans in Cleveland, it was estimated that only about 2,800 attended the most recent Sunday Buckeyes game at League Park. The editorial concluded, "Leave us remember, friends, without the Negro baseball, there would never have been a Jackie Robinson or a Larry Doby in the major leagues. You owe your support to the Cleveland Buckeyes and to the teams in Negro baseball."[52] Despite this call for fans to patronize both teams, the *Call and Post* was even guilty of paying more attention to the Indians than they did the Buckeyes. The newspaper was torn between supporting the disorganized and dying institution of Negro League baseball and the promise of black progress through integration into white baseball.

Even an integrated major league exhibition game drew almost five times as many fans as a Buckeyes game during the same week. Young estimated in his column that an Indians exhibition game against the Brooklyn Dodgers in July drew about 25,000 African American fans in what he called a "technicolor" crowd. He said the Buckeyes probably struggled to get even 5,000 fans for a game at that point in time.[53] In a separate story about the game, Young said that it was the four African American major leaguers — Larry Doby, Satchel Paige, Jackie Robinson and Roy Campanella — that drew the fans to the game. He estimated that of the 25,000 fans, about 3,000 came from out-of-town locales, such as Nashville, Chicago, Detroit, Youngstown, Dayton, Toledo and Erie. He said with those out-of-town fans subtracted, he estimated that one of every five African American residents in Cleveland saw the game.[54] The large number of both white and black fans at this game, coupled with the large number of out-of-town fans, showed that integrated major league baseball was important across the country and across racial boundaries. By the end of 1948, the Buckeyes would leave Cleveland for Louisville, Kentucky, a move barely acknowledged by the *Call and Post* at the end of 1948 or at the beginning of 1949.

Baseball became a symbol of racial progress for African Americans during the 1940s when teams like the Indians began to integrate. The *Call and Post* and the African American community in Cleveland chose to emphasize Larry Doby's positive qualities over Satchel Paige's because he represented more of the masculine attributes that they wanted to emphasize to whites. While Paige was a talented and legendary Negro League pitcher, by emphasizing his role in major league baseball African Americans ran the risk of his reputation off the field drawing attention away from the gains they were making on the field. Even though the Buckeyes had drawn decent-sized crowds for a time during the 1940s, the team was valued more for its entertainment qualities than for anything else. Baseball became so much more than a mere entertainment outlet for African Americans in Cleveland and across the United States. It was an important step towards broken barriers and integration into other aspects of society, such as education, business and government.

7

The End of an Era

The Buckeyes Collapse

Following the integration of major league baseball in 1947 and the Cleveland Indians' World Series victory in 1948, writers for the Cleveland *Call and Post* praised themselves for their role in the integration of the Indians and argued that the team's victories provided proof that African American baseball players improved the major leagues. As the writers continued their intense push toward further integration, the Negro Leagues were viewed as an antiquated system that should change the way it operated or disband completely. The Cleveland Buckeyes suffered extreme financial and legal troubles throughout 1949 and 1950, troubles the team could not overcome before it collapsed for good during the 1950 season. The *Call and Post*, specifically sportswriter John Fuster, who returned to the newspaper in 1949 when A.S. "Doc" Young left for the *Chicago Defender*, did everything in its power to increase the number of black players in the major leagues. Fuster turned his attention to the Negro Leagues and waged a campaign to add white players to the all-black teams. Even though the *Call and Post* exhibited support for integration in all aspects of society, it stopped short of advocating racial equality in the black press. Certain whites and blacks in the Cleveland community criticized the *Call and Post* for the lack of attention paid to newsworthy whites, but the paper stood firm and maintained its need to remain a black-only institution. While the paper's editorial page often included pieces promoting the support of black business, the Negro Leagues were noticeably absent from the list of businesses that should be supported. If there was an institution that could have used some support, it was definitely organized Negro League baseball.

By 1948 the Negro National League and the Negro American League struggled more than in previous years and teetered on the edge of collapse.

While the Negro Leagues had to contend with the increasing popularity of the integrated major leagues, they also had to deal with the departure of notable stars, poor promotion and the lack of home stadiums. The leagues suffered the loss of two of its biggest stars — Satchel Paige, who left to play with the Indians in 1948, and Josh Gibson, who died in 1947 at the age of 35 after battling numerous health and mental problems.[1] The Negro Leagues were at the mercy of the major leagues as far as playing venues were concerned. The leagues still rented major league parks, meaning that cancellation because of poor weather would not allow for makeup games due to scheduling conflicts. NNL and NAL teams needed to make a large profit from these games in order to pay stadium rental fees and still have enough left over to pay operating costs. If attendance was poor, teams may have just enough to cover the rent, leaving nothing for players, travel fees and promotional costs.[2] Fans of the Negro Leagues were left with two options — follow the team in person or through the black press. By the end of the 1948 season, the New York Black Yankees folded, as well as Effa and Abe Manley's Newark Eagles. The only reasonable solution for the remaining NNL teams and the NAL was to merge. On November 30, 1948, the NAL accepted the Philadelphia Stars, the Baltimore Elite Giants, the New York Cubans and the Houston Eagles (formerly Newark, under a new ownership group) into its fold. Teams like the Eagles and the Buckeyes, who were to play in Louisville, Kentucky, for the 1949 season, hoped to capitalize on a segregated South in order to improve business.[3]

While the *Call and Post* did little to acknowledge the Buckeyes' move, the writers appeared surprised and somewhat disappointed by the team's departure. The paper claimed the Buckeyes repeatedly said they would stay in Cleveland for 1949 despite suffering deep financial losses. The *Call and Post* blamed the loss of interest in the Buckeyes on the increasing popularity of Larry Doby and the Indians in the black community.[4] By July of 1949, the Buckeyes returned to Cleveland to play in a benefit game for the Karamu House community theater building in Cleveland. The *Call and Post* said, "Everybody can make mistakes, and Wilbur Hayes, eager-beaver general manager of Cleveland's erstwhile Cleveland Buckeyes, readily admits that he made a serious one when he took his popular aggregation of Negro stars off to Louisville with the expectations of bigger gates and lusher profits for his boss, Ernie Wright, Erie, Pa. sportsman."

Prior to the arrival of the Buckeyes back in Cleveland, Hayes wrote a note to the *Call and Post* that claimed his team was full of talented young players and addressed some of the larger problems the Negro Leagues faced. Hayes said that even though most people in America frequently discussed the collapse of the Negro Leagues, the young players on the Buckeyes did not believe it. These players thought that if they continued on their path in the Negro Leagues, they too would have a chance to play in the majors. The economic boom years of World War II were past, according to Hayes, and Negro League owners had to learn to succeed on a much smaller budget. In fact, that failure to adapt was what hurt the Buckeyes. Hayes said that when money became tight, the team cut costs and player salaries. Some players became frustrated and left for semi-pro teams while others remained with the team and were vocal about their frustration.[5] Here Hayes tries to defend some of the changes to the Buckeyes and made it seem as if many of the choices he made were unavoidable due to the larger problems that existed within Negro League baseball. Despite the problems of the Buckeyes, they still managed to raise $5,000 for the Karamu House and had an attendance of 5,541 for their doubleheader loss to the Indianapolis Clowns.[6] In his letter, Hayes referred to the "youngsters" who hoped to have a chance to play in the major leagues. By mentioning this, he admitted publicly what many other people were already starting to think — that the purpose of the Negro Leagues post-integration must be to prepare young players for the major leagues.

While the Buckeyes kept the severity of their financial problems under wraps for much of their existence in the 1940s, by 1949 their difficulties were impossible to mask when team owners Wilbur Hayes and Ernest Wright faced legal charges over unpaid bills. Wright faced court litigation, and Hayes was threatened with immediate arrest if he was to set foot in Cleveland after he ignored a summons from the Paramount Finance Company. Hayes borrowed $1,000 several years prior from the company and also mortgaged his 1942 Packard automobile in the transaction. Hayes only paid $267 of the loan back and took the automobile out of the state. Hayes was served his court summons as he attended pre-game festivities on the field for the benefit game for the Karamu House and later fled town, ignoring the summons. Landlord Samuel Klein also claimed Hayes owed him

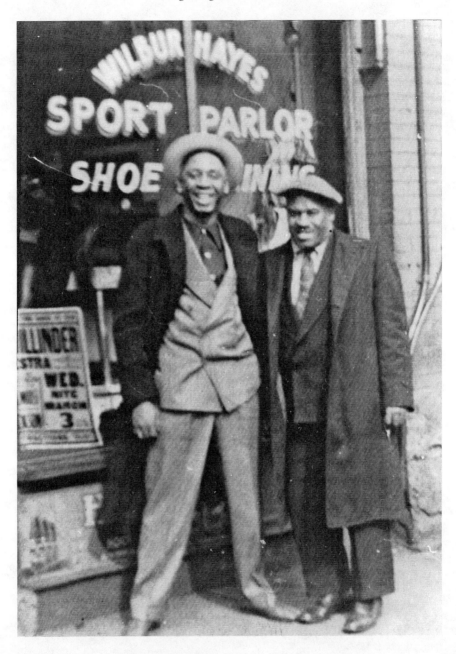

Former player and manager Alonso Boone (left) poses with general manager Wilbur Hayes outside of Hayes' business.

$450. Both Wright and Hayes were accused of not paying a $350 advertising bill. Marvin Cheecks, manager of the Majestic Hotel, said the Buckeyes racked up almost $500 in unpaid hotel bills. It was difficult for creditors to collect on money owed to them by the Buckeyes because the only asset the team was known to hold was its bus, and ownership of the vehicle was unclear. Hayes owned no property or other items that could be confiscated.[7] Former players also targeted Hayes, as pitcher Eugene Bremmer contacted the *Call and Post* to report his financial problems with the team. Bremmer claimed he quit the Buckeyes with four or five other players at the end of May 1949 because he was never paid. Bremmer's contract stated that he should receive a salary of $425 per month, but the only money Bremmer claimed he ever received was a $70 "loan" from Hayes. Bremmer was not exactly angered by the missing money; he was more upset with a ruling from NAL president and owner of the Chicago American Giants, Dr. J.B. Martin, that suspended Bremmer from league play because he "jumped the Buckeyes." Martin never talked to Bremmer but took the word of Wright and Hayes without further investigation. Hayes later defended himself against the accusations when he said Bremmer quit the Buckeyes not because of salary differences, but to pitch for a mixed-race team in Rochester, Minnesota.[8]

Despite their financial troubles, in 1950 John Fuster was sentimental regarding the Buckeyes, and was clear about what the future should hold for the team. Wright was no longer involved with the Buckeyes, as Hayes took sole control of the team. He told the *Call and Post* that his strategy to draw fans was to reduce ticket prices and increase the number of night games.[9] As John Fuster previewed the upcoming Indians season, he took a moment to reflect on the Buckeyes and preview their 1950 season. Fuster claimed that the *Call and Post* continually offered space to the Buckeyes, praising the team when they won and criticizing them when they lost. Even with all of the publicity the *Call and Post* gave the team, the Buckeyes were still unable to draw fans at League Park. When the Buckeyes left for Louisville in 1949, Fuster claimed fans in Cleveland were disappointed by their departure. He continued, "They had supplied Clevelanders with many seasons of fun and entertainment. They had sometimes provoked us, had sometimes presented us with bad umpiring and with other 'small time' mixups, but we loved them just the same. They were OUR TEAM."

Even though Fuster referred to the Buckeyes as "our team," he only seemed willing to refer to them in this manner after major league baseball had integrated. In 1942 when he wrote for the paper, he was much more concerned with integrating the Indians than he was celebrating the Buckeyes as "our team." Apparently, according to Fuster, Hayes openly claimed he was in a position to prepare young African American players for the major leagues and to date had sold four Buckeyes players to the Indians. Fuster said the Buckeyes had the paper's best wishes and added:

> We hope Wilbur does not bar any player good enough to make his team, whether he be white, or black or yellow; whether he be Catholic, Gentile or Jew. It would be hard to get the Negro owners to take that NEGRO prefix out of their league's name, but we hope they follow the lead of Branch Rickey and open positions on their teams to men of all races.[10]

Topics Fuster discussed in this preview article were issues that would dominate his and columnist Marty Richardson's coverage of the Buckeyes and the Negro Leagues throughout 1950. The *Call and Post* was mostly silent about the on-field activities of the Buckeyes, who folded by the end of the summer in 1950. Writers like Fuster and Richardson were quite vocal about what the Negro Leagues stood for and what they should accomplish in the future. According to the writers, the Negro Leagues should serve as a minor league system for the major leagues, preparing players for a future on a larger, integrated stage. In addition, the leagues should integrate and add white players to further prove the success of whites and blacks playing side by side. Fuster hoped the Buckeyes would still be able to draw crowds of about two or three thousand people during an upcoming season against the Indianapolis Clowns.

Even though he was far more concerned with increasing the number of African American players in the major leagues, Fuster still believed the Negro Leagues served a purpose, even if their responsibility was diminished. The fact remained that the major leagues needed a venue to prepare young players. Fuster believed the Negro Leagues were just as good of a location as high school, college, or the sandlots.[11] While Fuster wanted the Buckeyes to survive, he hoped their existence would be to stock the major leagues with talent rather than to provide entertainment for African American fans. Through his columns he made it clear that he did not want the Negro Leagues to continue as they had for the past decade; the leagues must change and develop. Fuster did not want fans to be disappointed by the disappearance of the Negro Leagues, but considered the leagues' demise to be another step on the road to progress. If the major leagues included both white and black players, perhaps the Negro Leagues should consider a similar move. Fuster implied that the black press did not work hard for integration just to see the continuance of a segregated league. He was also insulted by the term "Negro" as a subheading within his column stated, "Should Change Name Of League, The Word Negro Smacks Segregation In The Nth." Fuster argued that the major leagues did not place the term "white" before their league names; they just used "American League" and "National League." He suggested that the Negro Leagues "come up to date" and eliminate the term "Negro" before their league names. Fuster noted that so few fans attended Buckeye games that he could practically count all of the people in attendance by glancing around the stadium. He cited an average of 1,200 fans per contest, a figure he feared would barely pay the team's rent for the stadium. Even though integration was successful in the North, Fuster mentioned that perhaps an all-black team may be more successful in the South. "But up north, using the questionable success of the Cleveland Buckeyes as a yardstick, all–Negro baseball can be measured for its casket. It is just about dead." The solution in the North, according to Fuster, was for the Negro League teams to integrate. He addressed league president Dr. J.B. Martin and said that with integration of the Negro Leagues, "You will win support from America's black masses — and you can bet on that!"[12]

Despite the collapse of the Buckeyes and the aforementioned struggles of the Negro Leagues, the East-West All-Star Game, which existed annually until 1953, remained popular. The August 20, 1950, edition of the game drew 24,614 fans to Comiskey Park in Chicago.[13] In more profitable years, the game welcomed as many as 50,000 fans to the Chicago exhibition, but the 1950 game proved that fans were still interested. It was possible that many watching the East-West game at this point in time were more interested in seeing future major league stars than they were in cheering for the players of their hometown Negro League team.

Fuster and writers of the *Call and Post* continued their push toward the full integration of the major leagues as they encouraged teams to add more African American players to their rosters and sought to prove how much better the major leagues were because of integration. Prior to the 1949 season, writer Robert Benfield pointed out that the Indians now had eleven African American players between their major league team and minor league system, while the Brooklyn Dodgers, home of Jackie Robinson, had eight. Benfield praised other teams that were signing black players to their minor league rosters and said, "So, with more and more colored players breaking into the ranks of organized baseball, it appears that big league owners are finally realizing the true ability of Negro players and are employing full-time scouts to search for the best available talent." The *Call and Post* also pointed out that due to the high number of African American players in major league baseball for 1949, owners were sure to host record-breaking crowds, huge profits and extremely close pennant races.[14] Following the 1949 season, Fuster mentioned that every year since baseball had integrated there was an African American player on at least one of the championship teams. In 1947, Jackie Robinson was on the National League champion Brooklyn Dodgers (the New York Yankees won the World Series), in 1948 the American League and World Series champion Indians had Larry Doby, and in 1949 Brooklyn was again the National League champion (and again the Yankees won the World Series). Fuster hoped these victories would show major league teams that integration equaled a pennant. This would assuredly cause teams to add more African American players, and Fuster encouraged black fans to anticipate this day. Above everything else, baseball was a business, according to Fuster. Major league owners, in order to run their team efficiently, had to place the best players on the field. Since there were many talented African American players, soon every team in the majors would be integrated in order to remain competitive.[15]

Fuster also publicly criticized major league teams that had yet to integrate in the hopes of spurring change within their rosters. The New York Yankees, Chicago White Sox, Detroit Tigers, Philadelphia Athletics, Washington Senators, St. Louis Cardinals, Cincinnati Reds, Pittsburgh Pirates, Philadelphia Phillies and the Boston Red Sox (the last team to integrate, in 1959) were teams that had no African American players on their major league rosters or in their minor league systems. The Cleveland Indians, Brooklyn Dodgers, New York Giants and Boston Braves all had African Americans on their major league rosters, while the St. Louis Browns and Chicago Cubs had integrated their minor league systems. Fuster questioned the slow movement of integration as he said, "Now how in the Sam Hill can you have a 'great American game' when this game, in its highest bracket still almost completely ignores the talents of that vast and willing segment of American's population commonly called the American Negro?" He asked if owners were already "too rich" and said that only once all teams integrated would he see baseball as "the great American game."[16]

A great victory, as far as Fuster was concerned, was the fact that these new African American players were elected to the major league All-Star game by fans, both white and black alike. When voting for the All-Star game, fans traditionally chose the starting lineups for the American and National league squads, while managers and players choose the reserves and pitchers. For the 1949 game, Brooklyn Dodger Jackie Robinson was elected as a starter for the National League and Dodger Don Newcombe was the starting pitcher. Dodger Roy Campanella, a catcher, was a reserve, as was Larry Doby. By 1950 both Campanella and Robinson were voted to the starting lineups of the National League team, while Larry Doby was elected a starter for the American League squad, beating out legendary Yankee outfielder Joe DiMaggio.

Fuster criticized owners who did not recognize the popularity of African American players on teams when he targeted Warren Giles' Detroit Tigers. He noted that when the Indians arrived in Detroit with Larry Doby and new African American outfielder Luke Easter, at least 15,000 black fans came to watch them. Fuster asked, "Why can't this club make those 15,000 fans over into Tigers fans by signing some Negro players?" His suggestion implied that integrating the team was a smart business move, and that an integrated Tigers team would draw at least 15,000 more fans per game than they did currently. The *Call and Post* also criticized Clark Griffith, owner of the Washington Nationals/Senators, for making money off the appearance of Doby and Easter while he refused to sign African American players to the Senators. The article stated that Griffith was "unalterably opposed to colored players in the big leagues, except that he has never hesitated to take his share of the gate receipts made larger by the presence of Doby and Easter in the Indians lineup." The story claimed that many African American fans came to games with Doby and Easter, as well as a large amount of white fans from Virginia and North Carolina.[17]

Satchel Paige was nearly forgotten in the post-integration era, as Doby and new outfielder Luke Easter were promoted frequently by the *Call and Post* as the face of African Americans on the Indians. By the time Paige won the World Series with the Indians in 1948, he was already in his 40s — long considered the twilight years of a pitcher's career. Paige signed with the Indians for the 1949 season, and while he remained popular, he was almost more of an afterthought. Columnist Marty Richardson chose to offer a tribute to Paige at the end of the 1949 season when he claimed he wanted to memorialize the famous pitcher and encourage him to retire at the top of his game. Richardson praised Paige as the "greatest hurler of Negro baseball," which was a difficult field in which to play because "the ups and downs of playing Negro baseball would make one of the epics of Homer look like a child's jaunt around its nursery." Paige succeeded even as he dealt with the challenges of Negro League ball, like "bad hours, playing two games in different towns hundreds of miles apart in the same day, managers and owners who have little or no regard for their players, infrequent paydays and occasional 'skips' by the paymaster." Richardson pondered what could have been if Paige was allowed to integrate baseball years earlier. Because of Paige's popularity, he could have brought "millions" of additional fans into major league ballparks. Richardson said he hoped teams that suffered financial difficulties in the past twenty-five years would think about the money that Paige could have earned for them. Paige could have helped these teams win championships but was forced to settle for a spot on the Indians in the twilight of his career. Richardson added, "Satchel is the one dramatic example of the fact that Jim Crow is a Fool's Device." Richardson went on to call Paige a "four-inning pitcher" for the Indians, in reference to the fact that the team mainly used him as relief for a faulty starting pitcher. He believed the Indians needed more than just an additional relief pitcher at this point. Richardson said that Paige had two roads to choose from, one was retiring at the top of his game and the other was deteriorating until his legs could hardly support him anymore.[18]

The *Call and Post* seemed almost pleased that Paige was not asked back for the 1950 season when the newspaper headlined a story, "Paige's Release May Get Minoso Better Chance." Orestes "Minnie" Minoso was a young Cuban fielder who played on the Indians minor league team in the Pacific Coast League after he narrowly missed making the squad in 1949. Even though Minoso was not an African American, the *Call and Post* often grouped him with young black players in the Indians' farm system, the color of his skin more important than his racial or ethnic background. The paper hoped the new roster spot, cleared by Paige, gave Minoso a better chance of making the 1950 Indians.[19] A young player, such as Minoso, had the potential for a long, productive future in the major leagues compared to Paige, who probably had a couple of more years at the most. Minoso would ensure that black players would remain on the Indians throughout the 1950s and possibly into the 1960s and the number of African American players would not dwindle.

Another reason the *Call and Post* may have been pleased with the departure of Paige was the rather cloudy circumstances in which the pitcher was released from the Indians. New Indians president Hank Greenberg told Fuster that he released Paige because of the pitcher's "complete disregard for training rules and for train time and game time."[20] Fuster did express sadness at Paige's departure and his lack of knowledge at the pitcher's whereabouts at the start of the 1950 season following his release. Greenburg also told Fuster that the Indians' players liked Paige and that he thought Paige was a good man. Unfortunately, Greenburg said the situation on the Indians deteriorated to the point where there was one set of rules for Satchel Paige and another set of rules for the rest of the team. Paige was late for practices and would occasionally show up just in time for the start of a game. Even though he thought Paige could still pitch, Greenburg cut ties with him.

The *Call and Post* was likely glad to see the Indians cut ties with Satchel Paige after these perceived behavior issues became public knowledge. If he was breaking rules that white players were expected to follow, the paper was probably afraid of the image that behavior portrayed. Greenberg added that if Bill Veeck still ran the Indians, perhaps he would have tolerated Paige longer. The new Indians president stressed that the departure had nothing to do with money, because Paige's popularity brought ticket sales and these increased sales would have covered any salary increases.[21] If Paige had an unsavory reputation among major leaguers, for ignoring rules and skipping practices, Fuster and the *Call and Post* may have been afraid of the image this behavior portrayed to whites. Perhaps a young player like Minoso, who carried less baggage, was preferable to the controversial Paige.

Larry Doby and Luke Easter embodied many of the qualities of respectability that many in the African American community felt integrationist players needed to have. Even though Easter struggled offensively at times and battled a knee injury throughout the 1949 season, the *Call and Post* said that white newspapers finally agreed with them prior to the 1950 season that Easter was "Cleveland's 'hope' for the pennant this season." The newspaper also discussed the humble qualities of Doby after he modestly told the *Call and Post* a hitting streak that broke one of his slumps was merely luck. This caused Fuster to say, "Nobody gets that lucky," and "Greatness is a two-faced coin, on one side is humility."[22] At one point Fuster recollected Doby's first on-field appearance in July of 1947 and seemed almost disappointed that the young player was not more charismatic during his first Indians appearance. Fuster called Doby a "stranger in a strange, strange place" and said that he was unable to relax. The "poker-faced" Doby was accused of being aloof by fans and reporters due to his serious demeanor. Fuster claimed that African American fans saw Doby as "theirs" and expected the ballplayer to be as excited to meet them as they were him. These fans "wanted too much," according to Fuster. Doby was a young kid who felt alone in his new surroundings and had to face the challenges that all major league players faced, with the added stress of being one of the few black players in the league. Fuster explained, "He felt as only a Negro lad breaking into the white man's game of baseball could feel ... nervous ... tense with the desire to come through." Fuster fast-forwarded to the present and noted how much progress Doby had made while pointing out Doby's "aloofness" and "one-word conversations" were a thing of the past. Fans supposedly liked Doby and Doby liked the fans as he went about his business "with a complete lack of I-AM-MIS-TER-BIG."[23]

The *Call and Post* once drew a comparison between Doby and Jackie Robinson in a column entitled "Who's The Best?" as the two men's (almost identical) batting statistics were noted through August of 1950. Despite the similarities in their playing statistics, the author focused on the differing levels of attention afforded the two men. Robinson received a great deal of attention before he proved his abilities as a ballplayer simply due to the fact that he was the first African American in major league baseball. In a short amount of time, Doby was able to prove he was a talented ballplayer and a patient man. When he was hit by a Joe Dobson pitch in an exhibition game, Doby did not express anger. It was incidents like this, coupled with his home run power, that drew many fans' attention to Doby.[24]

"Beanings," like the one mentioned in this column, were a concern for African American players who integrated the major leagues. There were fears that pitchers would throw intentionally at hitters and that base runners would slide violently into black fielders simply because of their color. Doby created controversy in 1950 after he was nearly hit by a pitch from Detroit pitcher Dizzy Trout. *Cleveland Plain Dealer* writer Gordon Cobbledick criticized Doby for reacting in anger to the incident, which prompted Charles P. Lucas, the executive secretary for the Cleveland branch of the NAACP, to respond in the *Call and Post*. Lucas called Cobbledick a great sportswriter and said that he would usually encourage Doby to take his advice, but in this instance Lucas greatly disagreed with the veteran scribe. Even though Cobbledick admitted that white Indians player Joe Gordon reacted similarly to a brush-back pitch in the past, he argued that Doby should have reacted differently. Lucas said, "Here he infers that because Doby is colored, he shouldn't have reacted as white players would. This I contend is foolish deduction, Why should the color of a man's skin temper his normal response to a given situation?" Cobbledick said that even though other major league ballplayers have responded in a similar manner in the past, they were just ballplayers, while Doby is a "Negro ballplayer." Lucas said he believed the whole purpose of Cobbledick's statements to Doby was to carry an "ominous threat that Negro ball players were performing in the Major league by a thin thread."[25]

Lucas further disagreed with Cobbledick's assessment; he said that African Americans were now in the majors because of their hitting, running, and fielding abilities. There was no way that the major leagues could expel African Americans without generating wrath from the fans. Lucas believed that black players were not "in the major leagues on a rain check," and that there was no way league management could tactfully explain the rejection of players in the post-integration major leagues. Lucas said that Cobbledick's column implied that Doby needed to be a "good little boy" since so many people relied on him for more equality in their lives. He continued, "Let me state here and now that whether Doby is good or bad, these same people are demanding equal opportunities on their own. Who is going to rightfully penalize a whole group of people because of the action of one? What kind of democratic sportsmanship is that?" Lucas offered Doby his own advice; he told the young outfielder not to hide his natural human responses. He contended that if a pitcher threw at a white batter's head, nobody would question the white player's response if he acted in anger. Lucas even suggested that Doby carry his bat with him to the pitcher's mound to defend himself if necessary. Hopefully Doby would not need to take such drastic measures, but he should be ready for an esca-

lating situation just the same. Lucas said Doby needed to react like any
other ballplayer, and that fans would be proud of him. He added, "I don't
attempt to speak for all of them but I do know that some of them want
you to remain a Good Man and not a good boy."[26] Cobbledick criticized
Doby for entering a verbal altercation with Trout over the brush-back
pitch. What Lucas suggested here was quite an escalation as he implied
that Doby had a right to turn to violence by using his bat to physically
defend him. He also suggested that Doby's manhood was tied to his
response to threats by reminding him to be a "Good Man" instead of a
"good boy."[27]

Instead of suggesting more confrontational behavior as Lucas did,
sportswriter Marty Richardson chose instead to recommend proper behavior for African American fans when they attended Indians games. Richardson said he was compelled to write this column on fan behavior since many
in Cleveland's black community had never attended a game before and
therefore did not understand proper fan conduct. He observed, "Your buck
and a half, pal, did not purchase the park for you." Suggestions Richardson
offered included cheering without cussing and keeping comments directed
at players "decent." While loud, sometimes obnoxious, cheering was
acceptable at baseball games, it was important to make sure that no pro-
fanities were used. Richardson suggested that fans stay at home and watch
games on television if they were unwilling to be bumped or shoved while
at a crowded baseball game. He was concerned about fights that started
after fans randomly collided with each other entering and exiting the park.
Fans should also wait until they were home or at a local bar before they
consumed alcohol, since Richardson thought that alcohol contributed to
many of the problems at baseball games. He advised that fans avoid people
thinking, "Take him OUT of the Ball Park."[28] Richardson obviously
wanted African American fans to appear orderly and polite to the white
fans in attendance at the game. The implications by Cobbledick that black
players were in the major leagues by a "thin thread" likely played a role in
Richardson's recommendations. If fans did not cause disruptions in the
ballpark, it was further evidence that blacks and whites could enjoy baseball
together and proved that integration was successful.

Steve Estes addressed these issues of race and respectability in *I Am
a Man! Race, Manhood and the Civil Rights Movement* and discussed how
African Americans had to hide their "true thoughts and identities" through-

out the first half of the twentieth century. "It behooved black men to become invisible, lest they become highly visible examples of the racial rules that governed American Society," Estes wrote. If Doby were to remain invisible, then he wouldn't be such a glaring example of inequality in America, playing on a majority-white team in what was for a time an all-white league.[29] This offered a possible explanation of why a white writer, like Cobbledick, might want to monitor his behavior, while an African American writer, like Lucas, might be more willing to encourage Doby to fight back when targeted with a wild pitch.

Estes went on to discuss the experiences of African American men during World War II, where he referred to military service in general as a "rite of passage of manhood."[30] He added that African-American men were forced to deal with the "idealistic rhetoric" surrounding World War II, yet faced a racist reality when they returned home from the war in the 1940s.[31] Estes discussed the "Catch-22" that African American soldiers often found themselves in since they needed to exhibit their manhood in order to help the United States win the war, yet those same behaviors they were exhibiting were "dangerous to an American social order that rested on white male supremacy."[32] Playing sports in America is something that's considered masculine, and professional athletes often are challenged to exhibit their manhood. Because of this desire or need for white male supremacy, it would be difficult for an African American such as Doby to truly assert himself in a white world, or more specifically, a white baseball league. If he hit well against a white pitcher, he faced the chance of being knocked down by a pitch to make sure he knew his place. If he ever became angry or looked more dominant than some of the white males on the field, then he no longer knew his place and had left his prescribed role behind; the retribution could be fierce for a violation such as that. The whole experience was emotionally challenging for Doby, as observed by Veeck. "It was a very real and bitter and gnawing battle for Larry all the way. He had suffered such a shock that he was possessed by the idea that he had to fight the battle for integration for his kids, Larry Jr. and Christine, so that they would never be bruised as badly as he had been." It was as if Doby had already given up on his own happiness and was focused strictly on what it would be like for the next generation. Veeck goes on to say that the "inner turmoil" Doby experienced was such a drain on him that it kept him from being as successful of a ballplayer as he could have been.[33]

The *Call and Post* raised Veeck to hero status because of his role in integrating the Indians. He managed to avoid harsh criticism and was praised frequently by the newspaper and others in the Cleveland African American community. Early in 1949, Veeck received a merit award from the Urban League of Greater Cleveland for his "democratic action" of choosing athletes "based on account of ability and with utter disregard for color or creed."[34] In fact, when the *Call and Post* polled several Cleveland citizens early in 1949 on who they thought had accomplished the most for African Americans on a national level during the prior year, two people questioned believed it was Veeck. Jesse Butler, upon naming Veeck, said, "His liberalism in giving Negroes a chance to show their real ability as major leaguers helped spearhead the attack on racial discrimination and segregation in this country." Otis Hicks said that Veeck and Branch Rickey of the Dodgers both accomplished the most because "they set the standard in racial practice by giving our boys a chance to prove that they can compete as well as a player of any other race and opened the way for future boys in the major leagues."[35] Later that spring, Veeck was referred to as "Cleveland's No. 1 hero, civic or athletic" when he donated a large quantity of baseball equipment to young patients at Rainbow Hospital, a children's facility.[36] In addition to integrating the Indians on the field, Veeck also gained popularity for hiring world record-holding Olympic sprinter and hurdler and Cleveland native Harrison Dillard for the team's public relations department. The 26-year-old Dillard was a graduate of Cleveland-area Baldwin-Wallace College and planned to continue competing in track events while serving his duties with the Indians.[37]

Veeck worked to integrate all departments of employees at Cleveland Municipal Stadium, which led the *Call and Post* to brag, "With Bill Veeck, it is ability that counts; not race, creed, nationality or color." In addition to the African American players added to the team and the hiring of Dillard, Veeck had black policemen patrolling the park, as well as black ushers, vendors and members of the grounds crew. There were African American performance acts prior to the game, and the Indians' press box was one of the first in the country to admit black sportswriters and provide them with regular seats. Veeck was not always so forgiving to the *Call and Post*, however. Fuster said that when he approached Veeck for an interview during August of 1949, the Indians' owner took the opportunity to criticize the African American press. Veeck merely called the black press "okay" and said he wished they dedicated more space to deserving white players on the Indians as well as the black players. Fuster did not respond too harshly to Veeck but took the opportunity to disagree with him as he said that African Americans were unable to read about their communities' news in the white daily papers. He argued that there was very little news about Cleveland's black citizens unless it was an elite person or a spectacular story. Although Fuster did concede that the African American press returned the favor by printing very few stories about Cleveland's white residents, Fuster completed his thoughts by saying that perhaps one day the African American press will give the same types of headlines to white players like Joe Gordon and Ted Williams that they do to Larry Doby, Jackie Robinson, Roy Campanella, Don Newcombe and Satchel Paige.[38] Even though Fuster advocated integrating other African American institutions such as the Negro Leagues, he stopped short of promoting that same complete integration for the *Call and Post* and the African American press.

By 1949, Veeck's time in Cleveland was limited. He and his wife, Eleanor, were in the process of a divorce, and Veeck sold his commanding share of the Indians in order to split the proceeds with his wife. Veeck claimed that the publisher of the *Cleveland Press*, Lou Seltzer, offered to loan him the money so he could maintain control of the Indians. Veeck declined, since part of the money was to go to his children's trust funds. He added, "I suspect now that mixed in there, unconsciously, was the feeling that I had done everything that could be done in Cleveland and that the time had come to pick myself up and wander on."[39]

Wendell Smith of the *Pittsburgh Courier* had a different opinion of why Veeck left Cleveland and was challenged for this view in the *Call and Post* by Fuster. In his column, "Wendell Smith's SPORTS BEAT," Smith argued that Veeck left after "Cleveland politicians" forced him from town and added that "the people of Cleveland have grown 'lazy and placid,' they 'should hang their heads in shame.'" Smith also said that the people of Cleveland were "spineless" because they did not help Veeck when he needed them the most. The politicians that Smith referred to apparently tried to double the Indians' rent of Cleveland Municipal Stadium (owned by the city) and refused to provide enough police for security at Indians games. Smith added, "They did all kinds of petty things to make his life miserable." Smith went even further with his accusations and discussed this "vicious campaign" as he said:

Through devious ways, they organized a gang of hoodlums who are operating daily at the ball park. Their precise job is to harass Larry Doby, Satchel Paige and Luke Easter. No matter what these three players do, the mob is supposed to belittle them. The mob is spread throughout the crowd and whenever the opportunity presents itself, they hoot, jeer and razz Doby, Paige and Easter.

Smith contended that because Veeck could not handle fighting issues such as these while attempting to win a pennant, he left. Fuster disputed Smith's claims and said that Veeck was still "one of the most popular men in Cleveland" and added, "If the people of Cleveland could have read Mr. Smith's article, they would have laughed at it, perhaps, or they might have become angry about it." Fuster claimed Smith's comments did not appear in the edition of the *Courier* that was sold in Cleveland. He accused Smith (or one of his editors) of keeping the article from the people of Cleveland because the readers would know that the article's claims were false. Fuster continued:

> As one of those more than one million Clevelanders whom Mr. Smith has so glibly called "lazy and placid"—and as one of those more than 2,000,000 Clevelanders who last year paid their way into Cleveland Stadium to ... the Indians on to the 1948 world's championship, I resent Mr. Smith's uncalled for, vicious, and totally untrue statements.

Fuster added that when Doby made a great catch on August 12, 1949, against the Chicago White Sox, he received the greatest ovation he had ever heard at Cleveland Stadium. With regard to fan treatment of Indians players, Fuster said that he heard almost all of the Indians' players, both white and black, booed at one point or another with the exception of Satchel Paige. Fuster claimed he never heard anyone react negatively to the star pitcher. He thought that fans turned on Luke Easter because the tall slugger struggled when he joined the Indians from the Pacific Coast League. In twenty at-bats in Cleveland, Easter managed only two singles and no RBI. Since fans hoped the Indians would return to the postseason in 1949, Fuster thought they had little patience for a player that did not perform. Becuase there were no gangs of fans that harassed African American players, Fuster speculated that Smith wanted to sensationalize the situation. Fuster was glad to set the record straight and make sure the public realized there were no problems in Cleveland. He reminded readers that the *Call and Post* first brought Larry Doby to Bill Veeck's attention in 1947, as if this fact provided him additional credibility. Fuster added, "In Cleveland, we have Doby, Satchell [*sic*] Paige and Luke Easter — three Negroes on our team. In Pittsburgh — can the *Courier* write one line about one Negro player on the Pittsburgh Pirates?"[40]

This rant by Fuster included several points that deserve further examination. In his autobiography, when Veeck discussed his desire to sign an African American player to the Indians, he said he assigned scouts to search for the player. Veeck said, "I wasn't necessarily looking for the best player in the Negro leagues, but for a young player with the best long-term potential." He never mentioned the *Call and Post* as part of this search and said he focused on Doby because his "name kept floating to the top." He later had scout Bill Killifer follow him undetected to watch Doby perform in several of the Newark Eagles' games.[41] Also, there was no prolonged push in the *Call and Post* during 1947 for the Indians to offer a tryout to Doby or to sign him, unlike in 1942 when Fuster pushed throughout the season for tryouts for Parnell Woods, Sam Jethroe and Eugene Bremmer. The other surprising point about Fuster's anger at Wendell Smith occurred when he criticized Smith because the Pittsburgh Pirates had not integrated, as if it was Smith's fault. Smith was the person who suggested Jackie Robinson to Branch Rickey of the Brooklyn Dodgers and later traveled with Robinson to the player's first spring training in Florida in 1946.[42] In fact, during his first season with the Dodgers, Robinson had a guest column periodically in the *Courier*. It was possible that Fuster took personally Smith's article on Veeck's departure and the "lazy" African American community in Cleveland. He believed the *Call and Post* made many achievements throughout the 1940s for civil rights and Smith's comments made it seem as if not just Clevelanders but also perhaps the *Call and Post* itself was lazy and complacent. Fuster probably knew the national impact Smith had through his promotion of Robinson to the Dodgers. However, when Smith challenged the *Call and Post* on its own turf, Fuster was quick to point out the lack of progress Smith had made in his home city.

Fuster saw many changes in Cleveland and had much to be proud of throughout his tenure at the *Call and Post*, which lasted from 1942 to 1943 and resumed midway through 1949. Fuster was not at the newspaper for the Buckeyes' 1945 championship season or their World Series appearance in 1947. Until 1948, the press box at Cleveland Municipal Stadium was whites only; the reasoning was that only members of the Baseball Writers Association of America were allowed in the press box. Only writers for daily newspapers could be members of the Baseball Writers Association of America, which effectively excluded African American writers for black weekly publications. Fuster said the press box integrated through joint efforts by the *Call and Post* and by the first African American in the Indians' public relations department, Lou Jones. Even though Fuster cited the "courtesy and liberality among the Cleveland members of the Baseball Writers Association and among officials of the Cleveland Indians Baseball Co.," he said African Americans were not invited into the press box and added, "It took a lot of perseverance on our part before they finally saw the light." African American writers were now allowed in the press box and the team's locker room as well.[43] Fuster later compared himself to white New York Yankee and Massillon, Ohio, native Tommy Henrich, who was left off the Yankees' World Series roster in 1950 and had trouble convincing a guard stationed at the team's locker room that he actually played for the Yankees. Fuster said he was also blocked from the locker room multiple times in his career and was forced to defend his credentials as a reporter. He believed this was due to the fact that he was an African American and that the officer guarding the door mistrusted his claims that he was a legitimate sportswriter. Fuster found the situation demeaning and embarrassing and said:

> Down inside every time a cop stands unmoving in front of men when I attempt to pass into a locker room, every time some usher or orderly looks at me questioning when I present my credentials to sit in the press box at a basketball game or at a fight it puts a knot into my stomach, two knots into the muscles which control my jaws.
> It makes me mad.[44]

Fuster must have felt a sense of pride and vindication at the end of the 1949 season when Sam Jethroe, a player he promoted for a major league tryout in 1942, finally signed a major league deal with the Boston Braves. Fuster said the signing brought "great satisfaction to the *Call-Post* and to this writer" and that Jethroe was likely to be the starting center fielder for the Braves when they opened the 1950 season. Fuster discussed the failed 1942 tryout with the Indians and said that following the promotion of Jethroe, W.O. Walker, editor of the *Call and Post* and at the time of the tryout president of the National Negro Publishers Association, pushed for citizens committees across the country to hasten the integration of baseball.[45]

Fuster and the *Call and Post* were also proud of the Indians, as they referred to them as "our team," "our Indians" or even "champions of democracy" in the period that followed the team's integration. When the Indians opened their 1949 season, the city was still charged from the team's World Series victory the prior fall. Of the opening game of the 1949 season, writer Robert Benfield said in a front-page story, "It will be an all-American audience thrilling to the play of an all-American team. Negro fans, probably more than ever before attended a ball game in the history of the national pastime, will yell encouragement from the highest-priced boxes and the most remote bleacher seats. They'll come streaming into Cleveland from Cincinnati, Columbus, Toledo, Youngstown, and from small towns all over the state to hail the only team in the American League they feel justified in claiming as their own." Benfield even went as far as to say that he predicted an Indians-Dodgers World Series in 1949, the first between two integrated teams.[46] Of Indians fans, Fuster said, "Just as hundreds of white fans would today name Doby as their favorite Indian, so would some Negro fans name Al Rosen or Bob Lemon or Dale Mitchell as their favorite." He continued, "It took some time to bring many white fans around to the point where they accepted the Indians' Negro players fully and without reserve. It has taken longer to bring many Negro fans around to accepting the Indians, fully and without reserve — but the turning point has been reached by many, and for hundreds of others it is just around the corner."[47] This is another example of where Fuster not only pushed whites to accept integration at all levels of society, but where he also started to encourage African Americans to be more accepting as well.

Following the integration of the Indians, the *Call and Post* continued to advocate for a variety of issues in Cleveland and beyond, often blurring the lines between sport and the rest of society. Charles P. Lucas, executive secretary of the Cleveland branch of the NAACP, took the opportunity to address baseball issues in the newspaper, and John Fuster often tied baseball to a larger social picture. The *Call and Post* gave the people of Cleveland a chance to provide their opinions on the African American press and printed comments from several individuals. Overall, the people questioned supported the black press but thought reporters often paid too much attention to negative issues, like crimes, homicides and divorces. One woman complained that there were too many typographical errors, and a couple of people thought there wasn't enough attention paid to national issues. One woman said she wished she could find news not only important to African Americans, but also to citizens of other races.[48] W.O. Walker, much like Fuster said in defending the African American press to Bill Veeck, said, "If the Negro press has become the voice of the Negro, it is because it is the only clear warning our ship of fate can hear through the thick fog of uncertainty that shrouds our progress."[49]

Walker quoted Swedish economist Gunner Myrdal's comments on the black press, which stated, "The Negro press is far more than a mere expression of the Negro protest. By expressing the protest, the press also magnified it, acting like a huge sounding board." The media, according to Myrdal, told African Americans how to think and feel and convinced readers that everyone agreed with the perspective they advanced. Myrdal considered the black press "strongly opinionated" and thought that it was likely to become stronger in the future as African Americans continued to fight for equal rights in America. The black press was credited with encouraging northward migration, and in Myrdal's opinion, made African Americans aware of hypocrisy during World War II. The media made people realize the United States fought for freedom overseas while it limited the rights of certain groups of citizens within its borders. Myrdal thought the black press was extremely important because the writers instilled pride in their readers and made them aware of injustices they faced.[50] Walker seemed to agree with most of Myrdal's comments, and believed his opinion had validity because it came from "an unbiased source." Walker thought that a vigilant, strong black press was necessary in America as African Americans worked to improve injustices and inequalities throughout society. Walker promised readers that he would not allow his work toward change to challenge his objectivity in the pages of the *Call and Post*.[51]

While the *Call and Post* conquered topics such as the FEPC legislation, segregation in the Garfield Park city pool, and the issue of rent control in addition to their push for continued integration in baseball throughout 1949 and 1950, Charles Lucas felt the role of his organization in these developments should not be forgotten. In 1950, the Cleveland branch of the NAACP was awarded the annual Thalheimer Award, the highest honor bestowed on one of the organization's nearly 1,100 branches, for its work during the prior year. Cleveland's branch was recognized for its work in securing an anti-discrimination clause in the public housing act, its work toward the establishment of a Cleveland FEPC ordinance, and a drive against police abuses in Cleveland.[52] Of all the racial advances in Cleveland,

Lucas said, "In the face of all these positive trends, the benefactors seem to forget the forces which brought them about. There is an unmindfulness of the great role the Cleveland Branch of the National Association for the Advancement of Colored People has played in this human struggle. Surely, no one would make the foolish claim that it alone is responsible for the many advantages we enjoy today, but hardly any informed citizens would deny that the 38 year contribution by the NAACP was a major factor." Lucas went on to say that citizens of Cleveland needed to support the organization by becoming members and that the annual membership drive was so difficult "that it causes one to wonder whether or not there is a full realization of its (the NAACP's) great worth in the community."[53] Even though Lucas had a regular column in the *Call and Post* by 1950, writers like Fuster never gave he or the NAACP credit for the successful integration of baseball in Cleveland. In fact, throughout many of the *Call and Post*'s campaigns for equality in the city, the NAACP was not mentioned as playing a decisive role.

Throughout 1949 and 1950, the *Call and Post* continued to push for greater integration in major league baseball and often praised themselves for the newpaper's role in integrating the Indians. Even though the Cleveland Buckeyes still existed following integration, they were almost forgotten by the paper — pushed aside for a more democratic and integrated Indians team. Even though the *Call and Post* mostly ignored the Buckeyes, the newspaper did not want the team to disappear completely. Instead, it was suggested that the Buckeyes integrate and serve as a minor league system — a team that would give young African American players a chance to be noticed by the scouts of white teams. While John Fuster admitted the Buckeyes were at one point "our team," by 1949 that phrase instead referred to the Indians. They were more than just a baseball team; they were in fact a "model of democracy." Larry Doby and Luke Easter became the human representatives of this democratic entity, and the two men were often closely scrutinized for their behavior and their attitude by both the white and black press. Even though the *Call and Post* campaigned for integration in all aspects of society, the newspaper stopped short of endorsing the integration of the African American press. As W.O. Walker quoted in his column, the African American press was "the greatest single power in the Negro race." A force this powerful and this important to the developing civil rights movement could not risk changing the formula that to this point was so successful.

8

Pioneer or Footnote?

Eddie Klepp and the 1946 Buckeyes

Throughout 1949 and 1950 John Fuster dedicated several of his columns to critiques of the Negro Leagues. One of his frequent complaints was the fact that the Negro Leagues remained segregated; they did not add white players to their rosters as the major leagues added black players to theirs. What Fuster neglected to acknowledge in his columns was the fact that the Buckeyes integrated in 1946, the first Negro League team to do so. The player to earn the honor of Negro League integrator was a man by the name of Eddie Klepp.

Klepp was a mediocre left-handed sandlot pitcher from Erie, Pennsylvania, who played in only a handful of professional baseball games before his return to anonymity. He was the type of player that nobody's heard of, and nobody really cares to know more about. How much can be said about a man's professional baseball career when that stint consisted of only three games? However, there was much, much more to Eddie Klepp. Singer-songwriter Chuck Brodsky wrote a song to immortalize the forgotten pitcher, "The Ballad of Eddie Klepp."*

The war had finally ended and America had changed
It had beaten back the Nazis but the Jim Crow laws remained
There was talk of staging marches & talk of civil rights
There was talk about a Negro playing baseball with the Whites

He walked into the clubhouse and the card players quit playing
Everybody stopped in the middle of whatever they were saying

*"The Ballad of Eddie Klepp," copyright Chuck Brodsky. From the album *The Baseball Ballads* (2002). Courtesy of Chuck Brodsky, www.chuckbrodsky.com.

It was just like when the sheriff walks into the saloon
He said, "My name is Eddie," as he looked around the room

"This man's here to play baseball," the manager said to the team
"We're all gonna have to live with this ... aw, that's not what I mean ...
You know what I mean"— and they all did ... it went without saying
The card players looked at their hands and they went on with their playing

They ran him off the field before a game in Birmingham one night
Made him sit up in the grandstand in the section marked "For Whites"
In his Cleveland Buckeyes uniform, it was a new twist on the law
The marshalls kept their eyes on him and the hecklers ate him raw

Eddie Klepp, he should've run the bases in reverse
A White man in the Negro Leagues, that had to be a first
He could not ride the same busses, or stay in the same motels
He could not eat in the same restaurants, you couldn't have mixed clientele

So while Jackie played for Brooklyn and wore the Dodger Blue
Eddie crossed the color line, the one without a queue
A White man in the Negro Leagues, might as well have been a Jew
Now you mention the name of Eddie Klepp and most everyone says, "Who?"

The year was 1946 and Jackie Robinson played with Montreal in the Brooklyn Dodgers' farm system and drew the attention of the media from across America. At the same time, Klepp crossed the color line to join the Negro American League's Cleveland Buckeyes, with significantly less fanfare than Robinson. In fact, Klepp was barely acknowledged in the black press in Cleveland, an intriguing fact considering that writers with the *Call and Post* intensely lobbied for an integrated Buckeyes squad by 1949. After the Cleveland Indians won the World Series in 1948 with prominent African American players like Larry Doby and Satchel Paige, the *Call and Post* saw integrated teams like this as the future of baseball and a way to further race relations across the country. What was unusual was the fact that John Fuster, the sports editor at the *Call and Post* in 1949 and 1950, continually called for an integrated Buckeyes team that could show the world that blacks and whites could successfully play together. Fuster expressed his distaste for segregated Negro Leagues, and hoped to integrate baseball at all levels. So why did the *Call and Post* practically ignore Klepp in 1946, and why did Fuster pretend as if he never existed a few years later? There are few definitive answers, but many plausible reasons.

First it is important to learn more about Klepp as an individual and about his rather limited experience with the Buckeyes since it is possible that his personal background played a role in the *Call and Post*'s opinion of him. Klepp was born in either 1919 or 1920, one of six children from a Polish family. Eddie's father, who friends called "Gust," was a meat cutter prior to the Depression; afterward, he found work as a welder. According to an interview with Eddie Klepp's sister Theresa DiPlacido, Gust loved baseball and shared this love with his children by taking them to watch sandlot Glenwood League games in Erie. Soon, Eddie started throwing rocks around at the neighborhood field in order to build arm strength. In 1937, when Klepp was eighteen, his father was killed in a tragic industrial accident. His family claimed there was so little left of Gust after the accident, his remains could fit in a wicker basket. This event appeared to be the turning point in Eddie Klepp's life. Within three months of his father's death, he had his first run-in with the law.[1]

Within ten years of his father's death, a time span that included his short stint with the Buckeyes, Klepp had more than a dozen incidents with law enforcement officials. In 1937, 1939 and 1940 he was charged with larceny. In 1941 he spent five weeks in jail while he awaited trial for burning down his uncle's shack, a prank supposedly gone very wrong. After this he was charged with disorderly conduct. He was jailed again in 1943 for disorderly conduct and five times in 1944 for larceny, assault and battery, and adultery. Just one short month before he joined the Buckeyes for spring training, he spent ten days in jail again for larceny. Six weeks after the Buckeyes released him, he was forced to return to Erie to await trial for burglary, larceny, and receiving stolen goods.[2]

Klepp's ex-wife Ethel once said, "Sometimes, you could see the Devil in his eyes." However, she maintained that Klepp was only mean to her twice. The pair had a child together and married in 1941 but separated by the end of the year. Ethel and Eddie would reunite for short periods of time, but eventually separated for good. Whenever he paid Ethel a visit, something (often home appliances) mysteriously came up missing from Ethel's home. Ethel said, "I wouldn't take my watch off except to shower ... or he would have taken that, too." In 1997 Eddie Klepp's adult son said he heard his father was a pretty good baseball player "as long as he could stay sober through the seventh inning."[3]

Unfortunately for Klepp, the Buckeyes likely needed someone who could stay sober throughout the entire game. In 1945 the Buckeyes did the unthinkable; they upset the powerhouse Homestead Grays in the Negro League World Series, four games to none. When they signed Klepp before the 1946 season, they hoped to add fortification to a pitching staff that was strong during their championship season. The 1946 staff had more problems than one white sandlot star could solve. Starter Eugene Bremmer injured his right hand during spring training and struggled to remain healthy throughout much of the year. Willie Jefferson spent much of the season playing in Central America while his brother George dealt with a sore arm for much of 1946. In addition to the pitching staff, the Buckeyes had to play without star infielders Parnell Woods at third base and Avelino Canizares at shortstop.[4]

When the Buckeyes invited Klepp to spring training in Birmingham, Alabama, it seemed like a pretty good gamble. The signing would attract publicity and provide the team with a promising left-handed pitcher;

Even though the 1946 Cleveland Buckeyes did not win the Negro League World Series, they were the first Negro League team to integrate. Eddie Klepp, a sandlot pitcher from Erie, Pennsylvania, joined the team for half of the season. Top row, from left: Gene Smith, Chet Brewer, Clyde Williams, Sam Jones, Alonzo Boone, Herb "Doc" Bracken, Ross Davis, Joe Atkins, unidentified. Middle row, from left: Vibert Clarke, Clyde Nelson, Johnny Cowan, Lefty Williams, Gene Bremmer, Jesse Williams, Willie Grace. Bottom row, from left: unidentified, Al Smith, Archie Ware, Quincy Trouppe, Leon Kellman, Sam Jethroe, unidentified.

Klepp had a 26–5 record for North East AC in the Glenwood League in Erie. If Klepp played well, he could help the team repeat its World Series title. If he played really well, Buckeyes owner Ernest Wright and general manager Wilbur Hayes could attempt to "sell him off for a goodly price to one of the major league ball clubs." With increasing competition from Mexican and Latin American leagues, Wright and Hayes had to think creatively when filling holes on the team's roster. They discovered Klepp when the Buckeyes faced North East AC in an exhibition game after the 1945 season when he "handcuffed" Cleveland for three innings.[5]

Klepp did not get much of a chance to showcase his abilities during spring training in 1946. The Birmingham police intervened during an exhibition game at Rickwood Field between the Buckeyes and the Birmingham Black Barons. The two officers that came to the park said that "the Birmingham city ordinance prevented the participation of or contesting against white and colored athletes." *Call and Post* writer Jimmie N. Jones tried to convince the police to allow Klepp to sit in the dugout during the game. The police refused and said Klepp had to remove his Buckeyes uniform and exit the park or they would prevent the game from taking place. Klepp left, changed clothes at his hotel and returned to the field to watch the game from a box seat behind the Buckeye dugout. Again he was approached by the police and was forced to sit in the white section for the rest of the game. Ernest Wright actually traveled to Birmingham to address the situation and brought Klepp north with him after the game to finish his pre-season preparation. Wright said, "If Branch Rickey and others of organized baseball can choose material for their liking in order to produce a winning ball club and without question of race or color despite the Southern 'Jim Crow' tradition, then why can't I do the same?"[6]

Despite the racism Klepp faced in Birmingham, it appeared that he fit in well as a member of the Buckeyes. By all reports he liked his teammates and they liked him. Several veterans of the team were natives of Erie, like Klepp, and made him feel at home. Veteran pitchers took him under their wings and supposedly "made him one of the most promising prospects of the pitching staff."[7] One of Klepp's roommates during his short tenure with the Buckeyes was outfielder Willie Grace. Grace said he liked the twenty-six-year-old pitcher and once loaned Klepp a suit of clothes "so he'd look decent." Grace thought Klepp was comfortable around black men, and said, "There wasn't a racist bone in him. He smoked and drank with the rest of the players, while it lasted."[8]

It did not last long. There was little fanfare in the *Call and Post* when Klepp signed with the team, and there was even less when he pitched. By early June he made his debut against the Indianapolis Clowns when he entered the game with the bases loaded. Goose Tatum hit the ball up the middle toward the pitcher's mound and it got away from Klepp, scoring two runs. The next batter hit a long single, and two more runs scored. When the dust settled, the Buckeyes had lost the game, 11–8.[9] During that same week, Klepp managed to notch his first win, against the Chicago American Giants. He held the game to a tie until the Buckeyes were able to gain the lead.[10] This was basically the first and last mention of Klepp in the *Call and Post.* The team attempted to rebuild for the second half of the season and brought in several rookie pitchers to help battle against the league-leading Kansas City Monarchs.

Wilbur Hayes gave Klepp his unconditional release on June 2, 1946. Manager Quincy Trouppe said that Klepp showed promise during spring training but "failed to measure up to the fast Negro American league standards" and needed more experience. Willie Grace also cited a lack of talent for Klepp's failure. When asked about the pitcher in 1997, Willie Grace said, "He couldn't have pitched in the league nowhere — he really wasn't fast enough. We had guys who could throw like a rifle shot." *Call and Post* writer Cleveland Jackson thought Klepp seemed bitter when he was questioned about his release from the Buckeyes. Klepp claimed he was only allowed to pitch seven innings during spring training and implied he was ill-prepared for the start of the 1946 season. Klepp said he wanted to continue his baseball career but had no immediate plans for the remainder of the 1946 season. He was willing to sign with another Negro League team and said his experience in the league was "very cordial.[11]

Jackson wanted Klepp to sign with another Negro League team in 1946 and said if he failed to sign with another black professional team, "it will mark a quiet end to one of the most liberal individual efforts ever attempted in American baseball." Jackson commended Klepp for his tolerance of the "taunts, insults and threats" from Southerners when the Buckeyes held their spring training in Alabama. Klepp "showed true blue" as he remained with the team despite the harsh treatment from vocal Southerners. Even though Jackson said Klepp was not ready for professional baseball, his contribution should not be forgotten. Jackson added, "But in the hearts of every true American sportman, there is an indelible feeling that little Eddie Klep [*sic*] is ready for the highest award in sportsmanship. He is a great little guy."[12]

So the question remains, why did the *Call and Post* virtually ignore Klepp when he signed with the team in 1946? It could be that writers realized Klepp was not as talented as the other players and would not last with the Buckeyes. Why make a big deal out of a pitcher that probably was not good enough to last through an entire season? If he failed, it may appear as if the racial aspect of the signing was to blame rather than the talent factor. Also, the sports editor with the *Call and Post* in 1946, Cleveland Jackson, seemed less interested in baseball than the other sports editors at the paper during the 1940s. He also appeared less interested in sports as a venue for racial advancement than other writers. His columns had less of a political bent than a Fuster or an A.S. "Doc" Young column, and many of his personal columns focused on other sports rather than baseball. This general difference in editorial style could be to blame for the lack of attention paid to an integrated Buckeyes squad. Or was the slight, particularly in later years, due to Klepp's character and the fact that he was continually in trouble with the law? Despite the legal troubles Klepp faced immediately before and after his time with the Buckeyes, there was never a mention of his arrests or the charges he faced.

In 1949 and 1950 John Fuster, an activist sports editor who dedicated half of the sports pages to baseball and racial activism through sports, ignored Klepp completely. This happened despite the fact that Fuster continually harped on the Buckeyes for their segregated existence and pushed the team to integrate. He often ignored the Buckeyes in favor of the integrated Indians squad, and defended his views in the pages of the sports section. Fuster viewed the Buckeyes as a type of farm team for the Indians, and in 1950 said he hoped Wilbur Hayes did not refuse to sign any player due to his skin color, ethnicity, or religious background. Of the Buckeyes, Fuster said, "They follow the lead of Branch Rickey and open positions on their teams to men of all races."[13]

Fuster still believed the Negro Leagues served a purpose, even if that purpose was significantly diminished.

> If Negro players are to be developed for the organized baseball they must have a starting point. Will it be high school ball? Or college ball? Or sandlot ball? Or shall it be the Negro American League?[14]

He also expressed open distaste for the term "Negro Leagues," and said the word Negro denoted segregation. By 1949 Negro League baseball struggled to draw fans and earn money, and was obviously dying. Fuster said that instead of complaining about this development, people should be celebrating. He clarified that he was not against African Americans or other non-whites in baseball but believed teams should be balanced by both white and black players. Fuster again pointed to the work of the black press in integrating baseball and did not want to see the existence of a segregated league after writers worked so hard. He thought the Negro Leagues were "just as un–American as lily-white baseball and it is much more silly."[15]

The problem with a comment like this was that all-black baseball was eliminated four years prior to this article, yet Fuster never acknowledged Klepp's existence and the Buckeyes' contribution to integration. It was quite possible that Fuster did not realize Klepp played with the team. He left the *Call and Post* after the 1942 season and did not return to the newspaper until 1949. There was so little fanfare over the Klepp signing that if Fuster worked out of town at the time, he may have missed it. It was also possible that Fuster was fully aware of Klepp's short tenure and he chose to ignore it. While the experiment was not exactly a failure, it was far from a complete success. If Fuster highlighted the failure of Klepp, it would portray the wrong idea — that integration was unsuccessful and teams were better off segregated.

Another distinct possibility was that Fuster chose to ignore Klepp because of his checkered background. When African American writers pushed for the integration of major league baseball throughout the 1940s, they were cautious when it came to choosing potential integrators. Players were chosen not just for talent but for their qualities as men. It was important to choose a player who was not controversial and could be viewed as an educated family man. It was a theory in line with the "politics of respectability," that a player who was a good man as well as a talented athlete could uplift the entire African American community. These most respectable members of black society would serve as models, as a visible representation to the white community that African Americans were worthy of integration. The *Call and Post* printed stories that advised the black community on proper fan behavior at Indians games. African American fans were to limit their alcohol consumption and not lose their tempers at the game, no matter what took place on the field. Perhaps Fuster was concerned about the image Klepp portrayed to both white and black society. The young pitcher was always in trouble with the law and had a problem with drinking, possibly even during games. Perhaps this was not the model of integrated society Fuster hoped to emphasize.

There was not much known of Klepp after his stint with the Buckeyes. He obviously jumped from job to job throughout his life since he listed clerk, laborer, truck driver, painter, waiter, bowling alley "pin sticker" and baseball player as careers throughout his life. Klepp died in November of 1981 in Los Angeles and was cremated in a pauper's ceremony. His ashes were eventually returned to Erie and buried with Eddie's brother Julius in 1986. As of 1997 there was no mention of Eddie at Julius' grave; there was just a small marker that noted his brother.[16]

Even though Eddie Klepp faced discrimination in the South, it was nothing compared to what confronted African American men like Jackie Robinson and Larry Doby. If Robinson or Doby had been the lone black man on a team of white men in Birmingham, Alabama, you can bet that a confrontation with police would have gone much further. Klepp was ordered to remove his uniform and sit in the white section of the stadium; a black man probably would have been arrested and might have faced the possibility of physical violence. Robinson and Doby endured taunts and jeers from crowds and at times fellow players, yet still managed to succeed on the field. Klepp, by all accounts, was treated fairly by players and fans alike, yet still struggled on the field. While pioneers Robinson and Doby faced far more challenges than Klepp, at the same time Klepp and the Buckeyes should be recognized for their unique contribution to race relations during the 1940s. Even though writers at the *Call and Post* clamored for a situation like Klepp's, they instead chose to pretend as if he never existed.

Conclusion

The integration of major league baseball in 1947 is often underscored or swept aside in the collective memory of the civil rights movement. Sporting events tend to be viewed as leisure activities, activities that have no bearing on the daily lives of average citizens. When the activist African American press chose an American institution to target during the 1940s, they focused their sights on baseball. These black newspapers hoped that the successful integration of baseball, a public and popular sport in the United States, could translate into social and economic progress in other walks of life. In their minds integrated baseball teams were the first step toward an integrated society.

Baseball was likely the focus of their efforts because, at the time, it was more popular than football or basketball. It is interesting to note that major league baseball was integrated in the nineteenth century; it was only due to a "gentleman's agreement" between team owners at the dawn of the twentieth century that led to its segregated status. This is a point that's rarely addressed in the media reports of the 1940s, that these writers actually encouraged the re-integration of baseball rather than first-time integration. When the Negro Leagues were formed by Rube Foster in 1920, it gave talented African American players a professional venue to showcase their skills. Cleveland, an active site for sandlot baseball for both white and black players, entered its first team in the Negro Leagues in 1922.

Cleveland hosted ten different Negro League teams during the 1920s and 1930s; the city never had a team that lasted for more than two seasons during that time period. Most of these teams had poor won-lost records and had difficulties finding a quality venue to play their home games. Reasons such as these led to diminished fan support and eventually the demise of the team. This pattern continued until 1942, when Ernest Wright and

Wilbur Hayes formed the Cleveland Buckeyes. The Buckeyes fielded talented teams with star players and benefited from a populace that was more likely to have the disposable income to attend games because of the war industries. The *Call and Post* offered constructive criticism to the Negro Leagues in both the 1930s and the 1940s, but during the 1940s the newspaper also started to focus its attention on integrating the major leagues.

In 1942 the *Call and Post* repeatedly encouraged the hometown Indians to consider a tryout for three Buckeye players: Sam Jethroe, Eugene Bremmer, and Parnell Woods. The paper continued to question Indians owner Alva Bradley of his intentions regarding integration, yet Bradley never offered a formal tryout. He scouted Jethroe, Bremmer and Woods at that year's East-West All-Star Game but never made any overtures to sign the players. Bill Veeck seemed interested in integration upon his arrival in Cleveland in 1946. He told the *Call and Post* that he would consider adding African American players to the Indians and did so before the *Call and Post* had a chance to start a public campaign to encourage integration.

While newspapers like the *Call and Post* voiced support of black businesses, they were unable to offer unequivocal support to the Negro Leagues following integration and eventually called for the demise or at least a restructuring of the leagues. Because of disorganization and poor publicity, the African American press was the primary outlet for fans to gain information on their favorite Negro League teams. Fans could not follow teams through the pages of white daily papers and did not have the opportunity to listen to Negro League games on the radio. At times, teams struggled to provide the black press with game and player statistics. If fans had no place to turn for information on Negro League teams, and the information they did find was more than likely negative, it is easy to see why fans may have lost interest in some of the Negro League teams in Cleveland. If the Indians were integrated and information on the team was more accessible, it may be the reason fans gravitated to them. As more star players left the Negro Leagues for the major leagues, fewer superstars were around for fans to watch. As the Jackie Robinson and Larry Doby signings became a rallying point for African American communities, it was just one more reason why the integrated major leagues were preferable to the antiquated and segregated Negro Leagues.

Cleveland was a great example of how this combination of events led to the demise of the city's Negro League team, the Cleveland Buckeyes.

From its inception, the Buckeyes were poorly promoted and had a confusing schedule that often mixed league games with meaningless exhibition contests. While writers at the *Call and Post* supported the Buckeyes, they made a point of telling readers that segregated baseball was an injustice and encouraged tryouts for Buckeye players with the Indians. These writers likely realized baseball was a business, one whose success was contingent upon a team's ability to win ball games. Many players in the Negro Leagues were as talented, if not more talented, than many of the major league players. African American writers knew that if they could prove to owners that an influx of talented black players could help their teams win and put additional black fans in the stands, the earning potential was limitless.

Once such a public and "American" institution was integrated successfully, it would aid the argument that integration was beneficial in all aspects of society. The *Call and Post* viewed itself as much more than an average media outlet by the 1940s, as did many African American publications. Writers at the paper knew they could use their power of communication to mobilize the citizenry of Cleveland and assist these same people in their daily lives. While the *Call and Post* was not the only source of influence in Cleveland during the 1940s, the newspaper used its connection with the public to inform and encourage change. With the support of the public the newspaper was able to encourage members of the Cleveland city and Cleveland Indians establishment to make these proposed changes a reality. Once this goal was achieved, the Buckeyes were almost completely forgotten.

Epilogue

Sam Jethroe left the Negro Leagues in 1948 and went to play for the Brooklyn Dodgers' Montreal club, the same team Jackie Robinson played for in 1946. Jethroe stayed in Montreal for the remainder of 1948 and 1949, before Branch Rickey sold his contract to the Boston Braves. Jethroe became the first African American player with the Braves and was named Rookie of the Year with the team in 1950, the oldest player to earn the honor, at the age of 33. Jethroe led the major leagues in steals that season with 35, and batted .273 with 18 home runs and 100 runs scored. Dodger pitcher Don Newcombe played with Jethroe in Montreal and said the outfielder "was the fastest human being I've ever seen." Buck O'Neil once said that when Jethroe came to the plate, "the infield would have to come in a few steps or you'd never throw him out."[1] Jethroe actually had the chance to integrate two different major league teams. After playing as Boston's starting center fielder for three years, Jethroe joined the Pittsburgh Pirates in 1954, when he and Curt Roberts integrated the team. Jethroe retired in 1958 with a career .261 average.[2]

Even though Jethroe was not considered a pioneer in the same manner as Jackie Robinson and Larry Doby, he made an incredible contribution to African American baseball players nearly forty years after he retired. In the mid–1990s, Jethroe filed suit in federal court against major league baseball and its players association. His contention was that baseball's segregationist policies prior to 1947 kept Jethroe and other Negro League players from earning a major league pension. Major league baseball first offered pensions in 1947, and players needed four years of service in the majors to qualify. (The modern agreement states that players only need to play one day in the major leagues to earn a pension.) Jethroe spent three years and seventeen days with the Braves and Pirates, which meant he fell just short of pension eligibility. Jethroe appeared to lose the battle when his suit was dismissed on October 4, 1996, by U.S. District Judge Sean McLaughlin in Baltimore. Even so, major league baseball decided to grant pensions to Jethroe and dozens of other Negro League players in 1997. To qualify, a player needed to play at least four years combined in the major leagues and Negro Leagues, and he would receive about $10,000 per year. Jethroe died a few years later from a heart attack on June 16, 2001, at the age of 84 in Erie, Pennsylvania.[3]

Sam Jethroe, nicknamed "The Jet," was a star outfielder with the Buckeyes. He became the oldest man to win Rookie of the Year honors in major league baseball when he earned the title at age 33 in 1950 with the Boston Braves.

Sam "The Jet" Jethroe was considered by major league teams on several occasions before he finally made it to the majors in 1950. He was summoned to Fenway Park in 1945 for a tryout with the Boston Red Sox but ended up playing for the city's other team, the Braves. Jethroe was scouted by the Cleveland Indians at the East-West All-Star Game in 1942 in what was billed as a tryout by the *Call and Post*. He seems to be forgotten by many when integration is discussed, despite the fact that he integrated two different major league teams. Also ignored was his contribution to many aging Negro League players who were able to receive a pension decades after they last played baseball. Even though his lawsuit was dismissed, the attention that it brought likely prompted major league baseball to take action.

Appendix 1

Rosters of All Cleveland Negro League Teams

1922 Tate Stars
Candy Jim Taylor 3b/p/M
John Barnes (Fat) c
George Boggs p
Robert Bonner 1b
Fred Boyd rf
Finis Branahan p
_ Branham (Slim) p
Walter Cannady (Rev) p/of
_ Chantman p
Eppie Hampton c
George Henderson (Rube) rf/ss
_ Howard p
Claude Johnson (Hooks) 2b
John Wesley Johnson p
Wade Johnson lf/p
Eugene Keeton p
James Leonard (Bobo) cf
Edward McClain (Boots) ss
Bob McClure p
Mitch Murray c
Alton Norman ss
Eugene Redd ss

Curtiss Ricks p/of
Fulton Strong p

1923 Tate Stars
Robert Baldwin ss
John Barnes (Fat) c/1b
Finis Branahan p
_ Branham (Slim) p
_ Cordova (Pete) ss
Ernest Gooden 2b/ss
G.E. Gray (Dolly) 1b
Don Hammond 3b
Vic Harris rf/lf
George Henderson (Rube) of
Logan Hensley (Slap) p
Harry Jeffries 3b
Claude Johnson (Hooks) 2b
James Leonard (Bobo) cf
William McCall (Bill) p
Bob McClure p
Willie Miles lf
Otto Ray c/of
Mathis Williams (Matt) 3b

1924 Browns
Solomon White (Sol) M
John Barnes (Fat) c
Charles Beverly p
Robert Bonner 2b
_ Browne (Hap) p
Albert Clark p
James Ellis ss
_ Fields p
Slyvester Foreman (Hooks) c
Bill Francis 3b
Herman Gordon p/of
Leroy Grant 1b
_ Hamilton p
Don Hammond ss/p
Vic Harris lf
_ Hayes (Buddy) c
Logan Hensley (Slap) p
Eugene Hunter p
Harry Jeffries of
John Wesley Johnson p
William Joseph ss
James Leonard (Bobo) cf
Dudley McAdoo (Tully) 1b
Edward McClain (Boots) cf/2b/ss
Willie Miles cf
W. Morrison 1b
Carl Perry 2b/ss/3b
Otto Ray c/1b/p
Wilson Redus rf
Curtis Ricks 1b
Harold Ross p
John Shackleford 3b
Orville Singer rf/cf
_ Stovall p
Harold Treadwell p

Ruby Tyree p/rf
_ Walters p

1926 Elites
Frank Duncan (Pete) rf/M
Candy Jim Taylor 3b/p/M
Grover Alexander (Buck) p
Robert Baldwin 2b/ss
John Barnes (Fat) c
Howard Black p
Robert Bonner c/1b
Finis Branahan p
George Brannigan p
Ernest Duff c/2b
_ Fields p
_ Goldie 1b
J.H. Hamilton (John) 3b/2b
Art Hancock p
Andy Harris 3b
Sam Jackson c
John Wesley Johnson p
James Leonard (Bobo) cf
Willie Miles cf/lf
Dempsey Miller (Dimp) p
Edward Milton cf/of
Ralf Moore (Squire) p
_ Nehf of
Alton Norman ss
William Owens ss/3b
Joe Ransom c
_ Redwine p
William Robinson (Bobby) lf/ss
Jerry Ross p
Charles Spearman 3b/of
William Spearman p/rf
Smith Summers (Tack) lf/of

Roy Tyler of
Eddie Walls p
Eddie Watts 1b
Edward Woolridge ss
Charles Zomphier 2b/rf/p

1927 Hornets

Frank Duncan (Pete) cf/M
John Barnes (Fat) c
_ Bonds c
George Grannigan p
Nelson Dean p
George Dixon c
Ernest Duff rf/of
Bill Evans cf/ss
B. Gibson p
_ Givens ss
_ Goldie 1b
James Gurley p
Art Hancock 1b/lf
James Leonard (Bobo) of/1b
Willie Miles 3b/of
Dempsey Miller (Dimp) p/lf
Ralph Moore (Squire) p
Orville Riggins ss/1b
William Ross p
Bob Saunders 3b
William Spearman p
Frank Stevens p/1b
Theodore Stockard 3b
Smith Summers (Tack) lf
Dan Thomas 3b
Eddie Watts ss/2b
Edgar Wesley 1b
Charles Zomphier 2b/3b/1b

1928 Tigers

Sam Crawford p/M
Frank Duncan (Pete) M
Perry Hall 2b/3b/M
John Barnes (Fat) c
George Boggs p
Tom Cox p
Homer Curry (Goose) p/lf
Saul Davis ss/2b
A.C.Davis inf
Nelson Dean p
S.R. Dewitt (Eddie) 1b
George Dixon c
John Dixon (Johnny Bob) p
Ernest Duff 1b/cf
Chancellor Edwards (Jak) c
Robert Gans (Jude)
Eppie Hampton c
Tom Jackson p
_ Jauron p
Harry Jeffries 3b
John Wesley Johnson p
Oscar Johnson (Heavy) rf/1b
_ Kirby p
James Leonard (Bobo) 1b
Edward Milton 2b/cf/1b
Ralph Moore (Squire) p/of
Grady Orange of
A. Owens ss
William Ross p
Orville Singer cf
Owen Smaulding p
Frank Stevens p/cf/rf
_ Stevenson (Lefty) p
Theodore Stockard ss
Smith Summers (Tack) lf/rf/2b

Pete Willett 3b/ss
George Williams ss
Raymond Williams (Red) ss
James Womack 1b
_ Woodard inf
Edward Woolridge 1b/lf
Charles Zomphier 3b/2b

1931 Cubs
Clifford Bell (Cliff) p
Alonzo Boone p
Black Bottom Buford 2b
Richard Cannon p
Comer Cox (Hannibal) rf/lf
George Dixon c
A. Gillespie p
Joe Hewitt 2b/of
Milt Laurent 2b/utl/p
Dempsey Miller (Dimp) p
J. Owens of
Leroy Paige (Satchel) p
Bill Perkins c
Robert Pipkin (Lefty) p
Jack Ridley cf
Branch Russell 2b
Orville Singer lf
Robert Smith c/lf
Zack Spencer p
Sam Streeter p
E.C. Turner (Pop) 3b
Jesse Walker (Hoss) ss
Jack Wallace 3b
Jim West 1b
Joe Wiggins 3b
Nish Williams c/rf
Jim Willis p

Henry Wright (Red) p
Charles Zomphier 2b

1932 Cubs
Don Bennett rf
Ameal Brooks cf
Jim Brown 1b
Roy Brown p
Tom Cox p
Benny Fields 3b
Albert Morehead c
Clarence Ora lf
Guy Ousley ss
Andrew Porter p
Sammy Thompson (Runt) 2b
Cristobal Torriente p/1b
Jim Williams (Bullet) p

1932 Stars
_ Case rf
Alfred Cooper (Army) p
Anthony Cooper ss
_ Davis (Big Boy) p
Nelson Dean p
Benny Fields of
Chick Harris (Popsickle) 1b
George Mitchell p
Carroll Mothell (Dink) 2b/p
Bill Perkins c
Wilson Redus lf
William Robinson (Bobby) 3b
Branch Russell rf/2b
Orville Singer cf
Joe Ware lf/cf
Fietman Wilson c

1933 Giants
Ernest Carter (Spoon) p
Dewey Creacy 3b
Oland Dials (Lou) rf
David Harvey (Bill) p
Clarence Lewis (Foots) 1b
Leroy Morney ss
Clarence Palm (Spoony) c
Wilson Redus lf
_ Simpson cf
Bobby Williams 2b

1934 Red Sox
Bobby Williams M
Jesse Brooks 3b/c
Bill Byrd p
Anthony Cooper ss/3b
S. Davidson 3b
John Dixon (Johnny Bob) p
Dennis Gilcrest rf/c
Thomas Glover p
C.B. Griffin (Clarence) of
Charlie Hughes 2b
_ Hurd of
Norman Jackson (Jelly) rf/ss
Bill Johnson ss
B. Jones c/of
Reuben Jones rf/lf
Holsey Lee (Scrip) p
Clarence Lewis (Foots) ss
George McAllister 1b
C. Milton inf
Andrew Patterson (Pat) 2b
Willie Powell p
Wilson Redus lf
James Reese p
Roy Roberts p

William Robinson (Bobby) 3b
_ Robinson (Babe) p
John Henry Russell 2b
_ See rf/p
Felton Snow 3b
Leroy Taylor cf/lf
Guy Williams 3b

1939 Bears
Alonzo Mitchell (Hooks) 1b/p/M
Herman Andrews (Jabo) p
Herbert Barnhill c
Alonzo Boone p
Charles Bruton (Jak) p/of
Walter Burch c/of
Howard Cleveland (Duke) cf
Ralph Cole rf
M.D. Cox (Alphonse) p
Willie Ferrell (Trueheart) p
Albert Frazier 2b
_ Green (Honey) p
Leo Henry (Preacher) p
Leroy Homles (Phillie) ss
Herman Howard (Red) p
Ernest Jones ((Mint) 1b
Clarence Lamar ss
John Lyles ss/of
Jack Moore of
Raymond Owens (Smokey) p
John Ray of
Joseph Royall (John) lf
Lacey Thomas p/of
Henry Turner lf/c
_ Tyler of
David Whatley lf
Parnell Woods 3b

1940 Bears
James Williams (Jim) of/M
Ted Alexander p
Herbert Barnhill c
Ed Bordes ss/inf
_ Broom p
Howard Cleveland (Duke) rf
Ralph Cole lf
Albert Frazier 2b
Leo Henry (Preacher) p
Clarence Lamar ss
_ Manuel (Clown) of
Alonzo Mitchell (Hooks) p
Raymond Owens (Smokey) p
John Ray cf
Walter Robinson (Skin Down) 3b
Kenneth Robinson 1b
Sam Sampson 2b/of
Andrew Sarvis p
Henry Turner c/of
Henry White p
Parnell Woods 3b

1942 Cleveland and Cincinnati
   Buckeyes
Alonzo Boone p
Charles Boone (Lefty) p
Eugene Bremmer p
Chet Brewer p
George Britt (Chippy) c
George Brown of
Ulysses Brown (Buster) c
Walter Burch c/p
Thad Christopher lf/rf
Howard Cleveland (Duke) of
Willie Cornelius (Sug) p
John Cowan 3b

Lloyd Davenport (Ducky) of
Willie Grace of
J. Harris (Sonny) of
Billy Horne 2b
Willie Hubert p
Livingston James (Winky) ss/2b
Willie Jefferson p
Sam Jethroe cf/lf
John Lyles ss/2b
Fred McKelvin p
Raymond Owens (Smokey) p
Ray Robinson p
Dode Smith p
Eugene Smith (Gene) 3b
Raymond Taylor c
Archie Ware 1b
Herman Watts p
Jesse Williams c
Emmett Wilson of
Parnell Woods 3b

1943 Buckeyes
Sam Barber p
Alonzo Boone p
Eugene Bremmer p
Chet Brewer p
George Britt (Chippy) c
Thad Christopher rf/c
Howard Cleveland (Duke) lf
Ross Davis p
Willie Grace of
_ Grimes of
Napoleon Gulley p
Lovell Harden p
Billy Horne ss
Johnny Lee Hundley c/of
Willie Jefferson p

Sam Jethroe cf/3b
Johnny Johnson p/of
John Lyles inf
Willie McCarey p
Marshall Riddle 2b
Quincy Smith of
Theolic Smith p/of
Raymond Taylor c
Henry Turner c/of
Archie Ware 1b
Parnell Woods 3b

1944 Buckeyes

Alfred Armour (Buddy) lf
Rainey Bibbs inf
Eugene Bremmer p
George Britt (Chippy) c
John Brown p
Walter Burch c/2b
Frank Carswell p
John Cowan 2b/3b
Jimmy Crutchfield of
Lloyd Davenport rf
Willie Grace of
Jefferson Guiwn c
Lovell Harden p
Billy Horne ss
George Jefferson p
Willie Jefferson p
Sam Jethroe cf
Wilbur King (Dolly) inf
_ McCreary lf
Sherley Petway (Charlie) c
Harmon Purcell 3b
William Rowe (Schoolboy) p
Archie Ware 1b
Jesse Williams c

Parnell Woods 3b
Norman Young (Harvey) ss

1945 Buckeyes

Alfred Armour (Buddy) lf
Earl Ashby c
Eugene Bremmer p
George Brown p
Avelino Canizares ss
Frank Carswell p
John Cowan 2b/3b
Lloyd Davenport rf
Roosevelt Davis (Rosey) p
Willie Grace of
Jefferson Guiwn c
Napoleon Gulley p
Lovell Harden p
Billy Horne 2b/ss
George Jefferson p
Willie Jefferson p
Sam Jethroe cf
Willie McCarey p
Quincy Trouppe c
Archie Ware 1b
Jesse Williams c
Parnell Woods 3b

1946 Buckeyes

Hoses Allen (Buster) p
Alfred Armour (Buddy) lf/3b
Alonzo Boone p
Charles Boone (Lefty) p
Herbert Bracken (Doc) p
Eugene Bremmer p
Chet Brewer p
John Brown p
Walter Burch c

_ Bush p
Walter Calhoun p
Frank Carswell p
Elijah Chism (Eli) of
Vibert Clarke p
John Cowan 2b/3b/ss
Frank Flemming p
Willie Grace rf
Tommy Harris c
Billy Horne ss/2b
Willie Jefferson p
George Jefferson p
Sam Jethroe cf
Curtis Jones (Bud) p
Leon Kellman 3b/c/p
Steve Keyes (Zeke) p
Eddie Klepp p
Perez Larrinago 2b/ss
Nath McClinnic of
George Minor of
John Henry Oliver ss
Jimmy Reynolds 3b
Vicial Richardson ss
_ Singleton p
Al Smith 3b
Quincy Trouppe c
Archie Ware 1b
Andy Watts 3b
Jesse Williams c
Sam Woods p
Ralph Wyatt ss

1947 Buckeyes
Quincy Trouppe c/M
Joe Atkins lf/rf
Alonzo Boone p
Herbert Braken (Doc) p

Ramon Bragana p
Eugene Bremmer p
Chet Brewer p
Frank Caldwell p
Vibert Clarke p
John Cowan 2b
Ross Davis p
Willie Grace rf
Tommy Harris c
Sam Jethroe cf
Samuel Jones (Sad Sam) p
Leon Kellman 3b
Nath McClinnic of
George Minor of
Clyde Nelson 3b
Al Smith ss
Eugene Smith p
Archie Ware 1b
Ted Toles p
Jesse Williams ss/of
Clyde Williams p

1948 Buckeyes
Alonzo Boone p
Eugene Bremmer p
Chet Brewer p
John Brown p
Frank Carswell p
Vibert Clarke p
Willie Grace rf
James Greene (Joe) c/of
Tommy Harris c
George Jefferson coach
Sam Jethroe cf
Samuel Jones (Sad Sam) p
Leon Kellman 3b/2b
Ernest Long p

Nath McClinnic of
George Minor of
Clyde Nelson 3b/2b
Henry (Hank) Presswood 3b/ss
Othello Renfroe (Chico) ss/2b
William Reynolds (Bill) 2b/ss
Al Smith lf
Eugene Smith p
Harold Thompson p
Archie Ware 1b

1949 Louisville/Cleveland Buckeyes

Quincy Barbee (Bud) of
Pablo Bernard ss/inf
Alonzo Boone p
Lincoln Boyd of
T.J. Brown (Tom) ss/3b
Vilbert Clarke p
Rayford Finch p
Willie Grace cf/rf
Tommy Harris c
David Hoskins lf/cf
George Jefferson p
Paul Jones p
Leon Kellman 3b
Ernest Long p
Charles Marvray of
George Minor of
Charles Murray
Alberto Osorio p
Clyde Parris 3b
William Reynolds (Bill) 2b
John Scott rf/lf
William Scruggs (Willie) p
Eugene Smith p
Archie Ware 1b

Isaac Weston (Deacon) p
Parnell Woods 3b
Calvin Wynn of

1950 Buckeyes

Alonzo Boone p/M
Otha Bailey (Bill) c
Sam Barber p
Pablo Bernard 2b
Samuel Brewster of
T.J. Brown (Tom) 3b
Charles Bruton (Jack) 3b/2b
Johnnie Bryant of
Joseph Caffie (Clifford) lf
Wesley Calhoun rf
Kenneth Carter c
Leonard Colliers p
Robert Cunningham p
Albert Ellis p
Frank Evans cf
Rayford Finch p
_ Flourney p
Samuel Fowlkes p
Clyde Golden p
Willie Grace of/p
Wiley Griggs 3b
_ Hardy (Doc) 2b
Charles Harvey ss
Dallas Jackson ss
Eddie Jamison c
George Jefferson p/of
Charles Johnson 2b/3b
Rudolph Johnson (Rudy) of
Charles Jones 3b
Paul Jones p
Walter Kelly p
Curtis Livingston of

Ernest Long p
_ Lyons p
Lorenzo Marsh c
Charles Marvray of/1b
Bob Mitchell p
Excell Moore p
Charles Murray
Leonard Pigg c
Curtis Pitts c
Henry Presswood inf
Marvin Price 1b
William Reynolds (Bill) 3b/2b
Thomas Russell p
Robert Scruggs p

William Scruggs (Willie) p
Eugene Smith p
Artis Stewart p
Norris Stiles p
Earl Suttles 1b
John Thomas p
Joe Trawick 2b
Willie Turnstall p
Marvi Williams 2b
Stuart Williams ss/2b
Clyde Williams p
_ Wilson p
Clarence Wynder c
Bob Young ss/2b/3b

Names from the 1922, 1923, 1924, 1926, 1927 and 1928 teams came from the *Cleveland Gazette* and Dick Clark and Larry Lester, eds., *The Negro Leagues Book* (Cleveland: Society for American Baseball Research, 1994).

Names from the 1931, 1932, and 1933 teams came from the *Chicago Defender, Cleveland Gazette,* and Clark and Lester's *The Negro Leagues Book.*

Names from the 1934, 1939, 1940, 1942, 1943, 1944, 1945, 1946, 1947, 1948, 1949, 1950 teams came from the *Cleveland Call and Post,* the *Pittsburgh Courier,* and Clark and Lester's *The Negro Leagues Book.*

Appendix 2

Cleveland Negro League Participants in the East-West All-Star Game

(All Cleveland players played for the West team, with the exception of the 1949 Louisville/Cleveland Buckeyes)

Year	Site	Team	Player(s)
1933	Chicago, Illinois	Cleveland Giants	Leroy Morney
1934	Chicago, Illinois	Cleveland Red Sox	Andy Patterson
1939	Comiskey Park	Cleveland Bears	Parnell Woods
1939	Yankee Stadium	Cleveland Bears	John Lyles, Raymond "Smokey" Owens
1940	Chicago, Illinois	Cleveland Bears	none
1942	Comiskey Park	Cleveland-Cincinnati Buckeyes	Sam Jethroe, Eugene Bremmer
1942	Municipal Stadium, Cleveland	Cleveland-Cincinnati Buckeyes	Parnell Woods, Sam Jethroe, Eugene Bremmer
1943	Chicago, Illinois	Cleveland Buckeyes	Theolic "Fireball" Smith
1944	Chicago, Illinois	Cleveland Buckeyes	Sam Jethroe, Buddy Armour, Archie Ware, Eugene Bremmer
1945	Chicago, Illinois	Cleveland Buckeyes	Lloyd Davenport, Archie Ware, Quincy Trouppe, Eugene Bremmer
1946	Griffith Stadium, Washington, D.C.	Cleveland Buckeyes	Archie Ware, Sam Jethroe, Willie Grace, Quincy Trouppe, John Brown, Vibert Clarke

Year	Site	Team	Player(s)
1946	Comiskey Park	Cleveland Buckeyes	Archie Ware, Sam Jethroe, Willie Grace, Quincy Trouppe
1947	Comiskey Park	Cleveland Buckeyes	Sam Jethroe, Quincy Trouppe, Chet Brewer
1947	Polo Grounds	Cleveland Buckeyes	Leon Kellman, Sam Jethroe, Quincy Trouppe, Vibert Clarke
1948	Comiskey Park	Cleveland Buckeyes	none
1948	Yankee Stadium	Cleveland Buckeyes	Willie Grace, Vibert Clarke, Leon Kellman
1949	Chicago, Illinois	Louisville/Cleveland Buckeyes	Dave Hoskins, Leon Kellman
1950	Chicago, Illinois	Cleveland Buckeyes	none

Names for the East-West All-Star Game participants came from the *Chicago Defender*, the *Cleveland Call and Post*, the *Pittsburgh Courier*, and Larry Lester, *Black Baseball's National Showcase: The East-West All-Star Game, 1933–1953* (Lincoln: University of Nebraska Press, 2001).

Chapter Notes

Introduction

1. Rob Ruck, *Sandlot Seasons: Sport in Black Pittsburgh* (Urbana: University of Illinois Press, 1993), 3, xi.

2. "The Official Site of the Cleveland Indians," News: Cleveland Indians News, <http://cleveland.indians.mlb.com/news/article.jsp?ymd=20061204&content_id=1750392&vkey=news_cle&fext=.jsp&c_id=cle> (15 April 2007).

3. *To Promote Amicable Relations: 30 Year History of the Cleveland Community Relations Board* (Cleveland: The Board, 1975), 3, located at the Western Reserve Historical Society, Cleveland, OH. At times, the Community Relations Board was also referred to as the "Amity Board."

4. "Prime Sport News — A Stadium for Cleveland?" *Cleveland Gazette*, 28 April 1928, 2; "Color-Line Luna Park Pays!" *Cleveland Gazette*, 22 September 1928, 2. The *Gazette* was a much smaller newspaper than the *Call and Post*, as its weekly issues averaged just four pages. Even though the *Gazette* survived until 1945, it published issues somewhat sporadically between 1941 and 1945. The *Call and Post* started in 1927 from the merger of two smaller Cleveland weeklies, the *Call* and the *Post*. William O. Walker became the editor in 1932 and took the paper's circulation from 300 to 10,000. For more information on the *Call and Post*, please read "The Encyclopedia of Cleveland History: Cleveland Call & Post," Encyclopedia of Cleveland History, <http://ech.case.edu/ech-cgi/article.pl?id=CCP>. For more information on the *Gazette*, please read "The Encyclopedia of Cleveland History: Cleveland Gazette," Encyclopedia of Cleveland History, <http://ech.case.edu/ech-cgi/article.pl?id=CG2>.

Chapter 1

1. Kenneth L. Kusmer, *A Ghetto Takes Shape: Black Cleveland, 1870–1930* (Urbana and Chicago: University of Illinois Press, 1976), 204–205.

2. Robert Peterson, *Only the Ball Was White: A History of Legendary Black Players and All-Black Professional Teams* (Oxford: Oxford University Press, 1970), 80.

3. Peterson, *Only the Ball Was White*, 88–91. During this portion of the book, Peterson also mentions that league attendance averaged 1,650 per game in 1923.

4. Peterson, *Only the Ball Was White*, 92–93. When the NNL failed in 1948, the NAL absorbed the few surviving teams. The second incarnation of the NNL and the NAL were on reasonably solid financial footing from the late 1930s through World War II.

5. Leslie Heaphy, "Cleveland Tate Stars," in *Batting Four Thousand: Baseball in the Western Reserve*, Brad Sullivan, ed. (Cleveland: Society For American Baseball Research, 2008), 34–36; Allen Harrison Dorsey, "Prime Sport News — Big Doings in 'Chi,'" *Cleveland Gazette*, 4 February 1922, 1. Reference to $1,000 entry fee.

6. Allen Harrison Dorsey, "Prime Sport News — The League's New Vice President," *Cleveland Gazette*, 18 March 1922, 2; Allen Harrison Dorsey, "Prime Sport News — The League's New Vice President," *Cleveland Gazette*, 18 March 1922, 2.

7. Russell H. Davis, *Black Americans in Cleveland* (Washington, D.C.: The Associated Publishers, 1972), 272–273. Total population in 1910 was 560,663, while African Americans were 8,448. In 1920, total population was 796,841, while African Americans were 34,451. In 1930, total population was 900,492, while African Americans were 71,899. In 1940 total

population was at 878,336, while the African American population was 84,504.

8. Allen Harrison Dorsey, "Prime Sport News," *Cleveland Gazette*, 11 February 1922, 3.

9. Allen Harrison Dorsey, "Prime Sport News — "Dizzy's" Opinion," *Cleveland Gazette*, 28 January 1922, 2.

10. Allen Harrison Dorsey, "Prime Sport News — "Dizzy's" Opinion," *Cleveland Gazette*, 28 January 1922, 2.

11. "Prime Sport News — The Kansas City Team Wins One," *Cleveland Gazette*, 22 July 1922, 3.

12. Advertisement, "Your Last Chance," *Cleveland Gazette*, 7 January 1922, 1.

13. Advertisement, "Don't Get in Line," *Cleveland Gazette*, 21 January 1922, 1.

14. Allen Harrison Dorsey, "Prime Sport News," *Cleveland Gazette*, 11 February 1922, 3.

15. Allen Harrison Dorsey, "Prime Sport News — Tates Trim Massillon," *Cleveland Gazette*, 6 May 1922, 3.

16. Allen Harrison Dorsey, "Prime Sport News — Asks Receiver for Tates," *Cleveland Gazette*, 27 May 1922, 3.

17. "Prime Sport News — Col. J.E. Reed's Alleged Demand," *Cleveland Gazette*, 17 June 1922, 3.

18. Allen H. Dorsey, "Prime Sport News — Another Tate Baseball Co. Meeting," *Cleveland Gazette*, 24 June 1922, 3.

19. "Prime Sport News — Trouble Looms Big for the Tate Stars," *Cleveland Gazette*, 26 August 1922, 3.

20. George Tate was president of the team, Jason Pitts served as vice president, Coleman A. Lewis was secretary, Reed was treasurer, and Tony Strunko, the white businessman, was considered a "director" of the club.

21. "Prime Sport News — Trouble Looms Big for the Tate Stars," *Cleveland Gazette*, 26 August 1922, 3.

22. Larry Lester, Dick Clark, and NoirTech Research, Inc., "Negro League Teams in Cleveland." Statistical spreadsheet supplied by Ike Brooks, unpublished source.

23. "Prime Sport News — Tate Baseball Co. Affairs a Mess," *Cleveland Gazette*, 25 November 1922, 3.

24. "Prime Sport News — The Tates Out of the League," *Cleveland Gazette*, 30 December 1922, 3.

25. "Prime Sport News — Fireworks at Foster Banquet," *Cleveland Gazette*, 17 February 1923, 3.

26. "Prime Sport News — Tate's Stars Looming Again; President Tate Talks," *Cleveland Gazette*, 17 March 1923, 3.

27. "Prime Sport News — Tate Base-Ball

Co. Stockholders Rebel," *Cleveland Gazette*, 5 May 1923, 3.

28. "Prime Sport News — Tates to Rejoin the League," *Cleveland Gazette*, 30 June 1923, 2.

29. "Prime Sport News — Stars Win Both Games," *Cleveland Gazette*, 7 July 1923, 2.

30. "Prime Sport News — Refused to Play Before Small Crowd," *Cleveland Gazette*, 23 July 1923, 2.

31. Larry Lester, Dick Clark, and NoirTech Research, Inc., "Negro League Teams in Cleveland." Statistical spreadsheet supplied by Ike Brooks; "Prime Sports News — Tate Stars May Join," *Cleveland Gazette*, 24 November 1923, 2; "Prime Sport News — The Tate Stars Are No More," *Cleveland Gazette*, 22 March 1924, 1.

32. "Prime Sport News — Browns Win Initial Contest," *Cleveland Gazette*, 19 April 1924, 2; "Prime Sport News — The Browns 'Trimmed,'" Cleveland Gazette, 10 May 1924, 2; "Prime Sport News — The Browns Playing Better Ball," *Cleveland Gazette*, 31 May 1924, 2. The Browns played their first games of the season against several white semi-pro teams from the Cleveland area, but lost their first official Negro League match of the season against the Detroit Stars in Detroit.

33. "Prime Sport News — The Browns Win Two, Again!" *Cleveland Gazette*, 7 June 1924, 2.

34. "Prime Sport News — Browns Playing Great Ball," *Cleveland Gazette*, 21 June 1924, 2.

35. "Prime Sport News — Browns Beaten Again," *Cleveland Gazette*, 5 July 1924, 2.

36. "Prime Sport News — The Browns Win Both," *Cleveland Gazette*, 19 July 1924, 2.

37. "Prime Sport News — Champion Monarchs Play Here," *Cleveland Gazette*, 26 July 1924, 2.

38. "Prime Sport News — The Browns Won One, Anyhow," *Cleveland Gazette*, 2 August 1924, 2.

39. "Prime Sport News — Browns Trimmed Again," *Cleveland Gazette*, 28 June 1924, 2.

40. Lester, Clark, and NoirTech, "Negro League Teams in Cleveland." Statistical spreadsheet supplied by Ike Brooks.

41. "Prime Sport News," *Cleveland Gazette*, 3 January 1925, 2.

42. "Prime Sport News — The Cleveland Browns," *Cleveland Gazette*, 24 January 1925, 2.

43. "Prime Sport News — The Cleveland Browns," *Cleveland Gazette*, 24 January 1925, 2; "Prime Sport News — The Browns or 'Stars' Bumped," *Cleveland Gazette*, 9 May 1925, 2.

44. "Prime Sport News — Browns, Hooper and Yancy," *Cleveland Gazette*, 9 May 1925, 2.

45. "Prime Sport News — The Browns Expose," *Cleveland Gazette*, 16 May 1925, 2; "Prime Sport News — Truth About The Browns?" *Cleveland Gazette*, 30 May 1925, 1.

46. Lester, Clark, and NoirTech, "Negro League Teams in Cleveland." Statistical spreadsheet supplied by Ike Brooks; "Prime Sport News — Cleveland Elite Baseball Team," *Cleveland Gazette*, 10 April 1926, 1.

47. "Prime Sport News — Cleveland Elite Baseball Team," *Cleveland Gazette*, 10 April 1926, 1.

48. "Prime Sport News — The Elites or Derelicts — Which?" *Cleveland Gazette*, 26 June 1926, 1.

49. "Prime Sport News — The Worm Turned Once, Anyhow," *Cleveland Gazette*, 3 July 1926, 1.

50. "Prime Sport News — The Elites Lose and Win and Well Earned and Deserved Praise," *Cleveland Gazette*, 4 September 1926, 2.

51. "Prime Sport News — Cleveland's League Team," *Cleveland Gazette*, 26 February 1927, 2.

52. "Prime Sport News — Cleveland's New Club," *Cleveland Gazette*, 12 February 1927, 2. Other public figures included Landon O'Neal as vice president, J.C. Hicks as secretary, Dr. Joe T. Thomas as treasurer, and Alex Brown as assistant treasurer. The board of directors included Dr. L.I. Rodgers, W.C. Petite, W. Pearson and L. Brown. J.A. Jones was the purchasing agent for the team.

53. "Prime Sport News — Hornets Win, Score 6 to 5," *Cleveland Gazette*, 29 July 1927, 2.

54. "Prime Sport News — Our Local Baseball Team," *Cleveland Gazette*, 26 March 1927, 1.

55. "Prime Sport News — Cleveland's New Club," *Cleveland Gazette*, 12 February 1927, 2.

56. "Prime Sport News — The Buckeyes Won One, Anyhow," *Cleveland Gazette*, 14 May 1927, 2.

57. "Prime Sport News — Dropped From Our National League," *Cleveland Gazette*, 16 July 1927, 2.

58. "Cleveland Hornets' New Backer," *Cleveland Gazette*, 17 March 1928, 2.

59. "Prime Sport News — Barkin Backer of Tigers," *Cleveland Gazette*, 24 March 1928, 1; "Prime Sport News — Barkin Backer of Tigers," *Cleveland Gazette*, 24 March 1928, 1. Barkin was involved in the hardware business and was a catcher in Class A baseball.

60. "Prime Sport News — The Cleveland Tigers," *Cleveland Gazette*, 17 March 1928, 2.

61. Advertisement, "Color-Line Luna Park," *Cleveland Gazette*, 31 July 1926, 1.

62. "Prime Sport News — A Financial Failure," *Cleveland Gazette*, 15 December 1928, 2.

63. "Prime Sport News — A Stadium for Cleveland?" *Cleveland Gazette*, 28 April 1928, 2. The Indians played their first game at the Stadium in 1932. They used it primarily for weekend and holiday games until Bill Veeck moved the team there full time in the late 1940s.

64. Kusmer, *A Ghetto Takes Shape*, 58, 180.

65. "Prime Sport News — The Cleveland Tigers," *Cleveland Gazette*, 10 March 1928, 2; "Prime Sport News — Tigers Secure Slugger," *Cleveland Gazette*, 7 April 1928, 2.

66. "Prime Sport News — Tigers Secure Slugger," *Cleveland Gazette*, 7 April 1928, 2.

67. Bill Finger, "Passing In Review," *Call and Post*, 14 July 1934, 6. Terrell was also a pitcher in his youth, and worked as an assistant superintendent at the Cleveland "garbage plant"; "Prime Sport News — Barkin Backer of Tigers," *Cleveland Gazette*, 24 March 1928, 1. White umpires called most of the games for the Tigers that season; "Prime Sport News — Eight Players Signed By Tigers," *Cleveland Gazette*, 7 April 1928, 2; "Prime Sport News — Sport Items," *Cleveland Gazette*, 26 May 1928, 2; "Prime Sport News — Stars Wallop Tigers," *Cleveland Gazette*, 2 June 1928, 2; "Prime Sport News — The Tigers' New Managers," *Cleveland Gazette*, 9 June 1928, 2; "Prime Sport News — General Manager Williams," *Cleveland Gazette*, 9 June 1928, 2.

68. "Prime Sport News — General Manager Williams," *Cleveland Gazette*, 9 June 1928, 2.

69. "Prime Sport News — Turns In Perfect Ball Game," *Cleveland Gazette*, 22 September 1928, 2.

70. Kusmer, *A Ghetto Takes Shape*, 204–205.

71. "Prime Sport News — The Cleveland Cubs in the South," *Cleveland Gazette*, 2 May 1931, 2. The scores of both games were 7–1 and 5–0 in favor of the Cubs. The games took place in Nashville, Tennessee; Lester, Clark, and NoirTech, "Negro League Teams in Cleveland." Statistical spreadsheet supplied by Ike Brooks; the Cubs finished in second place in league standings for the 1931 season. They were owned by Tom Wilson and managed by Joe Hewitt, Nish Williams.

72. "Prime Sport News — Baseball Fans Riot in Ohio," *Cleveland Gazette*, 13 June 1931, 2.

73. "Prime Sport News — The Cubs Beaten, Twice," *Cleveland Gazette*, 27 June 1931, 2.

74. "Prime Sport News — The Grays vs. the Monarchs," *Cleveland Gazette*, 29 August 1931, 1; "Prime Sport News," *Cleveland Gazette*, 5 September 1931, 1; "Prime Sport News," *Cleveland Gazette*, 26 September 1931, 1; "Prime

Sport News — The Homesteads Win Big," *Cleveland Gazette*, 10 October 1931, 1. Against the Monarchs, the Grays won the first game, 9–1, and the Monarchs won the second one, 8–1. The Grays defeated the white team, 18–0.

75. "Fans Await Baseball Plans Here," *Chicago Defender*, 23 January 1932, 8; Lloyd P. Thompson, "East-West League To Employ Race Umpires In Major Games," *Chicago Defender*, 20 February 1932, 9.

76. "Cleveland to Welcome Jim Brown's Team," *Chicago Defender*, 7 May 1932, 8; "Cleveland's Boss," *Chicago Defender*, 30 April 1932, 8; "Franchise of Cleveland to Chicagoan's 9," *Chicago Defender*, 30 April 1932, 9.

77. "East-West's Cleveland 9 Easy Victor," *Chicago Defender*, 7 May 1932, 8; Lester, Clark, and NoirTech, "Negro League Teams in Cleveland." Statistical spreadsheet supplied by Ike Brooks.

78. "Baseball Players and Owners Must Compromise to Save Game for All," *Chicago Defender*, 21 January 1933, 9.

79. "'Help Cleveland,' Is Ball Magnates' Idea," *Chicago Defender*, 28 January 1933, 9.

80. Al Monroe, "Cleveland Seeks Star As Manager," *Chicago Defender*, 18 February 1933, 11. Also mentioned as possible managerial choices were Dixon, Gray and Crowford.

81. "Detroit Added To League," *Chicago Defender*, 25 February 1933, 8.

82. "That Help Cleveland Was to Get May Reach Detroit," *Chicago Defender*, 25 February 1933, 9; "Detroit Out Of Baseball," *Chicago Defender*, 13 May 1933, 8.

83. "Girl Ball Player Aids Cleveland 9," *Chicago Defender*, 17 June 1933, 8. The Giants beat the Canton Clowns, 14–8.

84. "Cleveland Man to Start Baseball 9," *Chicago Defender*, 8 July 1933, 8; "Cleveland Plans Big Sports Bill," *Chicago Defender*, 15 July 1933, 8. A big game between Pittsburgh Crawfords and the New York Black Yankees at the "Cleveland American league baseball park" on July 3. Track stars Jesse Owens and Ralph Metcalfe were to compete in a special race at the game.

85. "Columbus Drops Out Of League And Cleveland Gets Its Berth," *Chicago Defender*, 26 August 1933, 8. It does not appear Isabelle Baxter made it to the new team; "Chicago Leads League as End of Race Nears," *Chicago Defender*, 9 September 1933, 8; "Cleveland to See Crawfords," *Chicago Defender*, 16 September 1933, 8; "Crawfords and Cleveland Win and Lose In Two," *Chicago Defender*, 23 September 1933, 8.

86. William Finger, "Passing In Review," *Call and Post*, 17 February 1934, 6; William Fin-

ger, "Passing In Review," *Call and Post*, 14 April 1934, 6; William Finger, "Passing In Review," *Call and Post*, 16 June 1934, 6.

87. William Finger, "Passing In Review," *Call and Post*, 17 February 1934, 6; William Finger, "Passing In Review," *Call and Post*, 24 March 1934, 6; "Bobby Williams Signed to Manage Cleveland Red Sox," *Call and Post*, 14 April 1934, 6. The Red Sox planned to train for the season in the South; Bill Finger, "Passing In Review," *Call and Post*, 21 April 1934, 6.

88. Bill Finger, "Passing In Review," *Call and Post*, 12 May 1934, 6. The *Chicago Defender* predicted that the Crawfords or the Chicago American Giants would be the best team.

89. "Cleveland Red Sox Home June Third," *Call and Post*, 26 May 1934, 6; "Centecs Beat Red Sox," *Call and Post*, 30 June 1934, 6.

90. Bill Finger, "Passing In Review," *Call and Post*, 8 September 1934, 6.

91. Bill Finger, "Passing In Review," *Call and Post*, 5 May 1934, 6.

92. Bill Finger, "Passing In Review," *Call and Post*, 4 August 1934, 6.

93. Bill Finger, "Passing In Review," *Call and Post*, 11 August 1934, 6.

94. Ibid.

95. Ibid.

96. Ibid.

97. Bill Finger, "Passing In Review," *Call and Post*, 27 October 1934, 6.

98. Bill Finger, "Passing In Review," *Call and Post*, 9 February 1935, 7.

99. Bill Finger, "Passing In Review," *Call and Post*, 12 September 1935, 7. *Cleveland News,* a white daily, ran an article that claimed the game was cancelled. The paper said they ran the story because they got a call from a "Mr. Williams," who told them the game was cancelled and to run the notice. Monroe Felton, the game's promoter, did not authorize such a cancellation.

100. Bill Finger, "Passing In Review," *Call and Post*, 27 April 1935, 7.

101. Bill Finger, "Passing In Review," *Call and Post*, 18 July 1935, 7; "Crawfords Win 2 From Chicago Here," *Call and Post*, 25 July 1935, 7; "Base Ball Enthusiasts Head For East-West Game In Chicago," *Call and Post*, 8 August 1935, 7. The Crawfords won both games of the doubleheader, 17–2 and 12–8. The East-West All-Star Game in Chicago was still able to draw large numbers of fans, even during the Depression. The game drew 15,000 people in 1933, 22,000 in 1934, and was expected to peak close to 40,000 in 1935.

102. "Baseball Club Opens Season Here, May 14," *Call and Post*, 23 February 1939, 10.

103. "Appoint Mitchell Manager Of Cleve-

land Baseball Club," *Call and Post*, 23 March 1939, 10. Bert Stokes, a Cleveland sports figure, was named a coach for the team. In 1939 Lem Williams worked for the city of Cleveland and was a member of various fraternal organizations in town; "Twirlers Report; Local Club Starts Grind; Wilbur Hayes Selected For Umpire's Post," *Call and Post*, 30 March 1939, 10; Ken Jessamy, "Yours For Sports," *Call and Post*, 6 April 1939, 10; "Cleveland 9 Wins 2 From Chicago Giants," *Call and Post*, 6 April 1939, 10; Bill Finger, "Passing In Review," *Call and Post*, 5 January 1935, 6. In 1935, Hayes also owned a shop where "one can have his suit cleaned and pressed, as well as their boots blacked."

104. Ken Jessamy, "Yours For Sports," *Call and Post*, 20 April 1939, 10.

105. "Cleveland Bears To Use Stadium As Home Grounds," *Call and Post*, 27 April 1939, 10.

106. Ken Jessamy, "Yours For Sports," *Call and Post*, 13 July 1939, 10.

107. "7,000 Fans Watch Cleveland Bears Win Doubleheader," *Call and Post*, 18 May 1939, 10; "Bears Win 6 Straight Games; Top Indianapolis 5–1, 10–8," *Call and Post*, 25 May 1939, 10; Ken Jessamy, "Yours For Sports," *Call and Post*, 25 May 1939, 10; "Cleveland Bears Lose 2 To Chi Team; Play Here June 18," *Call and Post*, 8 June 1939, 10.

108. "Kansas City Monarchs Open 3 Games Series Here, Sunday," *Call and Post*, 15 June 1939, 10; "Bears Top St. Louis Stars in Final of Three Team Doubleheader, 9 to 0," *Call and Post*, 29 June 1939, 10; "4 Cleveland Bears To Play In East-West Nine Classic," *Call and Post*, 3 August 1939, 10. Leo "Preacher" Henry received 190,323 votes, Parnell Woods received 115,577 votes and Raymond Owens received 104,597 votes; "Bears Play Last Home Game Of Season, Sunday," *Call and Post*, 17 August 1939, 10.

109. Ken Jessamy, "Yours For Sports," *Call and Post*, 10 August 1939, 10; "Cleveland Bears Nix Williams as Representative," *Call and Post*, 10 August 1939, 10.

110. Ken Jessamy, "Yours For Sports," *Call and Post*, 24 August 1939, 10; "Bears Play Last Home Game Of Season Sunday," *Call and Post*, 17 August 1939, 10.

111. "No Semi.Pro Baseball Club; Reader Wants To Know Why," *Call and Post*, 25 January 1940, 10.

112. Ken Jessamy, "Yours For Sports," *Call and Post*, 25 April 1940, 6.

113. Ken Jessamy, "Yours For Sports," *Call and Post*, 25 April 1940, 6.

114. "Manager States True Status Of Cleve-

land Bears," *Call and Post*, 25 April 1949, 6. The Jacksonville Red Caps became affiliated with the Negro American League in 1938, and became a full member of the league when they moved to Cleveland for the 1939 season.

115. "Manager States True Status Of Cleveland Bears," *Call and Post*, 25 April 1949, 6. The Jacksonville Red Caps became affiliated with the Negro American League in 1938, and became a full member of the league when they moved to Cleveland for the 1939 season.

116. "St. Louis Stars To Test Bears In Opener At League Park May 26," *Call and Post*, 16 May 1940, 6. Mayor Burton once again threw out the first pitch of the home opener; "..And A Goodly Crowd Was There..," *Call and Post*, 1 June 1940, 6; "Bears Lose 7–1, 4–3 to St. Louis," *Call and Post*, 1 June 1940, 6; "Bears Explain Poor Showing Last Sunday; Bus Smash-Up Robbed Them Of Best Men; Says Manager," *Call and Post*, 1 June 1940, 7.

117. "Bears Explain Poor Showing Last Sunday; Bus Smash-Up Robbed Them Of Best Men, Says Manager," *Call and Post*, 1 June 1940, 7; "St. Louis Stars To Test Bears In Opener At League Park May 26," *Call and Post*, 16 May 1940, 6. By the way it was reported, the *Call and Post* made the accident story seem suspicious. The story's author made it clear that Williams did not mention the accident until reporters demanded an explanation for their poor play; Bob Williams, "Sports Rambler," *Call and Post*, 21 August 1943, 10A. In 1943 Ernest "Mint" Jones, first baseman for the Bears, wrote to the *Call and Post* from the Naval Barracks at Hingham, Massachusetts, to find out how to contact his old teammates; 16 May 1940.

118. Ken Jessamy, "Yours For Sports," *Call and Post*, 8 June 1940, 6.

119. Ken Jessamy, "Yours For Sports," *Call and Post*, 15 June 1940, 6. The Bears won the two games against the Crawfords, 1–0 and 11–9; "Rejuvinated (sic) Bears Win First Two Games; Alonzo Mitchell Takes Over Reins As Manager," *Call and Post*, 15 June 1940, 6.

120. "Harry Walker Proves Talk Does Pay; Spoke to 270,000 Fans This Year," *Call and Post*, 7 December 1939, 10. Walker also worked for the city of Cleveland. He lived with his wife and two daughters at 3247 E. 130th St; Bill Finger; "Passing In Review," *Call and Post*, 15 September 1934, 6; "Expect Record Crowd At Bears' Opener Sunday," *Call and Post*, 25 May 1940, 6; Ken Jessamy, "Yours For Sports," *Call and Post*, 8 June 1940, 6.

121. Ken Jessamy, "Yours For Sports," *Call and Post*, 13 July 1940, 6. Jessamy admitted that the Bears were likely handicapped by high prices at League Park (possibly field rental costs)

but that he still thought the team was able to earn a small profit. Jessamy also said that Cleveland fans rarely support teams without winning records.

122. Ken Jessamy, "Yours For Sports," *Call and Post*, 13 July 1940, 6; "Charges Cleveland Bears With Run–Out," *Call and Post*, 13 July 1940, 6. Walker claimed he tried to convince the team to add local player Jerry Williams.

123. "Locals To Play Puerto Rican 9 on August 11th," *Call and Post*, 3 August 1940, 7; "Local Nine Play Puerto Rican Champs Doubleheader At Stadium Sunday," *Call and Post*, 10 August 1940, 6; "Puerto Rican Team Disbands, Game At Stadium Is Kayoed," *Call and Post*, 17 August 1940, 6. Almost all of the players came from three local semi-pro squads, the Cleveland White Sox, the ABCs and Miles Heights; "Mystery Bride And Attendants At Stadium Event," *Call and Post*, 24 August 1940, 7.

Chapter 2

1. In 1942 the team officially split its home games between Cleveland and Cincinnati. The first season the team belonged only to Cleveland was 1943, but the ownership and many of the core players were in place by the end of the 1941 season.

2. Neil Lanctot, *Negro League Baseball: The Rise and Ruin of a Black Institution* (Philadelphia: University of Pennsylvania Press, 2004), 132.

3. Ibid., 59.

4. Randy Dixon, "The Sports Bugle," *Pittsburgh Courier*, 3 February 1940, Effa Manley Papers, Folder 3, National Baseball Hall of Fame and Museum, Cooperstown, NY.

5. Randy Dixon, "The Sports Bugle," *Pittsburgh Courier*, 11 May 1940, Effa Manley Papers, Folder 3, National Baseball Hall of Fame and Museum, Cooperstown, NY.

6. Al Sweeney, "As I See It," *Call and Post*, 28 March 1942, 10.

7. Larry Lester, *Black Baseball's National Showcase: The East-West All-Star Game, 1933–1953* (Lincoln: University of Nebraska Press, 2001), 6.

8. Wendell Smith, "A Strange Tribe," *Pittsburgh Courier-Journal*, 14 May 1938, in *The Unlevel Playing Field: A Documentary History of the African American Experience in Sport*, David K Wiggins and Patrick B. Miller, eds. (Urbana: University of Illinois Press, 2003), 135–136.

9. Ibid., 135–136.

10. John Fuster, "John Fuster's Sportlight," *Call and Post*, 6 June 1942, 10.

11. Al Sweeney, "Gamest Guy of the Year," *Call and Post*, 19 July 1941, 9A.

12. "Sunday is 'Alabama Day' at League Park as Hayes Tries Again With Double-Header," *Call and Post*, 21 June 1941, 10A.

13. Al Sweeney, "Hayes-Wright Purchase Interest In St. Louis Stars; Game Sun.," *Call and Post*, 5 July 1941, 9A.

14. Sweeney, "Gamest Guy of the Year."

15. "Wilbur Hayes Pens An Open Letter to Baseball Fans," *Call and Post*, 26 July 1941, 11A.

16. "Two More Stars Signed By Cleve-Cincy Buckeyes," *Call and Post*, 28 February 1942, 11.

17. Leroy (Satchel) Paige and David Lipman, *Maybe I'll Pitch Forever* (New York: Grove Press, 1961), 13.

18. Ibid., 14–15.

19. Ibid., 15, 18–20.

20. Ibid., 21.

21. Ibid., 30–31.

22. Al Sweeney, "10,000 Fans Roar Approval Of Paige's Mound Antics," *Call and Post*, 9 August 1941, 10A.

23. "St. Louis Stars Make Debut As the Local Entry in N.A.L.," *Call and Post*, 2 August 1941, 11A.

24. Wendell Smith, "Paige 'Thumbs Nose' at his Public Here," 1943, Wendell Smith Papers, Folder 3, National Baseball Hall of Fame and Museum, Cooperstown, NY.

25. Ibid.

26. Al Sweeney, "As I See It," *Call and Post*, 23 August 1941, 10A.

27. "Cleveland Nine To Be Named Buckeyes By Local Owners," *Call and Post*, 29 November 1941, 11A.

28. John Fuster, "John Fuster's Sportlight," *Call and Post*, 30 May 1942, 10.

29. Clarence L. Simmons, "Bucks Win One Then Lose One As 8200 Cheer," *Call and Post*, 6 June 1942, 10; John Fuster, "We Were on the Sidelines at League Park When the Buckeyes Played the Jacksonville Red Caps Last Sunday," *Call and Post*, 6 June 1942, 10.

30. Clarence L. Simmons, "Cold Weather, Clouds, Scare Crowd Away: Bucks Edge 2–1 Win In First One, Lose 2nd 3–0," *Call and Post*, 20 June 1942, 10; John Fuster, "Jefferson, Who Beat Monarch Ace Earlier In Season, Goes To The Mound For Cleveland," *Call and Post*, 13 June 1942, 10.

31. "Clowns Win 7 Out Of 8 to Keep Major League First Place," *Call and Post*, 4 July 1942, 10.

32. "Typical Weather for Cleveland, OH" <wwwa.accuweather.com/forecast-normals.asp?partner=accuweather&traveler=0&zipcode=44113> (31 January 2007); Kirk Lom-

bardy, correspondence with author, National Weather Service, Cleveland Hopkins International Airport, 30 and 31 January 2007.

33. John Fuster, "Slugging Josh Gibson and Famous Homestead Club To Play Bucks Here On July 19," *Call and Post*, 11 July 1942, 10.

34. "Wilbur Hayes Honored As Buckeyes Meet Jacksonville," *Call and Post*, 29 August 1942, 11.

35. "African Americans," Encyclopedia of Cleveland History, <*http://ech.case.edu/ech-cgi/ article.pl?id=AA*> (6 February 2007); Russell H. Davis, *Black Americans in Cleveland* (Washington, D.C.: Associated Publishers, 1972), 25. An influx of Southerners caused Cleveland's African American population to increase each decade around this time period, from about 72,000 African Americans in 1930, to 84,504 in 1940 and 147,847 in 1950, a figure that constituted 16.2 percent of Cleveland's overall population.

36. John Fuster, "Book Twilight Game For 30th; East-West Classic, July 18th," *Call and Post*, 20 June 1942, 10.

37. "Cleveland Baseball Capital July 18th East West Game," *Call and Post*, 27 June 1942, 11.

38. "Night Game at Cleveland August 18, Brings Stars of Negro Nat'l and American," *Call and Post*, 4 July 1942, 11.

39. John Fuster, "Game Score Is 9–2 And Army Navy Relief Score Is $9,499," *Call and Post*, 22 August 1942, 11.

40. Lester, *Black Baseball's National Showcase*, 2–3.

41. "Ace Battery, Owens-Brown Killed Instantly As Truck Rams Auto On Highway 20," *Call and Post*, 12 September 1942, 1.

42. "Buckeyes Stunned By Bad Fortune Lose Two Games," *Call and Post*, 19 September 1942, 10.

43. Fuster, "Jefferson, Who Beat Monarch Ace."

44. John Fuster, "John Fuster's Sportlight," *Call and Post*, 15 August 1942, 10.

45. Sam McKibben, "Paige Will Play No Jim-Crow Ball," *Call and Post*, 29 August 1942, 11. McKibben was the sports editor of the *Kansas City Call*; the story was reprinted in the *Call and Post*.

46. James N. Gregory, *The Southern Diaspora: How the Great Migrations of Black and White Southerners Transformed America* (Chapel Hill: University of North Carolina Press, 2005), 262–263.

47. Karen Ferguson, *Black Politics in New Deal Atlanta* (Chapel Hill: University of North Carolina Press, 2002), 5.

48. John Fuster, "John Fuster's Sportlight," *Call and Post*, 29 August 1942, 10.

49. Ibid.

50. John Fuster, "John Fuster's Sportlight," *Call and Post*, 20 June 1942, 10.

51. Lanctot, *Negro League Baseball*, 135.

52. John Fuster, "John Fuster's Sportlight," *Call and Post*, 27 June 1942, 10.

53. "Landis Lowers Gates And Six Major League Outfits Scout Two Negro Clashes," *Call and Post*, 25 July 1942, 10; "Boudreau, Bradley Say They Do Not Bar Race Players," *Call and Post*, 25 July 1942, 10; "Alva Bradley Says Indians Haven't Yet Made Arrangements to Try Negroes," *Call and Post*, 1 August 1942, 10.

54. "We Think Cleveland Indians Should Look Buckeyes Over," *Call and Post*, 25 July 1942, 10.

55. John Fuster, "Cleveland News Avoiding Major Leagues Question," *Call and Post*, 8 August 1942, 9; "Lewis Says It's Hot," *Call and Post*, 8 August 1942, 10; "We Have Carried the Battle and Worn Down the Enemy: Now We Need the K.O.," *Call and Post*, 1 August 1942, 10.

56. "Walker Makes Annual Address to Negro Newsmen," *Call and Post*, 13 June 1942, 1.

57. "President Walker Stresses Need For United Crusade For Negro Civil Rights," *Call and Post*, 30 May 1942, 13.

58. "Walker, News Association Head, Will Mobilize Forces," *Call and Post*, 29 August 1942, 11.

59. "The Courier's Double 'V' For A Double Victory Campaign Gets Country-Wide Support," *Pittsburgh Courier*, 14 February 1942, 1. This article was obtained on microfilm from Kent State University Library, Kent, Ohio.

60. "Ohio Cities Urged To Form Job Committees; Register Complaints With Call-Post," *Call and Post*, 27 June 1942, 1.

61. "Benswanger, of Pittsburgh Pirates Steals Show: He Tries Out 3 Stars," *Call and Post*, 1 August 1943, 10.

62. "Negroes Are Crazy About Baseball, But Will They Plague Magnates with Plugs?" *Call and Post*, 1 August 1942, 10.

63. John Fuster, "'Come And Get 'em,' Say Dr. Martin, Mrs. Manley," *Call and Post*, 8 August 1942, 10; "Wilbur Hayes Says Big League Move Helps Negro Ball," *Call and Post*, 8 August 1942, 10.

64. John Fuster, "John Fuster's Sportlight," *Call and Post*, 8 August 1942, 10.

65. "3 Seek Indian Tryouts," *Call and Post*, 15 August 1942, 10.

66. "Trio Is Not Good Enough For Big League Is Edict After Army-Navy Game Here," *Call and Post*, 12 September 1942, 11.

67. Mabray Kountze, "Are Big Leagues

Fooling Us?" *Call and Post*, 19 September 1942, 11.

68. Bob Williams, "Sports Rambler," *Call and Post*, 17 July 1943, 10A.

Chapter 3

1. William O. Walker, "Down the Big Road," *Call and Post*, 6 February 1943, 8B.

2. William O. Walker, "Down the Big Road," *Call and Post*, 27 February 1943, 8B.

3. Margaret Anderson, "Negro Newspapers Fight For Democracy Now," *Call and Post*, 6 March 1943, 8B.

4. P.B. Young Sr., "Says Negro Press is True Advocate of Freedom," *Call and Post*, 20 March 1943, 8B.

5. Bob Williams, "Sports Rambler," *Call and Post*, 15 April 1944, 9B.

6. "Lausche Plans Interracial Committee," *Call and Post*, 14 August 1943, 1.

7. Dr. J.B. Martin, "League President Predicts Survival of Negro Baseball," *Call and Post*, 6 March 1943, 10A.

8. "Hint Eastman Smiles On Negro Baseball For '43," *Call and Post*, 13 March 1943, 10A.

9. "Buckeyes Open Spring Training At Canton Park," *Call and Post*, 10 April 1943, 11A.

10. "Cullenbine's Sore Tootsies Preferred By Indians to Having Negroes; Bucks Open Season May 2 Against St. Louis Stars," *Call and Post*, 24 April 1943, 10A.

11. Art Cohn, "'Negroes Saved Boxing, Would Save Baseball,' Says Cal. Editor," *Call and Post*, 8 May 1943, 11A. This editorial is a reprint of one that ran in the *Oakland Tribune*. It was written by the newspaper's sports editor, Art Cohn.

12. "Negro Loops Ignore Shackle Order by Eastman, Plan Travel by Rail," *Call and Post*, 24 April 1943, 10A.

13. "Buckeyes Win In Dayton, Open Here Sunday," *Call and Post*, 1 May 1943, 10A.

14. "Lose to Red Sox, 8–5 in Free Hitting Game; Garner 15 Hits," *Call and Post*, 15 May 1943, 11A.

15. Bud Douglass, "Sports of All Sorts," *Call and Post*, 1 May 1943, 11A.

16. Bud Douglass, "Sports Of All Sorts," *Call and Post*, 29 May 1943, 11A.

17. Bob Williams, "Sports Rambler," *Call and Post*, 18 December 1943, 10A.

18. DeHart Hubbard, "Sports Opinion," *Call and Post*, 8 January 1944, 10A.

19. Bob Williams, "Sports Rambler," *Call and Post*, 12 February 1944, 10A.

20. Bud Douglass, "Expect Record Crowd Sun.," *Call and Post*, 5 June 1943, 10A; "'Fire-ball' Smith Hurls Shut-Out As Bucks Take Clowns In Double-Header," *Call and Post*, 5 June 1943, 11A; Bud Douglass, "Sports Of All Sorts," *Call and Post*, 12 June 1943, 10A; Bob Williams, "Sports Rambler," *Call and Post*, 17 July 1943, 10A. Cleveland won the first game of the doubleheader and "came near to winning" the second game. Paige did not get the win; there was no mention of Smith's performance.

21. Bud Douglass, "Buckeyes Win, Lose; But Baseball Gets Stern Rebuff," *Call and Post*, 26 June 1943, 10A.

22. Ibid.

23. Ibid.; Bud Douglass, "Sports Of All Sorts," *Call and Post*, 26 June 1943, 10A.

24. Bud Douglass, "Writer Lambasts [*sic*] Wildcat Players; Praises Arbiters," *Call and Post*, 3 July 1943, 10A; "American League Head Praises Conduct of Cleveland Umpire," *Call and Post*, 3 July 1943, 10A.

25. "Harry Walker to Umpire in Classic," *Call and Post*, 31 July 1943, 10A; Harry J. Walker, "Sidelights From The East-West Classic," *Call and Post*, 7 August 1943, 12A.

26. Bud Douglass, "Writer Lambasts [*sic*] Wildcat Players; Praises Arbiters," *Call and Post*, 3 July 1943, 10A; "American League Head Praises Conduct of Cleveland Umpire," *Call and Post*, 3 July 1943, 10A.

27. Bob Williams, "Sports Rambler," *Call and Post*, 28 August 1943, 10A.

28. Bud Douglass, "Writer Lambasts (sic) Wildcat Players; Praises Arbiters," *Call and Post*, 3 July 1943, 10A; "American League Head Praises Conduct of Cleveland Umpire," *Call and Post*, 3 July 1943, 10A.

29. William Brisker, "Buckeyes Suffer 'Breakdown' But Not In The Parks," *Call and Post*, 21 August 1943, 11A.

30. Bob Williams, "Sports Rambler," *Call and Post*, 17 July 1943, 10A.

31. William Brisker, "Buckeye Power Beats Black Crackers," *Call and Post*, 28 August 1943, 10A.

32. Bob Williams, "Our Mr. Hayes Tangles With Mexican Government," *Call and Post*, 17 July 1943, 11A.

33. Bob Williams, "Sports Rambler," *Call and Post*, 24 July 1943, 10A.

34. Bob Williams, "Sports Rambler," *Call and Post*, 4 September 1943, 10A; "Buckeyes Lost First Game But Nail Second 5 to 4," *Call and Post*, 4 September 1943, 11A. This "unpredictable" squad split its next doubleheader with the Birmingham Black Barons, before an estimated 10,000 fans at League Park. Due to the large migrant population from Alabama in Cleveland, many of the fans cheered for the visiting squad.

35. "Admirer, Critic Sees Too Much Bally-hoo In Negro Baseball, Hits Umpires," *Call and Post*, 14 August 1943, 10A. Letter reprinted from a local fan and Cleveland resident, Leo Rans-fer.

36. William Brisker, "Buckeyes Hammer Two Games From Red Sox," *Call and Post*, 7 August 1943, 10A; Bob Williams, "Sports Rambler," *Call and Post*, 7 August 1943, 10A; Bob Williams, "Notables Spur War Bond Drive at League Park," *Call and Post*, 18 September 1943, 10A; Morris Mills, "Wilbur Hayes Signs Crack Battery For New Buckeyes," *Call and Post*, 23 October 1943, 10; Bob Williams, "American League Players Favor Negro In Majors," *Call and Post*, 25 December 1943, 10A.

37. Bob Williams, "American League Players Favor Negro In Majors," *Call and Post*, 25 December 1943, 10A; Don Deleighbur, "Snubs Wendell Smith As Baseball Statistician; Hires White Agency!" *Call and Post*, 18 March 1944, 10B. Don Deleighbur was a pen name for Dan Burley of the *New York Amsterdam News*. Bob Williams, "Sports Rambler," *Call and Post*, 22 July 1944, 6B.

38. Bob Williams, "Sports Rambler," *Call and Post*, 25 March 1944, 9B.

39. "Cum Posey Answers Don Deleighbur's Tirade; Attacks Negro Press," *Call and Post*, 25 March 1944, 9B.

40. Bob Williams, "Sports Rambler," *Call and Post*, 15 January 1944, 10A.

41. Bob Williams, "'Negro Ball Player Must Come Thru Minors First' ... Alva Bradley," *Call and Post*, 15 January 1944, 10A.

42. "Says Bradley Ducks Issue of Negro In Pro Baseball," *Call and Post*, 19 February 1944, 10A.

43. "Buckeyes of Baseball All Set ... Hayes; Announces Fireball, Bremer [*sic*] Rejected," *Call and Post*, 22 January 1944, 11A; "Bracken, Bucks' New Pitcher, to Hurl for Navy," *Call and Post*, 4 March 1944, 9B; "Ware Acting Manager as Bucks Lose Woods to U.S.," *Call and Post*, 15 April 1944, 9B; Bob Williams, "Sports Rambler," *Call and Post*, 8 April 1944, 9B; Eddie P. Jennings, "Says Hayes Signs Best Players for Cleveland Team," *Call and Post*, 5 February 1944, 11A.

44. Eddie P. Jennings, "Buckeyes Should Be 1944 Champs," *Call and Post*, 19 February 1944, 10A.

45. Bob Williams, "Sports Rambler," *Call and Post*, 22 April 1944, 9B; Morris Mills, "Buckeyes Split Twin Bill with Clowns, Play Birmingham Champs, Sunday," *Call and Post*, 20 May 1944.

46. Morris Mills, "Buckeyes Split Twin Bill with Clowns, Play Birmingham Champs,

Sunday," *Call and Post*, 20 May 1944; Bob Williams, "Sports Rambler," *Call and Post*, 20 May 1944, 6B.

47. Bob Williams, "Sports Rambler," *Call and Post*, 27 May 1944, 8B; Bob Williams, "Bucks Defeat Barons Twice; Lead Race," *Call and Post*, 27 May 1944. The Buckeyes also announced that they hired a man named Eddie Kitchens to do publicity for the team.

48. Bob Williams, "Sports Rambler," *Call and Post*, 4 March 1944, 9B.

49. Bob Williams, "Sports Rambler," *Call and Post*, 1 July 1944, 6B.

50. Bob Williams, "Sports Rambler," *Call and Post*, 15 July 1944, 6B.

51. "Three New Players Added; Buckeyes Meet Chicago American Giants, Sunday," *Call and Post*, 12 August 1944, 6B.

52. DeHart Hubbard, "Program Proposed In Negro Baseball," *Call and Post*, 8 April 1944, 9B.

53. "Satchel Paige In Revolt but Both Teams Confident of East-West Classic Win," *Call and Post*, 12 August 1944, 6B. There were six Buckeyes named to the East-West All-Star Game: Parnell Woods, Sam Jethroe, Buddy Armour, Eugene Bremmer, Archie Ware and Billy Morne; Billy Young, "Voice in the Wind," *Call and Post*, 12 August 1944, 7B.

54. Bob Williams, "Sports Rambler," *Call and Post*, 19 August 1944, 6B; Bob Williams, "Sports Rambler," *Call and Post*, 26 August 1944, 6B.

55. Bob Williams, "Buckeyes, Chicago Play Twin Bills Sunday, Also Labor Day," *Call and Post*, 2 September 1944, 6B; Bob Williams, "Grays Trounce Buckeyes Twice," *Call and Post*, 16 September 1944, 6B. The Grays went on to play the Birmingham Black Barons in the Negro League World Series that year. Just before the series started, five Birmingham players were hospitalized after a head-on automobile collision in Alabama. "Five of Best Players on Birmingham Barons Injured, Crippled in Auto Smash-Up," *Call and Post*, 16 September 1944, 6B. The soon-to-be world champion Grays won the exhibition doubleheader, 10–4 and 9–5.

56. "Bucks Lead in Batting, Fielding; Jethroe Is League Champ," *Call and Post*, 14 October 1944, 6B; Bob Williams, "Satchel Paige to Seek Revenge from Buckeyes at League Park Sunday," *Call and Post*, 10 June 1944, 6. Archie Ware led all first basemen with a .987 fielding percentage, John Cowan led second basemen with a .947 fielding percentage, Parnell Woods led third basemen with a .948 average, and William Horne led shortstops with a .963 fielding percentage.

57. "Buckeyes Doing O.K. on Barnstorming Tour," *Call and Post*, 7 October 1944, 6B.

58. Bob Williams, "Negro Baseball to Select High Commissioner," *Call and Post*, 23 December 1944, 6B.

Chapter 4

1. Bob Williams, "Sports Rambler," *Call and Post*, 3 March 1945, 6B.

2. Bob Williams, "Sports Rambler," *Call and Post*, 10 March 1945, 6B.

3. Bob Williams, "Sports Rambler," Call and Post, 21 April 1945, 6B.

4. Bob Williams, "Demands House Probe of Jim-Crow Baseball," *Call and Post*, 5 May 1945, 6B.

5. "Buckeyes Split Two with Cubans, Good Spring Games," *Call and Post*, 14 April 1945, 7B.

6. "Bucks Set To Play In Cleveland, May 27," *Call and Post*, 19 May 1945, 6B.

7. "Jethroe Gets Tryout With Boston Red Sox," *Call and Post*, 14 April 1945, 7B.

8. "Discounts Tryouts, Says Negroes Were Humiliated," *Call and Post*, 5 May 1945, 7B.

9. Michael Madden, "He Ran Into a Fenway Wall; After Sox Tryout, Jethroe Became First Black Boston Player–As Brave," *Boston Globe*, 28 May 1993, 29.

10. Bob Williams, "Brilliant Opening Games Show Greatness as Buckeyes Prepare for Clowns Sunday," *Call and Post*, 2 June 1945, 6B.

11. Bob Williams, "Sports Rambler," *Call and Post*, 2 June 1945, 6B.

12. Bob Williams, "American Giants Here Sunday," *Call and Post*, 16 June 1945, 6B; Bob Williams, "Buckeyes Leading, Top American Circuit in Batting, Fielding, Clinch Grip on First Half Honor," *Call and Post*, 7 July 1945, 7B.

13. Bob Williams, "Sports Rambler," *Call and Post*, 9 June 1945, 6B.

14. "Disputed Umpire's Decision Almost Disrupts Buckeyes–Giant Series," *Call and Post*, 23 June 1945, 6B.

15. Bob Williams, "Sports Rambler," *Call and Post*, 30 June 1945, 6B.

16. "Cleveland Group Demands Apology," *Pittsburgh Courier*, 4 August 1945, 12. From the national edition of the *Courier*. Paid attendance for the game was 12,733, which brought a gate total of $14,708.25. "Bucks Defeat Baron Champs," *Call and Post*, 21 July 1945, 7B.

17. Bob Williams, "Attack on Umpire Mars Ball Classic," *Call and Post*, 21 July 1945, 1.

18. Bob Williams, "Suspends Player Who Slugged Umpire Here," *Call and Post*, 28 July 1945, 9A.

19. "Makes Apology to FOL For Player Conduct, Suspends Davis, Birmingham Player," *Call and Post*, 28 July 1945, 6B.

20. Bob Williams, "Sports Rambler," *Call and Post*, 18 August 1945, 6B.

21. "We Will Protest Striking Umpire, Holly Promises," *Call and Post*, 21 July 1945, 7B. After taxes, insurance, rentals, and "other expenses" were removed from the $14,708.25 gate total, the game netted $10,682 in profits. Holly said that the FOL's cut was $2,337.93. The funds went toward their building fund.

22. Bob Williams, "Suspends Player Who Slugged Umpire Here," *Call and Post*, 28 July 1945, 9A.

23. Kimberley L. Phillips, *Alabama North: African-American Migrants, Community, and Working-Class Activism in Cleveland, 1915–45* (Urbana and Chicago: University of Illinois Press, 1999), 4–5. Phillips provides excellent background information on the FOL and African American labor and activism in Cleveland.

24. "Buckeyes Defeat Old Satchmo, 3–2, Injured Ump Back," *Call and Post*, 28 July 1945, 1.

25. Bob Williams, "Give New Car To Wilbur; Bucks, Chicago Clash At League Park Sun.," *Call and Post*, 1 September 1945, 6B.

26. Bob Williams, "Sports Rambler," *Call and Post*, 15 September 1945, 6B.

27. Ibid.

28. Jimmy Jones, "Buckeyes, Grays Clash Here in World Series Title Tilt Tonight; Sunday," *Call and Post*, 15 September 1945, 7B.

29. "Sammy Jethroe Again Bucks' Most Valuable Player, League Leader in Almost Every Batting Honor," *Call and Post*, 15 September 1945, 7B.

30. Jimmy Jones, "Buckeyes Grab First Game of Series, 2–1, Carry On in Fight with Mighty Grays," *Call and Post*, 22 September 1945, 6B.

31. "Second Win for Buckeyes Is Like Story-Book Thriller; Bremer [*sic*] Wins Own Game, 3–2," *Call and Post*, 22 September 1945, 6B.

32. Wendell Smith, "The Sports Beat," *Pittsburgh Courier*, 22 September 1945, 12.

33. Jimmy Jones, "Series Victors of 4-In-Row Bucks Stand Out as All-Time Greats, Carswell Wins No. 4," *Call and Post*, 29 September 1945, 6B.

34. Harry Walker, "World Series — Dots And Dashes," *Call and Post*, 29 September 1945, 6B.

35. Bob Williams, "Sports Rambler," *Call and Post*, 29 September 1945, 6B.

36. Bob Williams, "Posey Nominates Jackson for Negro Baseball Commissioner," *Call and Post*, 6 October 1945, 6B.

37. "Fan Praises, Thanks Bucks as Champs," *Call and Post*, 6 October 1945, 7B.

38. Bob Williams, "Manager Quincy Trouppe, Man Behind the Scenes, Was the Deciding Factor," *Call and Post*, 27 October 1945, 6B.

39. Quincy Trouppe, *20 Years Too Soon: Prelude To Major-League Integrated Baseball* (Saint Louis: Missouri Historical Society Press, 1977, reprint 1995), 84.

40. Ibid., 85–86.

41. Don Deleighbur, "Negro Club Owners to Fight Robinson Deal," *Call and Post*, 3 November 1945, 6B; "Dr. Martin Speaks Up," *Call and Post*, 3 November 1945, 6B.

Chapter 5

1. Cleveland Jackson, "Headline Action," *Call and Post*, 16 February 1946, 9B.

2. Ibid.; Cleveland Jackson, "Mexican Baseball League Raids American Negro Teams," *Call and Post*, 23 February 1946, 9B.

3. Cleveland Jackson, "Headline Action," *Call and Post*, 16 February 1946, 9B.

4. Cleveland Jackson, "Mexican Baseball League Raids American Negro Teams," *Call and Post*, 23 February 1946, 9B.

5. Cleveland Jackson, "Mexican Baseball League Raids American Negro Teams," *Call and Post*, 23 February 1946, 9B.

6. "Mexican League Seeks Sam Jethroe, $15,000 Offered to Batting Star," *Call and Post*, 18 May 1946, 8B.

7. Michael Singer, "Negro Stars Find Baseball 'Paradise,'" *Call and Post*, 18 May 1946, 9B.

8. John Lee, "Sports Shorts," *Call and Post*, 3 August 1946, 8B.

9. Jimmie N. Jones, "Buckeyes Start Spring Training with Strong Squad; List 15 Games," *Call and Post*, 30 March 1946, 8B.

10. Jimmie Jones, "Canton, O. Rookie Catcher Cinches Buck's Post; Horn, Larrinago to Start," *Call and Post*, 13 April 1946, 8B.

11. "Buckeye Notes," *Call and Post*, 27 April 1946, 8B.

12. Cleveland Jackson, "'Lefty' Calhoun's Nifty Pitching Sparkles as Buck's Defense Lags," *Call and Post*, 11 May 1946, 8B.

13. "Buckeyes Encounter Colorful Clowns Next Sunday at League Park," *Call and Post*, 1 June 1946, 8B; Jimmie Jones, "Buckeyes Drop Twin Bill, 11–8, 7–3 to Indianapolis," *Call and Post*, 8 June 1946, 8B.

14. Cleveland Jackson, "Headline Action," *Call and Post*, 11 May 1946, 9B.

15. Ibid.

16. "Buckeyes Gain Split with Eagles 5–6, 9–0 as Umpire Forfeits 2nd Fray," *Call and Post*, 27 July 1946, 9B.

17. Cleveland Jackson, "Headline Action," *Call and Post*, 27 July 1946, 9B.

18. Jimmie N. Jones, "Champs Capture Single Victory in 5 aGmes [*sic*] Tour with Monarchs," *Call and Post*, 22 June 1946, 9B.

19. Ibid.

20. Jimmie N. Jones, "Buckeyes Rebuild for 2nd Half; Add 2 Pitchers, Puerto Rican Shortstop," *Call and Post*, 29 June 1946, 8B.

21. Cleveland Jackson, "Headline Action," *Call and Post*, 20 July 1946, 9B.

22. "Buckeyes Score 5 Runs on No Hits in Double Victory Over Chi. Giants," *Call and Post*, 13 July 1946, 9B.

23. Jimmie Jones, "Buckeyes-Red Sox Games Feature Elk's Day, June 30; Champs Open Second Half Against Chicago, July 14," *Call and Post*, 29 June 1946, 8B.

24. "Buckeyes Encounter American Giants in July 4th Twin Bill, League Park," *Call and Post*, 6 July 1946, 9B.

25. Cleveland Jackson, "Jesse Owens Beats George Case in $1,000 Match Race; Winning Time, 9.9 Seconds," *Call and Post*, 14 September 1946, 8B.

26. Cleveland Jackson, "Headline Action," *Call and Post*, 21 September 1946, 9B; Cleveland Jackson, "Headline Action," *Call and Post*, 9 March 1946, 9B; Cleveland Jackson, "Headline Action," *Call and Post*, 17 August 1946, 9B; Wilson Irving, "Call-Post War Time Baseball Effort Bears Fruit with Record Turnout," *Call and Post*, 4 May 1946, 9B; "Jackie Rates Our Front Page With His Homer," *Call and Post*, 27 April 1946, 1.

27. Cleveland Jackson, "Headline Action," *Call and Post*, 20 April 1946, 9B.

28. Cleveland Jackson, "Indian Owner Would Hire Qualified Negro Players," *Call and Post*, 27 July 1946, 9B.

29. Ibid.

30. "Bob Feller Pits Reputation Against Satchell [*sic*] Paige," *Call and Post*, 21 September 1946, 9B.

31. "Feller's All-Stars Whitewash Satchel Paige's Nine, 5–0; Lead in Series 2–1," *Call and Post*, 6 October 1946, 9B; Jimmie N. Jones, "Barnstorming with Major Leaguers, Boost for Sepia Stars into 'Big Time,'" *Call and Post*, 19 October 1946, 8B.

32. Cleveland Jackson, "Headline Action," *Call and Post*, 2 November 1946, 8B.

33. Cleveland Jackson, "Headline Action," *Call and Post*, 26 October 1946, 8B; Cleveland

Jackson, "Headline Action," *Call and Post*, 2 November 1946, 8B.

34. Cleveland Jackson, "Headline Action," *Call and Post*, 18 January 1947, 8B.

35. "Acquisition of Prize Rookies Boosts Buckeyes' Baseball Hopes for 1947; Joe Atkins at Third," *Call and Post*, 30 November 1946, 9B.

36. "Jethroe Turns Down Winter League Contract. Baseball Boom in Antilles," *Call and Post*, 14 December 1946, 9B.

37. Cleveland Jackson, "3 Buckeye Stars Seek Reinstatement from Baseball Ban," *Call and Post*, 22 February 1947, 8B.

38. Cleveland Jackson, "Avelino Carnizares [*sic*] Signs $8,400 Mexican Contract. Night Games Planned for League Park," *Call and Post*, 1 March 1947, 8B.

39. Jimmie N. Jones, "Buckeye Veterans Encounter Keen Competition as Rookie Stars Inaugurate Battle for Regular Posts," *Call and Post*, 22 March 1947, 8B.

40. Cleveland Jackson, "Buckeyes Pummel Black Barons 9–4 in Season's Opener," *Call and Post*, 10 May 1947, 8B; Cleveland Jackson, "Headline Action," *Call and Post*, 10 May 1947, 8B.

41. Cleveland Jackson, "Cleve. Buckeyes Take Twin-Bill From Red Sox 11–7, 4–3," *Call and Post*, 24 May 1947, 8B; "Buckeyes Face American Giants In Holiday Double Header," *Call and Post*, 31 May 1947, 8B.

42. "Buckeyes to Battle Black Barons for First Place in Sunday's Double Header at League Park," *Call and Post*, 7 June 1947, 8B.

43. "Buckeyes Pace NAL; Wilson Ties Harriston for Batting Lead: Jethroe Shines on Sacks," *Call and Post*, 26 July 1947, 8B; Jimmie Jones, "Cleveland, Memphis Pennant Hopes Strengthened by Monarchs,' Barons' Losses; Red Sox Seeks Revenge," *Call and Post*, 2 August 1947, 8B.

44. Cleveland Jackson, "Jethroe Sought by Boston Braves, Not Red Sox Reports Sports Writer," *Call and Post*, 14 June 1947, 8B.

45. Cleveland Jackson, "Pasquale Brothers Trail Archie Ware; Seek Bob Feller for Post-Season Tour in Mexico ... Rumored," *Call and Post*, 2 August 1947, 9B.

46. Cleveland Jackson, "Pasquale [*sic*] Brothers Trail Archie Ware; Seek Bob Feller for Post-Season Tour in Mexico ... Rumored," *Call and Post*, 2 August 1947, 9B.

47. Cleveland Jackson, "Headline Action," *Call and Post*, 14 June 1947, 9B.

48. "Parnell Woods Likes Play In South America," *Call and Post*, 4 October 1947, 9B.

49. "Spirited Play Keeps Buckeyes in NAL Lead, Jethroe Pilfers [*sic*] 16," *Call and Post*, 28 June 1947, 8B.

50. "Buckeyes Meet Black Barons July 4; Chi. Giants July 6, 8," *Call and Post*, 5 July 1947, 8B.

51. "Buckeyes Lose, Tie; Meet Yanks Sunday," *Call and Post*, 13 September 1947, 8B; "Baseball Standings Batting Fielding," *Call and Post*, 13 September 1947, 8B; "Buckeyes Head for World Series with Cubans," *Call and Post*, 20 September 1947, 8B.

52. "Buckeyes Lose, Tie; Meet Yanks Sunday," *Call and Post*, 13 September 1947, 8B.

53. A.S. "Doc" Young, "Buckeyes, Cubans In 'World Series' At Stadium, Sept. 23–25," *Call and Post*, 20 September 1947, 8B.

54. A.S. "Doc" Young, "World Series at League Park Sunday," *Call and Post*, 27 September 1947, 9B. Some sources discuss the numbering of the 1947 Negro League World Series differently. Some refer to the incomplete game at the Polo Grounds as Game 1, which made it seem like there were actually six games in the series. I refer to Game 1 as the first complete game in the series at Yankee Stadium, and number the subsequent games accordingly.

55. A.S. "Doc" Young, "World Series at League Park Sunday," *Call and Post*, 27 September 1947, 9B.

56. "Cubans Cop Series with 6–5 Win Over Bucks in Sun. Game," *Call and Post*, 4 October 1947, 8B.

57. A.S. "Doc" Young, "Sportivanting," *Call and Post*, 22 November 1947, 8B.

58. A.S. "Doc" Young, "Alonzo Boone Picked to Manage Buckeyes," *Call and Post*, 20 December 1947, 8B.

59. "Cleveland Buckeye Hurler Operates Slum House, Too," *Call and Post*, 12 April 1947, 10B.

60. Ibid.

61. "Veeck Tries to Unload Doby to Coast — Hunter," *Call and Post*, 27 September 1947, 10B.

62. A.S. "Doc" Young, "Doby to Remain in Cleveland Organization," *Call and Post*, 18 October 1947, 8B.

63. Ibid.; A.S. "Doc" Young, "The Answer: Boudreau's Back," *Call and Post*, 29 November 1947, 9B.

64. Bill Veeck and Ed Linn, *Veeck — As in Wreck* (New York: Bantam, 1962), 94.

65. Ibid., 97–98.

66. A.S. "Doc" Young, "Sportivanting," *Call and Post*, 8 November 1947, 8B.

67. A.S. "Doc" Young, "Sportivanting," *Call and Post*, 13 September 1947, 9B.

Chapter 6

1. Larry Doby, Interview by Fay Vincent, Fay Vincent Oral History Collection, National Baseball Hall of Fame and Museum, 2001.
2. "Doby Believes He Will Make Grade as Infielder with Tribe," *Cleveland Plain Dealer*, 4 July 1947, 20.
3. Paige and Lipman, *Maybe I'll Pitch*, 151.
4. Ibid, 160.
5. Veeck and Linn, *Veeck*, 173–174, 4.
6. Ibid, 178.
7. Ibid, 184.
8. Paige and Lipman, *Maybe I'll Pitch*, 216–217.
9. Ibid, 215–216.
10. *Call and Post*, 12 July 1947, 1.
11. Cleveland Jackson, "Larry Doby Breaks Into Lineup on First Day with Team; Plays at First," *Call and Post*, 12 July 1947, 1.
12. A.S. "Doc" Young, "Sportivanting," *Call and Post*, 17 July 1948, 6B.
13. Ibid.
14. Cleveland Jackson, "Headline Action," *Call and Post*, 19 July 1947, 9B.
15. "Paige Pitches Seven-Hitter to Nats, Wins 10 to 1; Doby's Hitting .284," *Call and Post*, 4 September 1948, 7B.
16. A.S. "Doc" Young, "Sportivanting," *Call and Post*, 18 September 1948, 6B.
17. Larry Doby, Interview by Fay Vincent, Fay Vincent Oral History Collection, National Baseball Hall of Fame and Museum, 2001.
18. A.S. "Doc" Young, "Sportivanting," *Call and Post*, 18 September 1948, 6B.
19. A.S. "Doc" Young, "'Gotta Go To School!' Satchel Says; Boudreau Elated Over Debut," *Call and Post*, 17 July 1948, 7B.
20. "'Hesitation Pitch' Is Balk with Men On–Harridge," *Call and Post*, 31 July 1948, 6B.
21. Melvin Ely, *The Adventures of Amos 'n' Andy: A Social History of An American Phenomenon* (New York: Macmillan, 1991), 132.
22. Ibid, 169.
23. A.S. "Doc" Young, "Sportivanting," *Call and Post*, 15 May 1948, 6B.
24. "3 Cheers," *Call and Post*, 24 July 1948, 7B.
25. "Here's Another Guess At Paige's Age!" *Call and Post*, 31 July 1948, 7B.
26. Janet Bruce, *The Kansas City Monarchs: Champions of Black Baseball* (Lawrence: University Press of Kansas, 1985), 100.
27. Veeck and Linn, *Veeck*, 187.
28. Ibid, 188.
29. A.S. "Doc" Young, "Indians Win American League Pennant! Larry Doby and Paige Help a Lot!" *Call and Post*, 9 October 1948, 1.
30. "5-Game Schedule," *Call and Post*, 15 September 1945, 7B.
31. "Hail the Champion Cleveland Bucks!" *Call and Post*, 29 September 1945, 1.
32. *Call and Post*, 16 October 1948, 1.
33. *Cleveland Plain Dealer*, 10 October 1948, 1.
34. Veeck and Linn, *Veeck*, 180.
35. Bob Williams, "Sports Rambler," *Call and Post*, 5 May 1945, 6B.
36. Bob Williams, "Sports Rambler," *Call and Post*, 9 June 1945, 6B.
37. Bob Williams, "Sports Rambler," *Call and Post*, 2 June 1945, 6B.
38. Bob Williams, "Give New Car to Wilbur; Bucks, Chicago Clash at League Park Sun.," *Call and Post*, 1 September 1945, 6B.
39. Bob Williams, "15,000 Fans Irate After Huge Player Kayoes Umpire," *Call and Post*, 21 July 1945, 1.
40. Bob Williams, "Sports Rambler," *Call and Post*, 15 September 1945, 6B.
41. Neil Lanctot, *Negro League Baseball: The Rise and Ruin of a Black Institution* (Philadelphia: University of Philadelphia Press, 2004), ix–x.
42. Ibid., 320–321.
43. Ibid., 323, 325.
44. Ibid., 330.
45. Ibid., 332.
46. "Negro Club Head Chides Robinson," Effa Manley Papers, National Baseball Hall of Fame and Museum, Cooperstown, NY, Folder 3.
47. Letter from Ernest Wright to Effa Manley, Effa Manley Papers, National Baseball Hall of Fame and Museum, Cooperstown, NY, Folder 3.
48. Cleveland Jackson, "Headline Action," *Call and Post*, 26 July 1947, 9B.
49. Charles H. Loeb, "Headline Action," *Call and Post*, 9 August 1947, 9B.
50. A.S. "Doc" Young, "Cleveland Indians' Pennant Chances Passed to Ifs-Ands-&-Buts Dept.," *Call and Post*, 10 April 1948, 7B.
51. A.S. "Doc" Young, "Sportivanting," *Call and Post*, 8 May 1948, 6B.
52. "What's Wrong With the Buckeye Fans?" *Call and Post*, 12 June 1948, 7B.
53. A.S. "Doc" Young, "Sportivanting," *Call and Post*, 24 July 1948, 6B.
54. A.S. "Doc" Young, "Dodgers-Indians Exhibition Draws 25,000 Negro Fans; Tribe Wins, 4–3," *Call and Post*, 24 July 1948, 6B.

Chapter 7

1. Lanctot, *Negro League Baseball*, 310.
2. Ibid., 317.

3. Ibid., 338, 340.

4. "Buckeyes Move to Louisville, Ky.," *Call and Post*, 12 February 1949, 6B.

5. "Hayes Tells What 'appened to Cleveland Buckeyes," *Call and Post*, 23 July 1949, 6B.

6. "Clowns Win Double-Header; Karamu House Nets $5,000," *Call and Post*, 6 August 1949, 7B.

7. "Indians May Be Losing, But Buckeyes' Bosses Facing Court Room Squeeze Play," *Call and Post*, 13 August 1949, 4A.

8. "Eugene Bremer [*sic*], Vet Buckeye Hurler, Has a Beef About Some Wages Due," *Call and Post*, 27 August 1949, 6B; "Bucks' Manager Says Bremer [*sic*] Did Not State Facts," *Call and Post*, 17 September 1949, 6B.

9. "Ernie Wright Out, Wilbur Hayes in As Operator of Buckeye Franchise," *Call and Post*, 18 February 1950, 1B.

10. John Fuster, "Some Characters And Some Events In Sports," *Call and Post*, 14 January 1950, 6B.

11. John Fuster, "Buckeyes Face Test At Stadium May 28," *Call and Post*, 20 May 1950, 1B.

12. John Fuster, "Let's Junk Negro Baseball Leagues," *Call and Post*, 8 July 1950, 1D.

13. "24,614 See West Top East, 5–3, At Chicago," *Call and Post*, 26 August 1950, 3D.

14. Robert Benfield, "Negro Star in Vanguard of Record Number of Players Joining Majors," *Call and Post*, 26 February 1949, 6B; "Negro Players Setting Terrific Pace As Minor Leagues Launch Drives," *Call and Post*, 7 May 1949, 6B.

15. John E. Fuster, "Some Characters And Some Events In Sports," *Call and Post*, 15 October 1949, 6B.

16. John Fuster, "We Call It A Great American Game," *Call and Post*, 13 May 1950, 1B.

17. John Fuster, "Fans Forgetting Color All-Star Poll Shows," *Call and Post*, 15 July 1950, 1D; "Doby and Easter Help Clark Griffith Coin Dough," *Call and Post*, 29 July 1950, 2D.

18. Marty Richardson, "Let's Have Some Sport," *Call and Post*, 27 August 1949, 7B.

19. "Paige's Release May Get Minoso Better Chance," *Call and Post*, 18 February 1950, 1B.

20. John E. Fuster, "Time Marches On But Not for Satch," *Call and Post*, 20 May 1950, 1B.

21. John E. Fuster, "Some Characters And Some Events In Sports," *Call and Post*, 15 April 1950, 1B.

22. Ibid.; John E. Fuster, "Greatness Is Two-Faced Coin, On One Side Is Humility," *Call and Post*, 3 June 1950, 1D.

23. John Fuster, "It Has Been a Long Trip, But Larry Has Come Home," *Call and Post*, 1 July 1950, 1D.

24. "Larry Doby vs Jackie Robinson: Who's the Best?," *Call and Post*, 19 August 1950, 1D. Through 97 games played, Robinson had 366 at-bats with 76 runs, 131 hits and a .358 batting average while Doby had 339 at-bats, 79 runs, 121 hits and a .357 batting average. This column was printed with John Fuster's header, but a disclaimer noted that he was on vacation and an unnamed staff writer authored the piece.

25. Charles P. Lucas, "The Civil Rights Watch Dog," *Call and Post*, 15 July 1950, 1B.

26. Ibid.

27. Ibid.

28. Marty Richardson, "Let's Have Some Sport," *Call and Post*, 27 May 1950, 2D.

29. Steve Estes, *I Am A Man! Race, Manhood, and the Civil Rights Movement* (Chapel Hill: University of North Carolina Press, 2005), 1–2, 6.

30. Ibid., 12.

31. Ibid, 37.

32. Ibid, 22.

33. Bill Veeck and Ed Linn, *Veeck*, 183–184.

34. "Paul Brown, Bill Veeck to Receive Citations at Urban League Meeting," *Call and Post*, 1 January 1949, 1.

35. Bill Crawford and Robert Benfield, "The People Speak Out," *Call and Post*, 19 February 1949, 4B.

36. "Bill Veeck Donates Baseball Equipment To Crippled Kiddies," *Call and Post*, 20 April 1949, 6B.

37. "Harrison Dillard Joins Tribe Public Relations Staff," *Call and Post*, 14 May 1949, 7B.

38. "With Bill Veeck, It Is Ability That Counts," *Call and Post*, 1 October 1949, 9B; John E. Fuster, "Some Characters and Some Events In Sports," *Call and Post*, 27 August 1949, 6B.

39. Veeck and Linn, *Veeck*, 213–214.

40. John E. Fuster, "Courier Wrong About Bill Veeck Being Run Out of Town, and Organized Gangs Of Hoodlums Riding Doby, Paige, Easter," *Call and Post*, 24 September 1949, 6B.

41. Veeck and Linn, *Veeck*, 178.

42. Jules Tygiel, *Baseball's Great Experiment: Jackie Robinson and His Legacy* (New York: Oxford University Press, 1983), 59, 100.

43. John Fuster, "No Longer 'Yea, Doby!' Now It's 'Yea, Indians!'" *Call and Post*, 26 August 1950, 1D.

44. John Fuster, "Call & Post Sports Editor Gets Personal," *Call and Post*, 14 October 1950, 1D.

45. John E. Fuster, "Jethroe, Boosted for Majors by *Call & Post* in 1942, 'Steals' His Way In at Last; Is Now a Boston Brave," *Call and Post*, 8 October 1949, 6B.

46. Robert F. Benfield, "Our Indians …

1949 Champions in Baseball … and in Democracy!" *Call and Post*, 23 April 1949, 1.

47. Fuster, "No Longer 'Yea Doby!'" *Call and Post*, 26 August 1950, 1D.

48. Bill Crawford and Robert Benfield, "The People Speak Out," *Call and Post*, 12 March 1949, 4B.

49. W.O. Walker, "Down the Big Road," *Call and Post*, 26 February 1949, 4B.

50. Ibid. In his book *The Southern Diaspora: How the Great Migrations of Black and White Southerners Transformed America*, James N. Gregory discussed the role of the *Chicago Defender* in encouraging Southern African Americans to move to the North.

51. W.O. Walker, "Down the Big Road," *Call and Post*, 26 February 1949, 4B.

52. "Local Branch Cited As Outstanding In NAACP," *Call and Post*, 1 July 1950, 1.

53. Charles P. Lucas, "The Civil Rights Watch Dog," *Call and Post*, 14 October 1950, 1B.

Chapter 8

1. Scott Moore, "Wild Pitch," *Washington Post*, 7 September 1997, F01.

2. Ibid.

3. Ibid.

4. Cleveland Jackson, "Headline Action," *Call and Post*, 20 July 1946, 9B.

5. Cleveland Jackson, "Erie, Pa. Southpaw is First White Player in Negro Baseball Circuit," *Call and Post*, 23 March 1946, 8B.

6. Jimmie N. Jones, "Ernie Wright Protests Klep's Eviction. Cites Branch Rickey," *Call and Post*, 13 April 1946, 8B.

7. Ibid.

8. Moore, "Wild Pitch," *Washington Post*, 7 September 1997, F01.

9. "Buckeyes Drop Twin Bill, 11–8," *Call and Post*, 8 June 1946, 8B.

10. "Buckeyes to Play Mighty Monarchs in Crucial Games, Sunday, League Pk.," *Call and Post*, 8 June 1946, 9B.

11. Cleveland Jackson, "Lone White Player In Negro Baseball Released by Bucks," *Call and Post*, 8 June 1946, 9B; Moore, "Wild Pitch," *Washington Post*, 7 September 1997, F01.

12. Cleveland Jackson, "Lone White Player In Negro Baseball Released by Bucks," *Call and Post*, 8 June 1946, 9B.

13. John Fuster, "Some Characters and Some Events in Sports," *Call and Post*, 14 January 1950, 6B.

14. John Fuster, "Buckeyes Face Test At Stadium May 28," *Call and Post*, 20 May 1950, 1B.

15. John Fuster, "Let's Junk Negro Baseball Leagues," *Call and Post*, 8 July 1950, 1D.

16. Moore, "Wild Pitch," *Washington Post*, 7 September 1997, F01.

Epilogue

1. "Touching Base With Memories," *New York Times*, 29 October 1983, 24; Richard Goldstein, "Sam Jethroe Is Dead at 83; Was Oldest Rookie of the Year," *New York Times*, 19 June 2001, A21; "Mariners' Sasaki named AL Rookie of the Year," CNNSI.com <*http://sportsillustrated.cnn.com/baseball/mlb/news/2000/11/06/sasaki_roy_ap/*> (9 March 2009). Kazuhiro Sasaki, a pitcher from Japan, won American League Rookie of the Year honors with the Seattle Mariners in 2000 at the age of 32. Jethroe maintained the title of major league baseball's oldest Rookie of the Year because he was believed to be 33 days older than Sasaki.

2. "Touching Base With Memories," *New York Times*, 29 October 1983, 24; Richard Goldstein, "Sam Jethroe Is Dead at 83," *New York Times*, 19 June 2001, A21.

3. Richard Goldstein, "Sam Jethroe Is Dead at 83," *New York Times*, 19 June 2001, A21; Kip Kuduk, "Negro League Players Will Receive Pensions," *Washington Times*, 20 January 1997, B4; Murray Chass, "Pioneer Black Players to be Granted Pensions," *New York Times*, 20 January 1997, C9. Mike Copper, "Document Alters What We Know About Sam Jethroe," GoErie.com <http://www.goerie.com/apps/pbcs.dll/article?AID=/20100409/BASEBALL04/304099943/-1/SPORTS> (9 April 2010).

Bibliography

Primary Sources

Chicago Defender, 1932–1933.

Cleveland Call and Post, 1934–1935; 1939–1950

Cleveland Gazette, 1922–1928; 1931–1933.

Cleveland Plain Dealer, 5 July 1947.

Cleveland Plain Dealer, 10 October 1948.

Doby, Larry. Interview by Fay Vincent. Fay Vincent Oral History Collection. National Baseball Hall of Fame and Museum, 2001.

Lombardy, Kirk. Correspondence with author via e-mail. National Weather Service, Cleveland Hopkins International Airport, 30 and 31 January 2007.

Manley, Effa. Papers. 3 files. National Baseball Hall of Fame and Museum, Archive Center, Cooperstown, NY

Paige, Leroy (Satchel), and David Lipman. *Maybe I'll Pitch Forever*. New York: Grove Press, 1961.

Pittsburgh Courier, 14 February 1942.

Pittsburgh Courier, 14 February 1945.

Smith, Wendell. "A Strange Tribe: On the Loyalties of Black Fans." *Pittsburgh Courier*, 14 May 1938. In *The Unlevel Playing Field: A Documentary History of the African American Experience in Sport*, David K. Wiggins and Patrick B. Miller, eds. Urbana: University of Illinois Press, 2003.

Smith, Wendell. Papers. 4 files. National Baseball Hall of Fame and Museum, Archive Center, Cooperstown, NY.

Trouppe, Quincy. *20 Years Too Soon:* *Prelude to Major-League Integrated Baseball*. St. Louis: Missouri Historical Society Press, 1977, revised edition 1995.

Veeck, Bill, and Ed Linn. *Veeck — As in Wreck*. New York: Bantam, 1962.

Secondary Sources

"African Americans." Encyclopedia of Cleveland History. <http://ech.case.edu/echcgi/article.pl?id=AA> (6 February 2007).

Bruce, Janet. *The Kansas City Monarchs: Champions of Black Baseball*. Lawrence: University Press of Kansas, 1985.

Clark, Dick, and Larry Lester, eds. *The Negro Leagues Book*. Cleveland: Society for American Baseball Research, 1994.

Davis, Russell H. *Black Americans in Cleveland*. Washington, D.C.: Associated Publishers, 1972.

Ely, Melvin. *The Adventures of Amos 'n' Andy: A Social History of an American Phenomenon*. New York: Macmillan, 1991.

Estes, Steve. *I Am a Man! Race, Manhood, and the Civil Rights Movement*. Chapel Hill: University of North Carolina Press, 2005.

Ferguson, Karen. *Black Politics in New Deal Atlanta*. Chapel Hill: University of North Carolina Press, 2002.

Gregory, James N. *The Southern Diaspora: How the Great Migrations of Black and White Southerners Transformed America*.

Chapel Hill: University of North Carolina Press, 2005.

Kusmer, Kenneth L. *A Ghetto Takes Shape:
Black Cleveland, 1870–1930.* Urbana:
University of Illinois Press, 1976.

Lanctot, Neil. *Negro League Baseball: The
Rise and Ruin of a Black Institution.*
Philadelphia: University of Pennsylvania
Press, 2004.

Lester, Larry. *Black Baseball's National
Showcase: The East-West All-Star Game,
1933–1953.* Lincoln: University of Nebraska Press, 2001.

Moore, Joseph Thomas. *Pride Against
Prejudice: The Biography of Larry Doby.*
New York: Praeger, 1988.

"The Official Site of the Cleveland Indians." News: Cleveland Indians News.
<http://cleveland.indians.mlb.com/new
s/article.jsp?ymd=20061204&content_
id1750392&vkey=news_cle&fext=.jsp
&c_id=cle> (15 April 2007).

Peterson, Robert. *Only the Ball Was White:
A History of Legendary Black Players and
All-Black Professional Teams.* New York:
Oxford University Press, 1970.

Phillips, Kimberley L. *Alabama North:
African-American Migrants, Community,
and Working-Class Activism in Cleveland, 1915–45.* Urbana: University of
Illinois Press, 1999.

Ruck, Rob. *Sandlot Seasons: Sport in Black
Pittsburgh.* Urbana: University of Illinois Press, 1993.

*To Promote Amicable Relations: 30 Year
History of the Cleveland Community Relations Board.* Cleveland: The Board,
1975.

Tygiel, Jules. *Baseball's Great Experiment:
Jackie Robinson and His Legacy.* New
York: Oxford University Press, 1983.

"Typical Weather for Cleveland, OH." Ac-
cuweather.com. <wwwa.accuweather.
com/forecast-normals.asp?partner=ac-
cuweather&traveler=0&zipcode=44113>
(31 January 2007).

Western Reserve Historical Society.

Index